British Romantic Drama

British Romantic Drama

Historical and Critical Essays

Edited by
Terence Allan Hoagwood
and Daniel P. Watkins

Madison • Teaneck
Fairleigh Dickinson University Press
London: Associated University Presses

© 1998 by Associated University Presses, Inc.

All rights reserved. Authorization to photocopy items for internal or personal use, or the internal or personal use of specific clients, is granted by the copyright owner, provided that a base fee of $10.00, plus eight cents per page, per copy is paid directly to the Copyright Clearance Center, 222 Rosewood Drive, Danvers, Massachusetts 01923. [0-8386-3743-4/98 $10.00+8¢ pp, pc.]

Associated University Presses
440 Forsgate Drive
Cranbury, NJ 08512

Associated University Presses
16 Barter Street
London WC1A 2AH, England

Associated University Presses
P.O. Box 338, Port Credit
Mississauga, Ontario
Canada L5G 4L8

The paper used in this publication meets the requirements
of the American National Standard for Permanence of Paper
for Printed Library Materials Z39.48-1984.

Library of Congress Cataloging-in-Publication Data

British romantic drama : historical and critical essays / edited by Terence Allan Hoagwood and Daniel P. Watkins.
    p.   cm.
    Includes index.
    ISBN 0-8386-3743-4 (alk. paper)
    1. English drama—19th century—History and criticism. 2. English drama—18th century—History and criticism. 3. Romanticism—Great Britain. I. Hoagwood, Terence Allan, 1952– . II. Watkins, Daniel P., 1952–
PR716.B75   1998
822'.709145—dc21   97-43701
                                                                                                 CIP

PRINTED IN THE UNITED STATES OF AMERICA

Contents

Acknowledgments	7
List of Contributors	9
Introduction	13
1. Romantic Drama and Historical Hermeneutics 　Terence Allan Hoagwood	22
2. "A Haunted Ruin": Romantic Drama, Renaissance Tradition, and the Critical Establishment 　Greg Kucich	56
3. Ideology and Genre in the British Antirevolutionary Drama in the 1790s 　Jeffrey N. Cox	84
4. Transitory Actions, Men Betrayed: The French Revolution in the English Revolution in Romantic Drama 　Kenneth R. Johnston and Joseph Nicholes	115
5. The English Pamphlet War of the 1790s and Coleridge's *Osorio* 　Marjean D. Purinton	159
6. Scott the Dramatist 　Daniel P. Watkins	182
7. Percy Bysshe Shelley's *The Cenci* and the Rhetoric of Tyranny 　Suzanne Ferriss	208
Index	229

Acknowledgments

THE EDITORS GRATEFULLY ACKNOWLEDGE *ELH* FOR PERMISSION TO REPRINT Jeffrey N. Cox's essay, "Ideology and Genre in the British Antirevolutionary Drama in the 1790s," 58 (1992): 579–610.

The editors also gratefully acknowledge permission to reprint several articles that first appeared in *The Wordsworth Circle*, 23 (1992): Greg Kucich, "'A Haunted Ruin': Romantic Drama, Renaissance Tradition, and the Critical Establishment," pp. 64–76, and Kenneth R. Johnston and Joseph Nicholes, "Transitory Actions, Men Betrayed: The French Revolution in the English Revolution in Romantic Drama," pp. 76–96.

Two additional essays, which have been substantially revised, and which now appear under different titles, also originally appeared in the same issue of *The Wordsworth Circle*, and the editors gratefully acknowledge permission to reprint them: Terence Allan Hoagwood, "Prolegomenon for a Theory of Romantic Drama" and Suzanne Ferriss, "Reflection in a 'Many-Sided Mirror': Shelley's *The Cenci* through the Post-Revolutionary Prism."

Contributors

JEFFREY N. COX is Professor of English at Texas A&M University, where he also serves as Director of the Interdisciplinary Group for Historical Study. He is the author of *In the Shadows of Romance: Romantic Tragic Drama in Germany, England, and France* (1987), the editor of *Seven Gothic Dramas 1789–1825* (1992), and the coeditor with Larry Reynolds of *New Historical Literary Study: Reproducing Texts, Representing History*. His book, *The Cockney School: Poetics and Politics in the Hunt Circle*, is forthcoming from Cambridge UP.

SUZANNE FERRISS is Associate Professor of Liberal Arts at Nova Southeastern University. Coeditor of *On Fashion* (1994), she has published articles on Romantic poetry and drama, feminist theory, and film. She is currently working with Shari Benstock on *A Handbook of Literary Feminism* and a companion anthology.

TERENCE ALLAN HOAGWOOD, Professor of English at Texas A&M University and Fellow of the Interdisciplinary Group for Historical Study, is the author of *Politics, Philosophy, and the Production of Romantic Texts* (1996), *Byron's Dialectic: Skepticism and the Critique of Culture* (1993), *Skepticism and Ideology* (1988), *Prophecy and the Philosophy of Mind: Traditions of Blake and Shelley* (1985), and other books. He is the editor of several previously rare works of eighteenth-century and nineteenth-century literature, including Violet Fane's *Denzil Place* (1996), Mary Robinson's *Sappho and Phaon* (1995), Robert Stephen Hawker's *Cornish Ballads* (1994), Charlotte Smith's *"Beachy Head" and Other Poems* (1993), Elizabeth Smith's *The Brethren: A Poem in Four Books* (1991), and Mary Hays's *The Victim of Prejudice* (1990). He is also the editor of a collection of essays by several hands entitled *Materialism and Textuality*, which appeared as the Spring 1997 issue of *Studies in the Literary Imagination*.

KENNETH R. JOHNSTON, Professor and Chair, Department of English, Indiana University, Bloomington, is the author of *Wordsworth and "The Recluse"* (1984) and *Young Wordsworth: Creation of the Poet* (forthcoming). He is also coeditor of, and contributed to, *The Age of William Wordsworth* (1987) and *Romantic Revolutions: Criticism and Theory* (1990).

GREG KUCICH, Associate Professor of English, Notre Dame University, is the author of *Keats, Shelley, and Romantic Spenserianism,* and many essays on Romanticism in *Keats-Shelley Journal, Keats-Shelley Review, The Wordsworth Circle,* and elsewhere. He is editor of *Nineteenth-Century Contexts.*

JOSEPH NICHOLES, now deceased, was Assistant Professor of English at Brigham Young University-Hawaii. He published numerous essays on Romantic and Victorian literature.

MARJEAN PURINTON, Assistant Professor of English, Texas Tech University, recently served as President and then Vice President of the South Central Women's Studies Association (1994–97). She has also been a Research Associate at the Five College Women's Studies Research Center at Mount Holyoke College (1993–94) and Coordinator of Women's Studies at Westfield State College (1994–95). She is the author of *Romantic Ideology Unmasked: The Mentally Constructed Tyrannies in Dramas of William Wordsworth, Lord Byron, Percy Shelley, and Joanna Baillie* (1994), and has published essays on Blake, Romantic drama, and early nineteenth-century women's fiction. She is currently writing a book about British Romantic drama and cultural Identity.

DANIEL P. WATKINS, Professor of English at Duquesne University, is the author of *Social Relations in Byron's Eastern Tales* (1987), *Keats's Poetry and the Politics of the Imagination* (1989), *A Materialist Critique of English Romantic Drama* (1993), and *Sexual Power in British Romantic Poetry* (1996). With G. A. Rosso, he is editor of *Spirits of Fire: English Romantic Writers and Contemporary Historical Methods* (1990).

British Romantic Drama

Introduction

THIS COLLECTION OF ESSAYS CELEBRATES A GROWING SCHOLARLY INTEREST IN the Romantic drama.[1] For more than a century—and until the recent resurgence of historicist scholarship in Romanticism—literary opinion understood Romantic literature to be synonymous with short lyric poems; the intellectual and thematic content of the Romantic lyric was characterized by subjectivity and individualism. At the same time, and contradictorily, the ideology of the Romantic lyric was seen as a device for sublimating circumstantiality into abstractions exempt from time and space. The conceptual field of Romanticism, contained within the charmed but tiny spaces of lyric poems, was shaped by these interests: the mind of the individual subject and the spirit of the universe marked the limits of Romantic literature and imagination.

Preserving this traditional view of Romanticism involved exclusions, of course: Jane Austen's novels were long understood as if they had been written at some time other than the early part of the nineteenth century; Scott's novels have sometimes been treated as elephantine anticipations of Victorian novels of history; the Gothic romances of Lewis and Maturin, besmirched by popularity, have been thrillingly déclassé entertainments for the lower orders. Coleridge's voluminous life's work in prose, chiefly on political subjects, was often seen as a mere excuse for his insufficient productivity in short lyric poems or as an idiosyncratic symptom which presciently anticipates the profound privacy of psychoanalysis. Other writers of prose—chiefly Hazlitt, Lamb, and DeQuincey—were long treated as a "quaint trio" of essayists, as John Kinnaird once observed.[2]

In such a climate of literary opinion, a genre so thoroughly public as the drama could hardly rise to the higher levels of critical appreciation. A phrase—"mental theatre"—which Byron used in a letter, with an entirely different sense, was seized as a category under which *some* verse plays (chiefly *Manfred* and *Prometheus Unbound*) could be retrieved. That rubric enabled readers to understand those plays as distended lyrics or collections of lyrics; those plays could thus be understood to confine themselves within the same conceptual limits as the Romantic lyric—for example, the mind of the individual subject and the spirit of the universe.

Especially when these few lyrical dramas are written by the same ineffectual angels whose lyrics had already been venerated for their subjectivity, the poetic dramas can be (and have been) handily appropriated under the same categories of personal feeling that define the salience of the short and personal lyric. Conspicuously public performances, with conspicuously public reference, by writers such as Elizabeth Inchbald, George Colman, Thomas Holcroft, or Mary Russell Mitford, however, hardly submit themselves to those same categories; such works can therefore hardly attain much appreciation under the authority of traditional critical categories such as those described above. These plays do not devote themselves to the individual subject and the spirit of the universe, at least not in the abstract and timeless ways that we have learned to revere in lyric poems.

Critical thinking about Romantic drama began to change in the early 1980s, when a materialist reassessment of Romanticism itself was begun. The most important work in this effort was Jerome McGann's *The Romantic Ideology*, which showed that Romantic individualism and idealism were inexorably tied to the social and historical conditions under which Romantic texts were produced.[3] McGann's demonstration of this fact encouraged a burst of critical and scholarly work that not only sought to expose and clarify the historicity of canonical texts but also began to discover the historical and cultural significance of heretofore marginalized texts.[4] More than any other genre, drama has been a major focus of interest in the historicist revaluation of Romanticism, perhaps because of its fascinating and complex strategies of registering the political, social, and cultural dynamics of British society. Historically minded critics have learned anew what Shelley, for instance, understood all along: drama is the most social of all art forms.

The importance of drama in the effort to map out the historical dynamics of Romanticism is seen not only in the numerous critical essays that have appeared in major journals over the past few years[5] but also in the proliferation of major book-length studies. Not only has Jeffrey Cox published an important edition of *Seven Gothic Dramas*, but critical studies using a historicist methodology have also been published by Daniel P. Watkins, Marjean Purinton, Julie Carlson, and Gillian Russell.[6] Although these works may vary in their emphases and conclusions, they share a common assumption about the historical richness and importance of Romantic drama, and they have helped to move critical discussion definitively away from the belief that lyric poetry is the heart and soul of Romantic cultural production.

Despite the proliferation of work on Romantic drama in recent years, much more both of a practical and theoretical nature remains to be done. With respect to practical criticism and scholarship, there are so many dramatic works of the period not yet known—let alone critically investigated—that the labor of discovering, introducing, and assessing it is enormous. It is as yet impossible to know which works may be historically—*and aesthetically*—most significant, because not enough is known about the range, nature, and complexity of Romantic dramatic expression. The theoretical work still to be done is no less daunting, as questions of ideology, historical definition, social relations, formal complexity, uses of the past, and more must be studied as the growing body of material facts bearing on Romantic drama become known.

The present volume attempts a systematic explanation of various dimensions of Romantic drama by foregrounding both the theoretical and practical questions bearing on Romantic drama in its historical situation. In this effort, the volume intentionally gravitates toward discussion of lesser known works of the period, rather than such major dramas as *Manfred* or *Prometheus Unbound,* because the poetic dramas by Byron and Shelley have already been the subject of many useful historicist investigations and because lesser-known works—for instance, the dramas of Scott, Wordsworth's *Borderers,* and the many revolutionary and counterrevolutionary dramas of the period—provide avenues into historical and ideological issues that cannot be adequately considered by exclusive attention to dramas long recognized as canonical. The historicist revaluation of Romanticism to which this volume is committed assumes that an understanding of the historical reach of Romantic cultural expression requires a concentrated investigation of works that challenge dominant forms of Romantic expression.

* * *

The volume's subtitle designates its concentric sets of concerns: from a narrowly literary point of view, the essays examine questions of genre, of the difference that genre makes in literary production and reception. More largely, as studies in culture, these essays examine the function, meaning, and cultural work of the dramas during the period. At the level of interpretation theory, these essays show how the genre of Romantic drama is especially important for the embodiment and analysis of a historical hermeneutic: the dramas *express* a historical construction of understanding, and they offer *subjects for* a historical act of understanding. Although the essays in the present volume do not club together to offer a single critical explanation of Romanticism and history, or accept uncritically all the claims of what might be called the New Romanticism, they do share a common concern with historical problems and Romantic literature that has been elaborated by McGann and others; and these essays are concerned especially with the way historical pressure helps to shape drama during the Romantic period and the way Romantic drama shapes and defines history.

These essays offer accounts of exemplary plays, and they explain the historical conditions that shape them, the historically important functions or interventions that the dramas constituted, and the corollary principles of a historical theory of meaning. For instance, Hoagwood's essay offers a detailed consideration of the Romantic theater, beginning with an account of the dramatists and the institutions that helped to shape and direct the theater in the period. He then brings this information to bear on a consideration of particular plays of the period, including Inchbald's *The Massacre,* Samuel Birch's *The Adopted Child,* George Watson's *England Preserved,* and Joanna Baillie's *Constantine Paleologus;* more largely he constructs a critical framework that enables a fundamental revaluation of Romantic drama along historical and cultural lines. Perhaps most importantly, he interweaves into the discussion of specific plays, writers, and institutions an argument about the sources and directions of meaning in Romantic drama. Drawing upon the ideas of Wilhelm Dilthey, he puts forth a theory of historical hermeneutic that focuses on the historical displacements of symbolic substitution. For Hoagwood, Romantic dramas represent the conditions of their own formation, not under the operation of a reflexive cleverness but in a profound and ubiquitous engagement with their own historicity.

Greg Kucich's essay begins by acknowledging the difficulties that twentieth-century critics often face when approaching Romantic drama. These difficulties, he argues, arise most often from the inability of criticism to explain the apparent contradiction between the dramatic aspirations of the Romantic period and the seeming abandonment of theatrical activity during the period. Kucich approaches this problem by examining Romantic dramatic theory, especially as it emerged in the period's influential periodical press, and he finds that the Romantics' profound ambivalence about dramatic production was a complicated outgrowth of their effort to situate themselves in England's dramatic history. The Romantics' formulations of dramatic history are implicated in Romantic sociopolitical struggles. Kucich argues that critics and dramatists of the period manipulate fragments of the British past, including dramas, and that these interpretative manipulations are part of the Romantics' own cultural and political enterprise. His study broadens the scope of critical investigation by recovering many of the actual historical pressures operating on English Romantic drama, and it will serve as a necessary starting point for future studies of the historical and cultural dimensions of Romantic drama.

Jeffrey Cox's study of antirevolutionary drama traces the social and literary history of a body of work that has been all but forgotten, making a strong argument that this work is of fundamental importance to an understanding of the political and literary situation of the 1790s. Cox examines various antirevolutionary plays—for example, *The Rovers* (rumored to have been written by Pitt), *The Fall of the French Monarchy, Maid of Normandy, Democratic Rage*—in the context of the political struggles of the 1790s to show their ideological impact on the shape and direction of political culture. He concludes that the conservative culture of the time found its strongest voice in melodrama, whose extreme popularity marked an ideological victory for conservatism by effectively shifting popular attention away from foreign and domestic politics to an apparently apolitical domesticity. At the same time, however, that victory also marked a cultural defeat because the popularity of melodrama contributed to the demise of those dramatic forms embraced by official culture, particularly neoclassical tragedy. Although they cannot be defined in any sense as Romantic, the antirevolutionary plays of the 1790s, Cox shows, helped to shape Romantic culture as well as the future development of the English drama and theater.

In their essay, Kenneth Johnston and Joseph Nicholes study five Romantic dramas about the English Revolution, showing that the political content of these dramas is directly relevant to British politics after the French Revolution. Concerned with such fundamental political questions as who had the right to rule in the Commonwealth, Romantic drama was potentially as important in the cultural history of their time as Shakespeare's history plays were in the sixteenth century. That they never in fact fulfilled their potential is itself a significant matter in the cultural history of the Romantic period. The works that Johnston and Nicholes examine—Charles Lamb's *John Woodvil*, William Godwin's *Faulkner*, Percy Bysshe Shelley's *Charles the First*, Mary Russell Mitford's *Charles the First*, and Robert Browning's *Strafford: An Historical Tragedy*—cover a range of political sensibilities, from conservative to progressive; and, even as they display a peculiarly Romantic political emphasis on the personal, they also reveal a range of political interests that historical criticism has only recently come to understand in Romantic literature. These dramas insist, for instance, that the actions of individuals are seldom *only* private, or without far-reaching consequences, and that personal life carries within it the pressures and principles of the age to which it belongs. Johnston and Nicholes's exemplary handling of issues at the level of historical conjuncture, and their sharp sense of the politics of the text, suggest fruitful ways that the reassessment of Romantic drama might be carried out.

Marjean D. Purinton's essay performs the much-needed service of situating Coleridge's *Osorio* amid the political pamphlet wars of the 1790s. Read in the context of the English pamphlet war, Purinton argues, *Osorio* presents a response to the French Revolution; that response is critical of both the Jacobins and Royalists, on the grounds that both sides pursue narrowly ideological programs that are prone to violence and that, therefore, inevitably impede true liberty. An alternative to such extreme political views, the play suggests, must begin with a radical reimagining of social and political systems; it must reject the ideological presuppositions of liberal and conservative structures of thought alike, replacing these with an unyielding commitment to mental freedom. On this view, even as the play rejects violent revolution, it endorses a revolution in human imagination, which alone can transform human existence and assure human liberty.

Daniel P. Watkins provides a historically informed introductory sketch of several of Sir Walter Scott's dramas in an effort to retrieve those plays for literary history and to suggest, more largely, that a critical investigation of the plays contributes importantly to a thoroughgoing historicist explanation of Romanticism. Scott's dramas, Watkins argues, are distinguished by their acknowledgment of the power and direction of historical change during the three hundred years immediately preceding Scott's own day; but even as they acknowledge certain specific dimensions of historical change, they attempt to preserve what Scott considered to be universal bedrock assumptions about human experience and meaning. Scott's plays—*Macduff's Cross, Auchindrane,* and *The Doom of Devorgoil*—are steeped in historical understanding and saturated with historical knowledge, and they seek ways to contain the flow of that understanding and knowledge and to define the significance of what cannot be contained. In short, they are historically charged dramas that are ambivalent about history, and in their ambivalence they (like many dramas of the period) tend to articulate a conservative vision of politics and culture. At the same time, however, that vision contains within it an anxious awareness of its own inevitable defeat.

Suzanne Ferriss studies Shelley's depiction of events from the Italian renaissance to show how Shelley's departures from his antecedent texts identify the French Revolution as the subtext of *The Cenci.* But Shelley's dramatic representation of events in France, Ferriss argues, should not be read naively as an endorsement, or condemnation, of revolution; rather, the play endorses revolutionary ideals while exhibiting a profound skepticism that these ideals may be incarnated in revolutionary action—political or poetic. In this respect, the play is truly a postrevolutionary work, not simply by virtue of its date of composition but also because of its problematic attitude toward revolution.

* * *

It is worth emphasizing, again, that neither the plays of the Romantic period nor the essays in this volume exhibit unanimity of theme, technique, argument, or assumption. The volume as a whole, however, does constitute an argument, and the coherence of that argument reflects a generalizable (though not unanimous) tendency among the British Romantic dramas. Simultaneously to avoid oversimplification and to adumbrate that coherence, it will be useful to articulate briefly the kinds of local difference and larger coherence that the following essays unfold. Again, we are convinced that the multeity and unity among the essays, their differentials and their continuity, arise from formal and conceptual features among the dramas themselves.

Some of the following essays (including Purinton's exposition of Coleridge's strategy of historical layering) assume authorial control and intentional design. Coleridge's play is shown to manifest a formal strategy contrived to embody an articulated awareness that is continuous with explicit arguments in polemical prose by Coleridge and likewise prose by Coleridge's contemporaries. In contrast, some of the essays (including Watkins's account of the ideological dimensions of Scott's dramas) disclose the determining power of tendencies and forces that often lie *outside* of authorial control, forces whose meaning was perhaps not available for conscious or complete articulation by the dramatist. Historical distance opens explanatory ranges that were not available in the same way to the consciousness of the very writers whose works bear such historical meanings. The plays studied by Johnston and Nicholes are important in this connection in a dual sense: each play takes a historical vantage on its plot materials (subjecting the English Revolution to a historical interpretation), but each play simultaneously *instantiates* a historically determined vantage which encloses (limits) playwright and play. The first historical vision falls under the limits of intentional design; it is a vision that is possessed by the playwright and play. The second sort of historical vantage, however, cannot be known within the limits of intentional design; it possesses both playwright and play.

Although *The Cenci* makes history its manifest subject, Ferriss's essay shows how the play's refraction of its historical materials is itself conditioned by historical determiners in ways that the drama and dramatist cannot express consciously and completely. Simply to designate the drama postrevolutionary is to place its historical subject and its authorial subject-form under interpretation. Both play and playwright are in this sense productions and therefore require both formal and etiological analysis.

Kucich's archival work in the periodical literature and Cox's study of many now-forgotten antirevolutionary dramas of the period are doubly informed in an important way: though the contemporary discourse about the drama frames and informs the dramas, that contemporary critical literature is itself situated in a historical field; the historical explanation of the Romantic critical literature was not available *to* that Romantic critical literature, though its own conceptual resources included its historical purchase on the dramatic tradition and its sociopolitical importance.

Hoagwood's essay adumbrates a set of conceptual forms that Romantic drama deploys in its own ideological critique. The intentional design of the drama is shown to thematize history and historically conditioned concept-formations. In a larger sense, however, Romantic drama is an instance *for* such an analysis. The sorts of alienated understanding that are voiced by various characters in the plays that Hoagwood discusses embody and dramatize a historical and social distance that is operative within the fictive relations of the drama, but the explanatory obsolescence that the characters experience, with respect to each other, implies a larger and more critical distance, which subsequent audiences must experience with respect to the dramas themselves. In this way, the plays make a theme of the problem of distantiation, but they also instantiate that problem. The sort of liberal humanism that would unfold (and thus reproduce) the author's mind, Hoagwood argues, can display the ideological criticism in much Romantic drama. To do so is to explicate the historical themes at a first level, inside the dramas and their frames of understanding. A historical hermeneutic is needed, however, to generate an ideological criticism *of* that drama, acknowledging the historical distances (and therefore meanings) that are opened when later generations (including ourselves) engage in interpretative acts from a position of historical removal.

At least two generalizable (but not ubiquitous) tendencies thus characterize many British Romantic dramas, including those mentioned in the following essays and many more that are not: a tendency to thematize history and historical change and a tendency to submerge social and political criticism under the symbolic form of historically removed scenes. Beyond these features of the dramas, no more specialized thesis is imposed on the essays in this volume; they do not, for example, illustrate collectively a contention about the discourse of power, or class-conflict, or textuality. The differentials that the dramas represent reproduce themselves in the multiplicity of polemical projections, but under this methodological variety, the historical preoccupations and historical importance of the Romantic drama do subsist, and we believe further that they emerge into greater clarity.

Notes

1. The extensive notes to the essays that follow list specifically many of these scholarly and critical studies of the Romantic drama. In addition, Hoagwood and Watkins have edited two earlier collections on English Romantic drama that form the basis of the present study. See "Forum: English Romantic Drama," in *Nineteenth-Century Contexts* 15, no. 2 (1991); and *Romantic Drama: Historical and Critical Essays*, in *The Wordsworth Circle* 23, no. 2 (1992).

2. John Kinnaird, comment made during a lecture in College Park, Maryland, 1974.

3. Jerome J. McGann, *The Romantic Ideology: A Critical Investigation* (Chicago and London: University of Chicago Press, 1983).

4. Marjorie Levinson, James K. Chandler, Alan Liu, and others have corrected and extended McGann's argument while focusing mainly on canonical writers and works. See, for instance, Levinson's *Keats's Life of Allegory: The Origins of a Style* (Oxford: Basil Blackwell, 1988); Chandler's *Wordsworth's Second Nature: A Study of the Poetry and Politics* (Chicago and London: University of Chicago Press, 1984); and Liu's *Wordsworth: The Sense of History* (Stanford: Stanford University Press, 1989).

5. See, for instance, Elaine Hadley, "The Old Price Wars: Melodramatizing the Public Sphere's Early-Nineteenth Century England," *PMLA* 107 (1992): 524–37; and Marilyn Gaull, "Romantic Theater," *The Wordsworth Circle*, 14 (1983): 255–63.

6. See Daniel P. Watkins, *A Materialist Critique of English Romantic Drama* (Gainesville: University Press of Florida, 1993); Marjean Purinton, *Romantic Ideology Unmasked: The Mentally Constructed Tyrannies in Dramas of William Wordsworth, Lord Byron, Percy Shelley, and Joanna Baillie* (Newark: University of Delaware Press, 1994); Julie Carlson, *In the Theatre of Romanticism: Coleridge, Nationalism, Women* (Cambridge and N.Y.: Cambridge University Press, 1994); and Gillian Russell, *The Theatres of War: Performance, Politics, and Society, 1793–1815* (Oxford: Clarendon Press, 1995).

1
Romantic Drama and Historical Hermeneutics
Terence Allan Hoagwood

I

Romantic drama was surely underrepresented in scholarly studies of the period's literature for several lifetimes,[1] but in the last decade, the topic and its keywords have proliferated at a surprising rate, like personal web pages, and perhaps for some of the same reasons. As our own culture's interest in literary works declines, and the hegemony of mass-mediated show business increases in corporate, educational, and political institutions, so that the presidential promise of a cathode-ray tube in every classroom is more popular than the older and more frankly carnivorous promise of a chicken in every pot, increasingly anxious and almost audienceless writers of literary scholarship turn, predictably, in larger numbers to the forms of more popular culture.

As I write, in 1996 and at a university, the popularity of a spectacle is more likely to be seen as an opportunity rather than (as it was generations ago) an index of vulgarity. When literary scholars sought respectability, as "English" was becoming a profession, it was high seriousness to which their public presentations aspired. A decade ago, Neil Postman wrote that Las Vegas was "a metaphor of our national character and aspiration," with "a thirty-foot high cardboard picture of a slot machine and a chorus girl." The city, like the society, is "entirely devoted to the idea of entertainment"; and Postman suggests that this idea is not limited to leisure activities. Ours is "a culture in which all public discourse increasingly takes the form of entertainment."[2]

In our own small way, Romanticists have joined that trend: in the 1980s, when Postman wrote that description of America, Romanticists, including Joan Mandell Baum, Richard Allen Cave, Jeffrey N. Cox, Marilyn Gaull, Erika Gottlieb, Terence Hoagwood, Alan Richardson, Daniel P. Watkins, and a host of others, announced that Romantic drama was a neglected genre.[3] The lack of publicity for Romantic drama was widely publicized. I joined the crowd of lone criers at increasingly popular gatherings—convention sessions and even whole conferences—and in densely populated collections of articles in which larger and larger choruses cried out multitudinously that when it came to Romantic drama, no one was paying attention.

In the 1990s, when Mary Shelley's *Frankenstein* was being surrogated by the smash hit *Mary Shelley's Frankenstein* and the typographic *Scarlet Letter* gave way to the cable version, Stephen Behrendt, Julie Carlson, Cox (again), Hoagwood (again), Marjean Purinton, Watkins (again), and others added yet more articles and books to the body of published announcements that Romantic drama was neglected.[4] The shelf began to creak with the weight of critical literature announcing that there was insufficient critical literature.

I write and rewrite these pages in the morning of a day on which my colleagues and I will debate and vote on the termination of assistant professors during budgetarily tight times. This circumstance may have some thematic or even causal continuity with this trend in critical literature.

As television commercials became campy (commercials about commercials), the reflexivity of spectacles about spectacles became a common topic in criticism of Romantic drama. With the popularity of C-SPAN and talk radio, and when G. Gordon Liddy and Mario Cuomo made career changes to become entertainers, criticism of Romantic drama emphasized politics, the anger of grievance groups, and, always, an interest in publicity.

To be underrepresented is to have an opportunity: in an important book on Romantic drama, Julie Carlson has suggested that opportunism is more than an ancillary purpose of many scholarly projects: "generally speaking, women and people of color . . . neither feel particularly constrained by their new access to universities and publishing houses nor view as an index of impotence the conviction that writing is a political act."[5] *Meet the Press. Crossfire.* Shields and Gigot. Opinion polls about opinion polls. Three features of the burgeoning criticism of Romantic drama reflect the popularity of publicity about publicity: ironic reflexivity about the spectacularity of the spectacle (see Woody Allen's *The Purple Rose of Cairo*); a frontal appeal to political anger (see, e.g., Watkins's "Violence, Class Consciousness, and Ideology"); and (always) the claim of neglect.[6]

I suggest that, in contrast to previous generations of literary critics, those of us working on Romantic drama now are not confronted by a lack of interest in the showbiz of Romanticism but rather by the danger that there will be no interest in, or comprehension of, anything else. There is, perhaps, a relationship between the McCarthy hearings and the themes of *A Man for All Seasons* (starring Charlton Heston), but this critical dimension of the film is not what made that Hollywood product popular. It was not the mass psychology of fascism but a set of love stories that movie audiences noticed in the Hollywood version of *Ship of Fools,* and this feature of the public taste may be one reason that Katherine Ann Porter's great novel has not attained the stature it deserves.

Among the multiple frames within which it is valuable to consider Romantic drama—including issues of stage production and the engineering of spectacle, or political topicality, or the anxieties of literary-historical revisionism, abusive treatments of aggrieved groups, or the similarity of plays to TV—the categories of history and historicity are especially important in several ways. These categories are characteristically *subjects* of romantic dramas, though it must be admitted that they become less popular as they are treated more trenchantly; and these categories also furnish critics with an Archimidean vantage on the meanings *of* the genre beyond the meanings *in* it. For example, under suppression in a time of severe political conflict and censorship, the drama's treatment of those events and crises is often figurative rather than explicitly topical. The troubled relationships of reality and fiction accordingly emerge as frequent thematic preoccupations, not because of idealism or psychology but because of materially conditioned restraint and duplicity.

Elizabeth Inchbald formulates these principles concisely. An actress who wrote tragedies and comedies prolifically (and two novels, *A Simple Story* and *Nature and Art*), Inchbald also translated plays from the German and French, and, furthermore, by 1808, she had edited more than one hundred plays to produce a collection of twenty-five volumes. Three years later, she had edited (in a collection of ten more volumes) about fifty modern plays; altogether she wrote more than a hundred essays of dramatic criticism.[7] In an essay on *Julius Caesar,* Inchbald raises the issue of censorship, political suppression, and their effects on the drama: "When men's thoughts are deeply engaged on public events," Inchbald writes, "Historical occurrences, of a similar kind, are only held proper for the contemplation of such minds as know how to distinguish, and appreciate, the good and the evil with which they abound." Audiences of playhouses are not wholly composed of such minds; "therefore, when the circumstances of certain periods make certain incidents of history most interesting, those are the very seasons to interdict their exhibition." Patterns of conflict in the political domain are recapitulated not only in the drama's subject matter, but also in its suppression: "the lovers of the drama will, probably, be compelled to accept of real conspiracies, assassinations, and the slaughter of war, in lieu of such spectacles, ably counterfeited."[8]

Inchbald's writing in that way about *Julius Caesar* suggests something important about drama and theater in the Romantic period. New (Romantic-period) plays and *also* plays from earlier historical periods were subjected to three important operations: they are interpreted to represent public and historical crises; those topics are represented figuratively rather than explicitly; and the relationships of fiction and reality become themes. Inchbald's reference to widespread violence indicates that these concerns are not purely intellectual. *Julius Caesar* was kept off the stage during the Revolutionary decades because the assassination of a monarch was not deemed to be a safe spectacle for public consumption.[9] New works representing revolutionary violence were likewise suppressed. For example, in 1792 Inchbald wrote a play, *The Massacre: Taken from the French*, about the September massacres in Paris in 1792; this work was printed in 1792 but not published and not produced on stage. In her preface to the printed text, she explains why the play did not appear on stage. She quotes Horace Walpole: "The subject is so horrid, that I thought it would shock, rather than give satisfaction to an audience"; the play was, therefore, deemed not "proper to appear on stage."[10]

The horrid behavior that is represented in the play is the intolerable violence of revolutionaries; the play is harshly and horribly critical of mob violence, and yet the fact that it represents such violence *at all* is enough to warrant its suppression. Further, the play's dangerous content brought a second-order suppression to bear on it as well. As James Boaden said, when he published a transcription of the play in 1833, "this play was suppressed, though printed, before publication, in deference to political opinions."[11]

Often, plays written during the Romantic period take in this suppression as a theme. Further, the fact of suppression gives rise to symbolic dodges on the part of writers, and these symbolic dodges in turn generate dramatic reflections on the figurality of dramatic representation itself.[12]

T. S. Eliot argued influentially that criticism should develop a self-conscious distance from the categories of understanding that predominate in the work under study.[13] But Inchbald's statement about political suppression and about the drama's figurations of the real (a symbolic suppression) might help to explain a paradox of long standing: although judgments of its artistic excellence vary notoriously according to the standards one brings to the appreciation of Romantic drama, a consensus that the Romantic drama is generally an artistic failure has sustained itself from the late eighteenth century into the twentieth. At the same time, however, there is no reasonable way to deny the importance of the drama in the cultural life of Europe and Britain in the period surrounding the French Revolution. I suggest that reasons for the preponderantly negative judgment include the plays' refusal to make themselves be about timeless truths and their simultaneous refusal to reduce themselves to the mindless emotional shock of a spectacle (as in what is called "entertainment"). "Censorship is the mother of metaphor," as Jorge Luis Borges has remarked;[14] and romantic drama is much more like a large system of metaphors for historically specific conflicts rather than an arcade of cheap thrills or a temple of eternal truth.

The steadily increasing popularity of the drama during the Romantic period was accompanied, even then, by an increasingly strident chorus of its decriers. Here again, Inchbald's dramatic criticism makes the important point: "It is said, that modern dramas are the worst that ever appeared on the English stage,—yet it is well known, that the English theatres never flourished as they do at present."[15] The consensus about the failure of the period's drama, considered as an art form, is contradicted widely—in the Romantic period as in our own, there is all the while a growing cultural preoccupation with this supposedly failed genre. While in *Mansfield Park* Sir Thomas Bertram is burning copies of *Lovers' Vows* (which, despite disapprobation like Sir Thomas's, was in a twelfth edition in 1799), Charles Lamb and Samuel Taylor Coleridge are publicly deprecating the state of theatrical art; J. G. Lockhart complains of a degradation of the genre; and the Examiner of Plays actively protects the public from perfidious productions by routinely censoring plays on remarkably wide grounds of religious or political problems. At the same time, Lamb and Coleridge continue to write dramas, and Byron writes stageworthy plays though denying that he does so. Byron also serves on the committee for Drury Lane, trying for years to promote the production of Joanna Baillie's plays, for example, while denying that he has an interest in the stage.[16] Among readers and theatergoers alike, the popularity of the drama was riotous.[17]

Loudly contradictory voices may in fact be valuable guides for a historical study of the genre of Romantic drama. Inchbald's statements about the reality of political tyranny and the suppression of plays coincides oddly with the reactionary voice of the censor, whose title was "Examiner of Plays"—George Colman the Younger. Colman was in the act of banning Mary Russell Mitford's *Charles the First* when he said something that—conservative as he was—confirms the point that Inchbald had made in a statement of protest: "the morbid matter," Colman said, "lies in the very bones and marrow of the historical facts."[18]

Of course, drama had always been a public medium, both in its medium of performance and in its subject matter as well. It remains so during the Romantic period, despite misleading clichés about "mental theater."[19] The censorship imposed on the drama by the vigilance of the Examiner of Plays intensified the suppression that the Licensing Act had imposed on the theater since 1737. For example, *King Lear* was removed from production,[20] because of its apparent applicability to George III, the current "old, mad, blind, despised, and dying King," to quote Shelley's description, in "England in 1819."[21] Shelley is clearly adapting a line from Lear, "A poor, infirm, weak, and despised old man" (3.3.20) while transferring Gloucester's blindness to the King. *Helvetic Liberty* was precluded from production at the licensed theaters "primarily because of its political content"; and in 1789, John St. John's *The Island of St. Marguerite*, which includes a mob bursting into revolutionary song ("Assert your freedom / Vindicate the Rights of Man"), was censored.[22]

The political content of dramatic art remained visible, however. Nelson's campaign on the Nile, for example, was elaborately produced on moving stages and with optical effects contrived by Philippe de Loutherbourg. "The Coronation" was lavishly staged at Drury Lane, on a set constructed by a thousand carpenters; and, with a very different ideological content, at Sadler's Wells (an unlicensed theater) *Gallic Freedom; or Vive la Liberté* was produced within two months of the fall of the Bastille in 1789.[23] In France, dramas and melodramas celebrated the ideology and the excitement of revolution; and Thomas Holcroft (who was tried for treason and imprisoned in the Tower in 1794) first used the term "melodrama" in English theater, with his translation of *A Tale of Mystery* in 1802.[24]

Beyond the plays that respond obviously and explicitly to the news of the day, other and more complex plays represent history and historical crises in more latent forms. In Germany, crowds were excited to riot at the first production of Schiller's *Die Räuber* in 1781, and Schiller "was prohibited the use of his pen, under pain of imprisonment," as announced in the Advertisement that appears in Alexander Tytler's translation into English in 1792.[25] From the moment that Tytler's translation appeared the *Robbers* was universally understood in England in terms of the French Revolution, despite the very different meanings that the play had had in Germany in 1781, eight years before the revolution. Tytler's language, in fact, positively calls for that interpretation—as he dies, Charles Moor encourages his loyal band to wage war "to vindicate the rights of man" (218). "No other play of the period had a comparable impact," as Jonathan Wordsworth has said.[26] In *Osorio* and *Remorse*, Coleridge adapts large elements from Schiller's prerevolutionary play in his own postrevolutionary setting.[27] Much of the revolutionary content of *Osorio* (1797) was erased before the play appeared publicly (in print and on stage) under the title *Remorse* in 1813, but that revolutionary content illustrates the same tendency that both Inchbald and Colman had described: the plays' ideological content and political importance are customarily displaced symbolically and dispersed across exotic, magical, or historically removed surface content. That ideological and political content is important in two ways: sometimes, it appears by explicit and intentional design ("Vindicate the Rights of Man," in *The Island of St. Marguerite*); sometimes that content is presented in latent form, as when, in Inchbald's *The Massacre*, the political valence does not protect it from suppression if the play deals with the violence of the French Revolution at all. Sometimes (as in Mitford's *Charles the First*) it is some other, earlier, but analogous revolutionary violence that is represented; or (as in Joanna Baillie's *Constantine Paleologus*) the insurrectionary conflict is resituated in a historically remote and exotic scene.

The central fact about Romantic drama is this suppression and consequent displacement of revolutionary sociopolitical content. This is the case whether we understand these sets of meanings to be products of conscious authorial intention or rather matters of the political unconscious. (For example, no one, not even the Examiner of Plays, thought that Shakespeare advocated the killing of George III in *Julius Caesar;* and yet the meanings of a production of that play were perceived, in the revolutionary decade, to include the *currently* feared revolutionary violence.) Historical forces and conflicts—even immediate conflicts—are less frequently portrayed literally (as in *The Fall of Robespierre* by Coleridge and Southey) after the Treason Trials of 1794. Instead, such issues are more often represented symbolically and moved into historically and geographically removed settings—in the period of the Crusades (as in Wordsworth's *The Borderers*); in Tudor England (as in Schiller's *Mary Stuart*); in central Europe during the Thirty Years' War (in Byron's *Werner*); in seventeenth-century England (as in Lamb's *John Woodvil*, Shelley's *Charles the First*, and Godwin's *Faulkener*); in sixteenth-century Spain (as in *Osorio*); in Rome in 1599 *(The Cenci);* and in a variety of yet more distant locations as well.

II

A clear example of political polemic that is not veiled at all, except in the most transparent satire, is the first act of *The Bugaboo. A Dramatic Poem. by R.S.*, published in 1817 by T. J. Wooler, in the first volume of *The Black Dwarf*. The characters—Curseallray, Cunning, Widemouth, Sir W. Blubber, and Smellplot—not only are vehicles for attacking government in comical verse, but the verse drama is also *meta*dramatic and metapoetic in its themes. It is introduced by a note (by "J. H. G.") claiming that this verse drama was written by the laureate (Southey), whose *Wat Tyler* had been recently republished, to his embarrassment. Internally, the play treats spies, traitors, conspiracies, and plots, while externally the tropes of duplicity are numerous as well. Southey did write *Wat Tyler*, though its republication in 1817 was a gesture of attack on him, because of his own reversed political position; Southey did not write *The Bugaboo*, which is, rather, satirically attributed to him by a mock-admirer who acknowledges that the piece is "of less poetical but of more political interest" [*The Black Dwarf*, 1 (1817):207].

This metadramatic and metapoetic preoccupation of the play is not unique to Wooler's satire, but it is characteristic in the dramatic writings of the period. The use (in politics, for example, as well as art) of deceptive and frequently symbolic screens is the subject of many plays of the period. To mention only one more example, *Pan Kives Ken Kow! Or, Three Kneelings and Nine Knocks!!! A Dramatic Entertainment in One Act* (also published by Wooler in 1817) sets itself in an Asian court; Chum Chi Fow Long Bum is "A Prince of Wang Wong," visited by Noddleguard (ambassador from Seagirt) who is accompanied by Quizall who is in turn accompanied by an Interpreter. Duplicity is a theme in two ways: the obvious satirical treatment of England and its diplomacy, under the comically exotic substitutes, is a transparent duplicity; and it is accompanied by a satirical display of trickery.

An earlier and equally transparent example of symbolic screening is the anonymous translation, *Dialogues of the Gods*, originally written in German by G. M. Wieland, which was published in English translation in 1795 by Joseph Johnson, the foremost radical publisher in England in the Revolutionary years. In this sequence, Jupiter, Juno, Semiramis, Henry IV, and Louis XIV discuss the celebration of the French Federation. The analogy with Shelley's mythological displacements in *Prometheus Unbound* and *Hellas* is obvious. To compare Shelley's lyrical dramas with *Dialogues of the Gods* is to allow some meanings to become more apparent. Shelley's dramas and Wieland's, like Wooler's in the *Black Dwarf*, include a reflexive theme, whereby their own signifying practices—speech, writing, forms of thought and art—are assimilated with openly political levels of reference. At the same time, and in the same way, political action is represented as a duplicitous and discursive practice.

Obviously satirical fictions such as *Pan Kives Ken Kow* and mythological figurations such as the *Dialogues of the Gods* illustrate two of the frequently used symbolic resources of the drama of the period. Another means by which dramatists of the period represent contemporary political conflicts under the safety of a symbolic screen involves the use of English history as a source of parallels for contemporary figures and events. An excellent example of this displacement into distant English history is George Watson's *England Preserved*.[28] Rather than treat Oliver Cromwell and the English Revolution directly as an analogy for the democratic revolutions of the eighteenth century, a fairly widespread symbolic choice whose dangers for playwrights are explained by Johnston and Nicholes in the present volume, Watson displaces his content yet again, choosing a different "Lord Protector"—the earl of Pembroke, who, in 1422, assumed that title as ward of the infant king. Lord Pembroke is furiously angry with his son, who has seditiously allied himself with French forces (which is what Charles James Fox, among others, was accused of doing in 1795, when the play was written). The earl's penitent son returns, however, loyally to the fold, saying, "Disgraceful day, / That saw us leagued with France!" (317). The earl of Chester warns that for too long England has been "to riot and rebellion loosed" (312). This play was written during a year of riot, sedition, charges of sedition, war with France, and treason trials. The events taking place while the play was written are obviously analogous with those historically removed actions that form its content. During the Protectorate, Cromwell did in fact achieve peace with France, Portugal, and also the Dutch States-General, and so Watson is able to produce the lord protector as an important model for peacemakers in the current war against France; but in the year of the Gagging Acts, he is also able to attack the bloodshed and futility of treason in ways that were beneficial for production at the Theatres Royal.

Raymond Williams has suggested (and Watkins has argued specifically in connection with Baillie's *DeMonfort*[29]) that historical forces express themselves in ways larger than authorial intention. The collapse of the feudal order and the emergence of industrial capitalism, Williams suggests, may underlie the anxieties, violence, fragmentation, and disorder that are so common among the Romantic dramas, with their settings among castles that decay, dungeons from which new forces burst free, and political battling in which (in disaster or triumph) they figure the anxieties and conflicts of the Revolutionary decades—whether by crafty authorial design or under the power of the "historical unconscious," which (in Watkins's argument) determines alike the play and the sensibility of its playwright. In either case, the plays can fruitfully be understood as figurations of historical conflict and change. I would add that this displaced content appears alike in the mythic displacements of *Prometheus Unbound* or the magical scenes of *Manfred,* no less than the manifestly historical preoccupations of other plays of the period.

Sometimes the symbolic displacements of the Romantic dramas involve conflicted systems of belief rather than persons or parties. Joanna Baillie's *Constantine Paleologus: or, The Last of the Caesars* presents the historical pattern of an imperiled monarch whose old order is under siege; like Coleridge's *Osorio* (and in fact like many works of the period, including Scott's *The Fire-King* of 1801), Baillie's play puts Moslems (in the act of besieging Christians) in a role analogous to the French Revolutionaries attacking the inherited monarchies of Europe. Baillie's play begins with the trope of historical change, which is voiced by loyalists of the emperor who are under attack:

> This dismal siege begin! 'Midst level ruin,
> Ah, see how sadly changed the prospect is
> Since first from our high station we beheld
> This dismal siege begin! 'Midst level ruin,
> Our city now shows but its batter'd
>   towers.[30]

The common topic of threatened wealth is raised: "What boots it now, encompassed thus with foes, / And death and ruin grinning at our side, / To set forth all this sumptuous garniture?" (448). The emperor uses the trope, common in the dramas of the period, which conflates material and political conflicts with mental and ideological operations: "Mine armourer, methinks, has better skill/To mar men's heads than save them" (449).

In this scene of fright and destruction, a citizen bursts into the imperial palace with a report of revolutionary violence, which is much like the messenger's description of Paris during the September Massacres of 1792 in Inchbald's *The Massacre.* In Baillie's play, "The citizens in crowds—the men and women—/ The very children too—mine eyes have seen it—/ In crowds they come" (450–51). In *The*

Massacre, violent crowds, including murderous children with knives who are stabbing other ten-year-old children, are reported to be overrunning the streets and even the prisons of Paris, murdering thousands in revolutionary fury. In Baillie's play, "the city / Is in commotion; e'en with flesh-forks arm'd, / and all the implements of glutt'nous sloth, / The people pour along in bawling crowds, / Calling out 'bread'" (451). In both plays, these mobs call on besieged royalty and aristocracy to surrender.

Inchbald's play, clearly, presents the French revolutionary violence literally, as a mob uprising in Paris in 1792; and her play was suppressed "in deference to political opinions." Baillie, whom Inchbald calls "a woman of genius,"[31] resituates the action in a scene at once historically removed and fictionalized; but the action, the historical pattern, and the meaning of the incident survive under this fictionalized and symbolic form. The analogy of *Constantine Paleologus* with *The Massacre* is a matter of their historical engagements, the political reference of the plays in their revolutionary and postrevolutionary time and place; the analogy of *Constantine Paleologus* with *Prometheus Unbound* and *Hellas* is a matter of the symbolic form within which that historical meaning is embodied.

A similar kind of displacement appears in Watson's play, *England Preserved*. Whereas *The Robbers*, *Bertram*, and *The Castle Spectre* remove the motif of rebellion and dispossession into a Gothic fantasy, Watson's play (like *The Robbers*, *Lover's Vows*, *Osorio*, *The Adopted Child*, and many other plays of the period) uses a drama of *historical* displacement. *England Preserved* also places the philosophical problem of perception, deception, illusion, and interpretation in a solidly political context.[32] William Mareschal's speech in which he calls his misguided alliance with the hostile French forces a form of "madness" continues in this way:

> as the eaglet gazes on the sun
> Till every object shows to him in fire,
> My fancy, warmed by Freedom's fiercest flame,
> Imaged her form, where she, alas! was not.
>
> (317)

No one seeing this play at Covent Garden in 1795 (in the time of the notorious treason trials), or reading it in Inchbald's edition in 1811 (during the war against France and in the year when mob violence erupted in Nottinghamshire and Yorkshire) would have understood those lines from *England Preserved* chiefly in reference to the play's ostensible setting between 1422 and 1428. The misguided and rebellious support of the French, in the apparent cause of freedom, which degenerated in actuality to another bloody tyranny, obviously had reference to current crises in the years in which the play was written, acted, and published. And so did the problem of political mistake, misinterpretation, delusion, and change of mind, as Watson treats it in this play.

William Moreschal's speech about the optical illusion caused by gazing on the sun is strikingly analogous with this precisely contemporary political argument: "Every one must, at least for the present, view the french revolution through a coloured medium," according to the *Analytical Review*'s article on John Moore's *A View of the Causes and Progress of the French Revolution*.[33] In Moore's words, "By contemplating political questions often in one point of view, men are very apt to be at last convinced that what is most favourable to their own private interest, is also most for the interest of the public"; the error of that apparent service to the cause of the people later becomes evident.[34] In act 2 of *England Preserved*, the machinations of the invading French leader, deceiving the English supporters of liberty, has obvious topical reference in 1795: Charles James Fox led the minority of opposition to Pitt's war against France, and he was widely seen as a supporter of the French who threatened invasion. Gillray's *French Telegraph making Signals in the Dark* (January 1795), for example, portrays Fox holding a beacon for the invading French fleet and directing them to London. Watson's play, under the guise of an incident in the early fifteenth century, portrays this position of the English lovers of liberty as a case of delusion.

Beyond the political allegory, the play raises an important metadramatic theme. Alone with his minion, the invading French prince scoffs at his own oath. When the English lovers of liberty arrive, the prince's minion says deceptively that France "rescued you from our oppression's gripe" (322); the French prince and his minion talk of "faith and truth" though they had scoffed at their own oaths. Watson's play treats unmistakably the issue of French revolutionary intentions with respect to England, when the English lovers of liberty naively ask, will you honor your "oath to keep our liberties entire?" (322). From the counterrevolutionary perspective of Watson's play, this question represents the quixotic delusion of radicals such as Richard Price, whose *Discourse on the Love of Our Country* (in 1789) had welcomed the French Revolution under the belief that its principles were consistent with the promise of liberty from the Glorious Revolution.

Happy expectations are undermined, in *England Preserved*, by the analogy of another English Revolution. Surrey says that lovers of liberty have, in the past, committed regicide (as Wordsworth likewise pointed out in his *Letter to the Bishop of Llandaff* of 1793, unpublished at the time); and he suggests that lovers of liberty are prepared to kill a king again. The executions of Charles I and Louis XVI were analogized frequently in the period,[35] and even before the execution of Louis XVI, George III was portrayed as anxious about whether he might suffer Charles's fate.[36] In a play produced so shortly after the execution of Louis XVI and the Reign of Terror, the meaning of this talk of regicide would be quite plain.[37] *England Preserved* repudiates the revolutionary violence as a profound mistake, a product of ideological delusion.

Individualistic appeals to enjoyment—with a concomitant emphasis on psychological rather than historical meanings—have perhaps predominated in America during the era of commercial television in part because literary criticism has had (consciously or unconsciously) a self-interest in the sale (literally and figuratively) of literary works. The historical distance of a literary work hardly seems like a selling point, from a marketing point of view; customers are thought to prefer a belief that the product is pertinent to themselves. Understanding of the historical displacements of the romantic drama has been delayed until fairly recently by a speciously personalistic construction of what the plays (including *Manfred* and *Prometheus Unbound*) are about. The category of "mental theatre" (a phrase which Byron used) and the medium of presentation (lyrical drama, closet drama, and otherwise drama to be read) have frequently been thought to sever the dramas' meanings from the public domain, making them interesting to new generations of customers by resituating their meanings and their medium in the private realm of mentality.

Byron and other playwrights of the Romantic period did not invent drama consigned to written rather than spoken form. Seneca's tragedies, by the traditional account of them, were composed as plays to be read rather than staged. But Byron's sentence, which uses the phrase "mental theatre" (in a letter to Lady Byron 14 September 1821), makes his public purposes explicit, as I have already pointed out. The medium of mental theater does not privatize its topics: it portrays ideology rather than psychology. Any student of the period even moderately conversant with its political philosophy—found, for example, in the work of Rousseau, Burke, Godwin, Condorcet, Holbach, Paine, Thelwall, and Coleridge—will be aware that the category of mental formations and reformations was normally understood as a *political* category. Political thought in the eighteenth century normally turned on the dialectical relationship of mentality and material conditions. An oft-cited example whose imagery is important in the Romantic drama is Rousseau's observation that "slaves lose everything in their chains, even the desire to escape from them."[38] Rousseau certainly refers to a mental phenomenon, though hardly in terms of merely private concerns. Godwin says, bluntly enough, that "the opinions of men [are], for the most part, under the absolute control of political institution."[39] To suppose that a mental theater somehow cannot (or even to suppose that Byron's mental theater does not) engage itself with social issues, even at the level of conscious authorial intention, would be an anachronistic mistake.

Other reasons, even beyond those that Byron suggests, can also help to explain why it is that the English or European stage would not admit drama of the sort that Byron describes. In its review of Elizabeth Inchbald's *Lovers' Vows* (a translation of Kotzebue's *Das Kind der Liebe* and the very book that Sir Thomas was burning in *Mansfield Park*—and I am especially pleased to mention Jane Austen because only a season ago, as I write, the moviegoing public enjoyed a commercial production entitled *Sense and Sensibility*), Joseph Johnson's *Analytical Review* observes "that tragedy, though supported by admirable talent, languishes in neglect . . . *Lovers' Vows* has not been more popular than *Castle Spectre*, and both must submit to the more attractive charms of *Blue Beard*."[40] The tendency of crowds to clamor for spectacles becomes a theme in Romantic plays that treat their own mode of representation metadramatically.[41]

When crowds clamor for the execution of Mary Stuart in Schiller's *Mary Stuart,* Schiller (who was invited by the French National Assembly to become an honorary citizen 1792) raises this issue about popular spectacles. His play invokes political meanings, obviously, but it also represents critically its *own* situation with regard to actual audiences. The beheading of the heroine, which the mob screams to see, is produced as an analogy for the September Massacres, the bloody purge of the Girondin, the execution of Louis XVI and Marie Antoinette, and the Reign of Terror. Plays like *Mary Stuart* treat critically their own audience's clamoring for brutish spectacle, but the clamoring crowds are also a massively *political* problem. The "rabble" in Inchbald's *The Massacre,* including the murderous children, is an obvious example. The spectacular representation and the political problem are analogues precisely because collective mental formations constitute their latent content and their enabling conditions.

A paradigmatic plot emerges among Romantic-period dramas, as I have suggested, appearing influentially in Schiller's plays—especially *The Robbers*. This fact of widespread reproduction of plot elements suggests something about the social and cultural scale of the preoccupations that the plays manifest. For example, the political conflict between brothers is widely reproduced in plays of the period, often generalized—as Schiller generalizes it—in tropes of dispossession, disinheritance, exile, and violent inversions of traditional hierarchies of power: in *The Robbers,* after hearing Francis's false account of Charles, and after she has repelled his attempt to seduce her, Amelia says, in soliloquy, "Out cast, did he say? the world is then unhinged:—Outcasts are kings, and kings are outcasts!" (25).

The issue of wealth is routinely coupled, critically, with inherited structures of power, and Amelia deprecates "the pageant triumphs of the rich and great"; in the next scene, Charles (also in soliloquy) says, "What a damn'd inequality in the lot of mankind!—While the gold lies useless in the mouldy coffer of the miser, the leaden hand of poverty checks the daring flight of youth, and chills the fire of enterprise" (26).

Besides Coleridge's adaptations of Schiller's plot, to which I have already referred, numerous plays (some of which are now scarcely remembered) reproduce its ingredients. In 1795, for example, Samuel Birch's play, *The Adopted Child,* appeared.[42] The play "exhibits a plot against the life of an heir to an ancient castle, that his destroyer might become possessed of the estate, and the person of the next female heiress," in the apt words of the article on Birch's play which appeared in the *Analytical Review* promptly after the production of the play at Drury Lane.[43] This play warrants some attention here, because, in an example that has received no critical attention for two hundred years, it illustrates clearly some of the recurrent features of the drama of the period—including the drama's preoccupation with the categories of history and the survival of the revolutionary anxieties under conditions of authorial, institutional, and symbolic suppression.

In *The Adopted Child,* Sir Bertrand with his cohort Le Sage seeks to seize ownership of Milford Castle. The rightful (hereditary) owner, Sir Edmund, had died from an accident at sea; his son had been saved from that accident by the honest innkeeper Michael, who did not know the identity of Edmund and his son. As Edmund lies dying on the beach to which Michael has hauled his drowning body, he entrusts Michael with a locked trunk containing the secret of the boy's identity. Michael of course leaves the secret locked in the trunk; he raises the boy as if he were his own son. When Bertrand and Le Sage arrive, the daughter of Sir Edmund (Clara) is living in a convent, and so the only occupants of Milford Castle are Mr. Record the steward and Lucy, a servant. A minion of Bertrand (named Spruce) arrives first; Record locks him in a room in the castle and goes to the honest innkeeper Michael for help and information. In his absence, Lucy releases Spruce and a flirtation ensues. Meanwhile, at the inn, Michael has revealed the secret of the boy's identity to his wife Nell. When Record returns, Lucy hides the flirtatious Spruce in a suit of black armor.

During the emergency of this threatened usurpation by Bertrand, Michael has lodged the boy in the convent where his sister Clara resides. Bertrand's minion Flint is on his way to that convent to seize the boy, but Michael intercepts him, learns that Bertrand plans to send the boy and the girl over the sea, and disguises himself in the garments of the minion whom he has waylaid. Michael takes the boy from the convent to Milford Castle where Clara is confronting Bertrand. On Michael's arrival, disguises are removed, secret documents are produced revealing Bertrand's plot and Edmund's will, the castle is restored to its heir, and "tenants of the estate" (villagers) arrive to defend the hereditary heir. The play closes in a happy song of restoration.

Clearly, at the level of plot this play tries to celebrate (or advocate) restoration of power to the ancien regime. In 1795, amidst Treason Trials, after the Reign of Terror, and during the escalating war with the revolutionary French, this doctrinal content is intelligible enough. Despite these obvious doctrinal intentions, however, the *Adopted Child* raises and reveals revolutionary anxieties that those intentions cannot entirely control. The usurper Le Sage, for example, calls Michael and the boy "usurpers" (8), generating a duplicity and reversal which is written large in the political history of the period. Who is usurper and who is usurped are questions over which there is profound disagreement. The troubled question of the will of the people, too, is made explicit: Record says that the villagers will "assert the right of our new baron against injury and oppression" (8). Referring to "rights" and to "oppression" in this way, the play engages itself in the conflicted discourse which had grown louder and yet more conflicted. Burke's *Reflections on the Revolution in France* uses the terms "rights" and "oppression" and describes the interest and the general will of the people in ways that exactly reverse their usage in the democratic documents he was concerned to oppose—the French *Declaration of Rights* and Price's *Discourse on the Love of Our Country*.

In other ways, too, the *Adopted Child* treats political conflict and its discourses in terms of calculated duplicity. In the armor in which Lucy hides the usurper's minion, Spruce, and in the disguise that Michael dons, posing as the usurper himself, the trope of deception is obvious; it involves likewise the heir to the baron living as a poor boy, unbeknownst to all, including Michael, who for years had not opened the trunk. This motif of noble offspring raised in the disguise of poverty is, of course, a traditional and even ancient commonplace: examples include Guiderius and Arviragus in *Cymbeline*. The *Pandosto* of Robert Greene and the story of Perdita in *The Winter's Tale* (Mary Robinson's most famous role) are also clear examples. The classical locus is *Oedipus Rex*, in the unknown and royal identity of the slayer of Laius. But the *Adopted Child* appropriates the motif in a way that is specific to its immediate time, as I shall try to show by placing the drama in its temporal context.

Near the end of the play, Michael defends his adopting disguise to confound the usurpers: "'Tis lawful in some cases to hoist false colours; and d—— if I must play the hypocrite, 'tis better to wear the villain's outside, so I am right and tight within, than to clothe a heart rotten at the core with the robes of honesty" (8). In its immediate context in the plot of the drama, this speech is surprising because it is needless; the clarity of the usurpers' evil and Michael's redemptive goodness, with respect to the rightful heir, hardly require an excuse within the moral frame of the play. In comedy, Aphra Behn's *The Rover*, among countless earlier examples, uses the trope of disguise and mistaken identity far more than the *Adopted Child*, and none of the characters who employ that stratagem needs to apologize for it. In tragedy, in *King Lear* the device of disguise is laden with positive moral agency. Michael's speech, however, has a contemporary application: it is also in 1795 that Coleridge, in his *Moral and Political Lecture*, denounces the government's use of disguised agents provocateur. In 1794, the government's Committee of Secrecy announced that it had detected a "traitorous conspiracy"; and the government, with some frequency, hired agents to enter excitable crowds, in disguise, and to incite riots, including the Church and King mobs that destroyed Priestley's house, library, and laboratory in Birmingham, and attacked Thomas Hardy's house while he was imprisoned in the Tower.

It is plausible that Birch places Michael's speech in the *Adopted Child* in 1795 to allude to the government's use of spies in that year and in the preceding year, in the collection of evidence for the treason trials of John Thelwall, Thomas Holcroft, and others; but such a claim about Birch's specific and conscious intention is not what I want to emphasize here. Instead, I mean to point out that the play's audience in 1795 received the play while this issue of disguised political agents was daily salient in the public mind. Like the regicide in *Julius Caesar* and like the madness and blindness of the king in *King Lear*, this traditional trope gathers meanings, in 1795, that are peculiar to that time. Produced, reproduced, and understood in its historical moment, the play represents a transfiguration of its traditional motifs.

In Inchbald's translation from Kotzebue, with her title *Lovers' Vows*, the power struggle is transposed to father and son, but this play reproduces the paradigm of dispossession, disinheritance, threatened violence, and sexual exploitation. Kotzebue's notoriously ambiguous or contradictory political intentions are not the issue that I would explore here; he was, and was thought to be, radical and reactionary at once or by turns.[44] Further, the play is already a corporate production, being a translation by Inchbald of a play by Kotzebue. It cannot be an apt icon of *any* sort of individualism or personalism in its meanings. And just as the play's plot embeds conventional elements, so, too, many of its meanings are generated and conditioned by its historical field rather than simply intentional design, construed as the conscious purposes of its maker.

In *Lover's Vows*, Frederick meets his mother begging in a road; he learns for the first time that he is the illegitimate son of Baron Wildenhaim. His mother is apparently starving. Attempting to rob the baron, Frederick "swore he'd have the baron's life, / Or else another dollar."[45] He is arrested and taken off to prison, after which a confrontation between Frederick and the baron ensues. Frederick angrily speaks of the riches, cruelty, and power of his father; the baron's abandonment of his seduced mother; and the extreme inequalities in wealth with which he is surrounded. His confession is furious—"I am a prisoner—I will not be free—I am a robber . . . I, in despair, will, to the last moment, call for retribution on my father" (4.2).

This sequence of intrafamilial political machinations and conflict is an old story. In *The Robbers*, Schiller also draws on an old form of story, whose earlier examples include the conflict of Edmund and Edgar in *King Lear*. The plots of Birch and of Kotzebue/Inchbald draw on patterns from Gothic and sentimental fiction, and they draw likewise on the form of story found most obviously in *Hamlet*. Kotzebue and Inchbald apply these old patterns of political conflict in pointedly contemporary ways. Greg Kucich has shown how Romantic-period critics, including Hazlitt, treated Kotzebue's plays as extreme in their representation of new and insurrectionary opinions.[46] Inchbald says that the contemporary "Dramatic Writer exists but under a despotic government."[47]

Maturin's *Bertram* makes use of the same cluster of plot elements and political themes, as Coleridge points out in his review of that play (substantially reprinted in *Biographia Literaria*). Bertram "out-herod[s] Charles de Moor in the Robbers";[48] the play presents a band of robbers, "thieves, pirates, and assassins," who enact political usurpation and murder. Coleridge points out that the play's motifs link it, in one sense, to earlier drama—he mentions the episodes of Edgar in *King Lear* and more generally "the *Libertine,* (Shadwell's adaptation of the *Atheista Fulminato* to the English stage in the reign of Charles the Second)" (2:221); but Coleridge begins with an explicit effort to differentiate the play from analogous dramas of early periods. *Bertram* is an illustration of "the modern jacobinical drama"; the popularity of this contemporary form, Coleridge writes, "consists in the confusion and subversion of the natural order of things . . . rewarding . . . those criminals whom law, reason, and religion have excommunicated" (2:221).

Usurpation, political violence, and a critique of power structures appear in "jacobinical drama," rather than a merely topical reference to particular events. Wordsworth's *Borderers* represents revolutionary action similarly. And a related cluster of plot elements appears in Baillie's *DeMonfort*. After he has killed his political rival, Rezenvelt, DeMonfort describes himself in terms allusive to the *Robbers* and much like those which Coleridge uses to disparage the genre as a whole: "I am a man, of holy claims bereft; / Out from the pale of social kindred cast; / Nameless and horrible."[49] Byron's *Werner* very evidently uses generically recognizable elements of plot and theme. Conflicts and central preoccupations are thematized culturally, across societies, and not merely within the textual limits of particular plays. In *Werner,* as in *Lovers' Vows* and the *Adopted Child,* the motif of the disinherited son, who has suffered hardship and consequently commits crimes, returns; like Frederick in the play of Kotzebue/Inchbald, Siegendorf has been a soldier and is now a beggar; like DeMonfort or like Charles de Moor, he is an "outcast"; like Frederick and Charles de Moor, he speaks angrily of "wealth in poverty";[50] and "bandit warfare" is a central element in the plot (as it is in the *Robbers* and *Bertram*). Byron explains the analogy of bandit warfare and national conquest far more explicitly than Schiller or Kotzebue or Maturin. The theme of the "disinherited prodigal" (581) is obviously a common motif, and so is the reunion of the lost son (in this case Ulric) with his mother (575). The motif of the mother-son reunion, under conditions of patriarchal oppression, is made explicit again in William Godwin's *Faulkener,* and so is the linkage of sexual exploitation with political conflict.

Plot features, which thus emerge as culturally thematic, appear likewise in Coleridge's *Zapolya*. In that play, Emerick is called "Emperor," a term whose connotations in the political world in which Coleridge writes were pointed out by Carlson in 1992.[51] Emerick kills his brother, the King Andreas. Intensifying the motif of abandonment by a patriarchal tyrant that appears in Kotzebue's play, Coleridge's tyrant attempts to kill Queen Zapolya and the infant Bethlen, while Emerick attempts to rape Lady Sarolta. (Later, Shelley's *The Cenci* in turn intensifies this linkage of political, sexual, and intrafamilial violence.) In *Zapolya*, the reunion of Bethlen with his mother is obviously analogous with the scene of Frederick and Agatha in Inchbald's earlier play, *Lovers' Vows*, and likewise in *Faulkener* and in *Werner*. The band of rebels, the conflict between brothers, the disinherited son, politically motivated murder, patriarchal control of women, assassins, and dungeons are also important elements of the plot in *Osorio*.

Dramas had always treated historical subjects, and they had always represented cultural features of the world in which they were made. Cultural products can scarcely avoid doing that. The British drama of the Romantic period exhibits, however, some tenacious and specifiable preoccupations. The assassin motif in *Remorse* or *Death's Jest Book* or the *Borderers* operates differently from the assassin motif in Middleton's *The Changeling* or in *Hamlet*; usurpation in the *Robbers* and in *Zapolya* differs from usurpation in *MacBeth* or *The Tempest*; the imagination of "slave shak[ing] off his chains" in Massinger's *The Bondman* differs from that imagination in *Osorio*; and its Elizabethan setting demands our recognition that *Mary Stuart* dramatizes the violence of political change differently from the Elizabethan plays that furnish the plots that the Romantic dramatist transforms.

III

The operative concept of historicity as a hermeneutic problem is a Romantic idea. In 1808 Friedrich Ast, for example, points out that historical meanings within a work become evident only when a critical understanding of the spirit of the age makes them evident; and in 1805 Friedrich Schleiermacher points out the extent to which historical meanings appear only under the analysis of historical differentiations: diachronically as well as synchronically, "all concepts proceed from contrasts. Perception becomes absorbed in inflection."[52]

The hermeneutic operation, which is an historicizing of the work and its meanings, cannot be strictly something that we in the twentieth century do to the particular Romantic works under analysis; that hermeneutical operation inhabits the Romantic works themselves, as their propositional content. The Kantian recognition that every understanding is mediated by categories of the faculty of understanding—even constituted by them—becomes, in the tradition of Romantic hermeneutics, a recognition that those categories themselves are historically conditioned.

This principle is retrospectively expressed in Dilthey's historicism. Whether or not writers express them consciously and intentionally, cultural products reveal the pressures, limits, and differences of their historically removed moment of production; and from this fact follows the insusceptibility of cultural products to abstraction—meanings can be differentiated but not abstractly formulated. At the same time that mental structures are subject to historical variability, historical structures and experiences themselves are interpretatively constituted in the first instance: "All exegesis of written works is only the systematic working out of that general process of Understanding which stretches throughout our lives and is exercised upon every type of speech or writing"; and therefore "the theory of interpretation becomes an essential connecting link between philosophy and the historical disciplines, an essential component in the foundation of the human studies themselves."[53]

Dilthey's description of historical hermeneutics is more than a prescription for scholarship in the humanities; it is a characterization of a principle in the cognitive content of nineteenth-century works themselves. Not only do the Romantic dramas, for example, come to us under the condition of their own historicity, but they thematize historicity as a condition. What appears in the narrowly factual domain of political history as a dissolution of traditional hierarchies (feudalism and monarchy) replicates itself in epistemological terms as a dissolution of the categories of certitude and, in aesthetics, a problematizing of the adequacy (or possibility) of representation. Dilthey's influential essay on the development of hermeneutic thought suggests that, prior to Schleiermacher's hermeneutics, historical interpretation tended to be contained in the notion of a "human nature, ever self-identical in its religious and ethical formation." In its earlier interpretative mode, meanings are understood to be "limited by place and time in a merely external fashion"; but from the vantage of historical understandings formulated after Schleiermacher's hermeneutics, "such a conception is non-historical" (Dilthey 109). Historicity constructs the human nature itself. The drama of Romanticism includes (as earlier dramas do not) a critique of its own epistemic relativity, considered as a product of its own historicity. It is a Romantic idea that history constitutes the categories of understanding and that *therefore* "all understanding remains partial and can never be terminated" (Dilthey, 113).

The viciousness of regress implied by Dilthey's formulation has much to do with the notorious anxiety and apparent nihilism of many Romantic dramas: Dilthey's sentence is not about the world, even about understandings of the world; Dilthey's sentence is about understandings of understandings of the world. The problem that Dilthey's essay declares is not safely philosophical: the proposition that historicity constitutes understandings *while* it undermines their authority is a Romantic idea, and it is a self-applicable proposition. But that concept of history is itself historically specific. A historical hermeneutic must seek to grasp both the concept and its historical distance (its datability). This idea also entails depersonalization: any idea is independent of any single author's cognized intentions; the notion of unconscious determinants of artistic creation implies as much; and this is also a Romantic idea (Dilthey, 113).

Two cases in point are especially instructive. As I have pointed out, Colman bans the production of Mitford's play, *Charles the First,* despite what he understands to be her loyalist purposes; his doing so exhibits his own awareness that meanings are not under the control of authorial intention. In the case of Inchbald's translation of the anonymous French play the *Massacre,* no meanings that are textually derivable can be assigned accurately to either author; and, further, the suppression of that play in response to others' political anxieties (as Boaden reports) removes the issues further from Inchbald's control and even further from the control of the anonymous French author. The play emerges from cultural matrices, and immediately it enters others. The determining power of these matrices of production and reception hopelessly escapes any hermeneutic of individual and authorial intention.

A heuristic dichotomy, therefore, between "history" as a set of conjunctural facts external to the dramas (for example, the imprisonment of Holcroft in 1794) and "history" as a description of the dramas' topicality (for example, the English Revolution in Mitford's *Charles the First*) rapidly becomes impertinent. The dramas characteristically worry their own representational status in part because they thematize the inevitable vanishing of their own frames of reference.

As I have tried to suggest, circumstances external to the Romantic dramas (including censorship, the Licensing Act, and the Gagging Acts) do condition the Romantic displacement of political themes. That act of displacement itself, however, gives rise to a shift in the meanings of the history that is thus represented in displaced forms.

The symbolic figuration of historical content discloses the figurality of that historical content itself. That is, symbolic displacement of historical conflicts reveals the extent to which the contents of external historical conflicts are themselves constructed in the first place, as products of variable interpretative systems that become visible only when they have vanished. Historicity's damaging implications for certitudes are raised by the symbolic strategies of the Romantic dramas. The plays raise this issue willy-nilly: the problem is a feature of the mode of representation and not only the content represented.

Tieck's *Puss in Boots* is an excellent instance of this duality, whereby the mode of figurative representation becomes the subject of the drama itself. *Puss in Boots* represents the act of representation as a problem; this is the strategy of the placement of the play within the play, allowing the drama's subject matter to be representationality itself. All the related issues—illusion, deception, trickery—are presented and interpreted in political context. As Burwick has said, "Tieck's satire implicates the illusory nature of all political authority."[54] To stop with the establishment of Tieck's intention would be to miss a larger and more important feature of the Romantic dramas and of their modes of meaning: it can be said with equal accuracy that Birch's play the *Adopted Child* and Mitford's *Charles the First* portray "the illusory nature of all political authority"; but both these plays manifestly do not want to mean any such thing. Those plays want to deplore instability, but, as Colman recognized, their submerged anxieties betray and foment exactly that which they would suppress.

In a reflexive operation that becomes common in the period, often a Romantic drama constitutes an interpretative act performed upon historical materials that are themselves represented as interpretative constructions: the *Geist* of the *Zeit* which is portrayed is manifestly placed in relationship with the *Geist* of the *Zeit* that portrays it. Movement among times becomes a topic and a theme, and so does the efficacy of times in the formation of systems of understanding. Categories of objective history are shown to be involved in the construction of subjects and of subjectively maintained thought-formations. As a result, no dichotomy of subject and object can adequately paraphrase the dramas' meanings—no story, for example, to the effect that *Manfred* severs the private mind of its hero or author from the soiled frustrations of Regency politics. In the characteristic mode of Romantic drama, subjectivity is represented as an inevitably objective problem; mutability in the context of historical categories and conflicts entails an epistemological problem no less than a political one.

Schiller expresses the poet's function in a way that clearly implies the inadequacy of the subject-object dichotomy as a model for dramatic (or generally literary) problems. The function of the poet, in Schiller's terms, is "Der Menschheit ihren moeglichst vollstaendigen Ausdruckzu geben" (to give to humanity its most complete possible expression);[55] but Schiller also subordinates aesthetic production, even when it is defined in that way, within the larger project of a struggle to form "that most perfect of all the works to be achieved by the art of man: the construction of true political freedom."[56] Thus, aesthetic forms are understood as total expressions of humanity, and at the same time aesthetic forms are subordinated in the larger cultural work of constructing political freedom. This relationship is expressed well by Elizabeth M. Wilkinson and Leonard A. Willoughby in their commentary on Schiller's *Aesthetic Education of Man:* "Schiller's whole purpose is not to fix the mind, but to keep it moving, and to keep it moving by changing the viewpoint."[57]

No human work is to be found external to a viewpoint, and no viewpoint survives. Dialectic, as Goethe once said, is "die Ausbildung des Widersprechungsgeistes" (the cultivation of the spirit of contradiction).[58] The supercession of political and other cultural formations is thematized in the same dramatic literature that (like Schiller's) intervenes within specific conflicts.

In his prospectus for the journal in which he was to publish both *The Aesthetic Education of Man* and *On Naive and Sentimental Poetry,* Schiller formulates the dialectical relationship that replaces the dichotomy of subject and object: "At a time when the nearby din of war alarms our country, when the clash of political opinions and interests renews this war in nearly all circles . . . it is salutary to invite the distracted reader to a totally different kind of colloquy." This proposed colloquy will furnish a critical vantage on the larger structures of historical change; it is not on current events considered as merely external and specific facts but rather on their enabling ideational constructions that "all true improvement of the social condition depends."[59] To perceive history as the Romantic-period writers suggest, as a structural form and a determining force rather than a collection of facts, implies the historicity of understandings no less than the historicity of that which is understood.

In this way, contradictions—including contradictions in and about the romantic dramas—become intelligible. The *suppression* of politically charged discourse designates precisely its *presence,* as an anonymous "Lover of Order" observed in 1795 in the course of explaining the importance of critical resistance to the Seditious Practices Act proposed by Lord Grenville and the Unlawful Assemblies

Act proposed by Pitt: "these bills are an unwilling homage, that the too-eager advocates of authority pay to the rising genius of freedom."[60] A proliferation of plays that avoid naming conspicuously contemporary conflicts (but use instead mythical or historically removed settings) is itself a sign of the times. The correlative theory of history and historicity appears in materialist form in Condorcet (and especially in his *Historical View of the Progress of the Human Mind*), and it appears in more idealist form in Hegel's *Philosophy of History:* "the influences that have formed the writer are identical with those which have moulded the events that constitute the matter of his story."[61] The concept of history, again to use Colman's words to a very different purpose from Colman's, "lies in the very bones and marrow of the historical facts."

These preoccupations condition the Romantic drama's treatment of its paradigmatic plot elements, as I have suggested, but they also condition its handling of ostensibly perennial motifs, including metadramatic reflection on the problem of representation itself. Tropes of illusion, disguise, the troubled transmission of meanings that can be effected by signs and signifiers, or their failure to transmit meanings, the appearance-reality problem, disguise, deception, trickery, doubt, error, and delusion of all kinds are nearly ubiquitous in the romantic dramas, as they are in earlier drama (and for that matter, later drama), too. Their function as bearers of meaning must be understood—can only be understood—by discerning their differentiated modes of operation in the romantic dramas themselves. In my judgment, it will not suffice to ascribe the period's different handling of these tropes in terms of historical generalization about the social and political history of the period. It will not do simply to say, for example, that the morbidity and sometimes the solipsism of the recurrently Gothic hero results from the fact that "it was a period of dissolution and chaos; and in such a period any emotional attitude which seems to give a man something firm, even if it be only the attitude of 'I am myself alone,' is eagerly taken up." Much as that description may accord with one's sense of the Gothic, it obscures the difference between the dramas of *this* period and any other. In fact, those words I have just quoted are from Eliot's description of the Elizabethan period, in his essay "Shakespeare and the Stoicism of Seneca"; its apparently equal relevance to the drama of a vastly different period should make us suspicious. I suggest that the Romantic dramas are (not always, not in every instance, but often and even paradigmatically) characterized by the dual and even dialectical operation of the category of history—"history" operating not only as an external setting in which the plays are made and performed, or an external set of facts designated by the plays, but also as an entirely inescapable condition of the plays themselves and their own modes of representation.

There are differences, for example, between the treatment of masking in *Le Misanthrope* or *Tartuffe* and in *DeMonfort*. Baillie's play makes an issue of its own entrapment in a thoroughly mortal frame of reference, and Molière's more confident drama does not. In *Le Misanthrope*, Alceste charges Philinte with hypocrisy and declares that speech should reveal truly the inner heart. Philinte says that we should sometimes hide what we feel, but Alceste is confident that a wise man can see through the masks of treachery. The play tropes frequently on role playing, on mere show, but always as something to be overcome by a discernment of truth whose fixity, and ultimate availability, are not questioned. The most frequent subject of the characters' metadramatic reflections is the pronoun "we," a pronoun whose undifferentiated plurality expresses the confidence of truths meant to be taken out of time.

Le Misanthrope clearly does worry questions of societal conflict, as in Alceste's ridiculed desire for retreat to Edenic isolation; but it is the *challenges* to certitude and stability that are impermanent. More characteristically among the Romantic-period dramas, it is certitude and stability that are ephemeral. In Molière's plays, the regnant social apparatus may appear threatened, but the threat is temporary and hardly more than a nuisance. In the Romantic–period dramas, the reverse is more often the case.

In *DeMonfort*, DeMonfort expresses in the alienation of a soliloquy his hidden dislike of Freberg, to whose revelry he has just consented to go (78–79). The Countess Freberg first appears on stage with a mask in her hand, emblematic of the trope of concealment and illusion that the play politicizes (78). Freberg and DeMonfort have a dialogue on the theme of true speech opening one's heart to one's friends, much like the corresponding dialogue between Alceste and Philinte in *Le Misanthrope;* but here the outcome of the exchange is the impossibility of knowledge, rather than its inevitability. Freberg says, "Wert thou my friend, / Wouldst thou not open all thine inmost soul, / And bid me share its every consciousness?" (80). This is very close to Alceste's speech in the first act of Molière's play. Here, however, DeMonfort replies,

> That man was never born whose secret soul,
> With all its motley treasure of dark thoughts,
> Foul fantasies, vain musings, and wild dreams,

> Was ever open'd to another's scan.
> Away, away! it is delusion all.

Two things differentiate this speech from the pessimism that darkens similar dialogues in earlier dramas: nothing happens to contradict this claim that all is delusion. In fact, the following scene intensifies the problem when Jane disguises herself from her own brother, behind a black veil, and elicits confessions and weeping from him under conditions of mistaken identity.

Further, the problem of delusion is politicized in *DeMonfort,* just as it is in Tieck's *Puss in Boots* (as Burwick points out). The unbridgeable gap between appearance and reality, outwardness and inwardness, is introduced and maintained as a political problem: "We mark . . . The gait disturb'd of wealthy honour'd men, / But do not know the cause" (79). As Watkins has shown, characters in this play (and perhaps even its author) do not know that historical forces determine the manifestations of this anxiety, which is nonetheless the romantic dramas' most consistent and powerful tone—and it is an anxiety of class-based conflict.

In this respect, we can distinguish Romantic dramas from other, earlier forms of dramatic and metadramatic treatments of illusion. Prospero's famous speeches of metadramatic metaphor in *The Tempest* (which is also a play about political usurpation) locate his (and "our") temporality against a stable screen of eternity.[62] The mutability of the pageant proceeds across a stage whose durability outside the temporal frustrations of the world is asserted, and more, assumed. In the Romantic drama, but not in the *Tempest,* the act of symbolic displacement—which is the behavior of a limited person in a specifiable time and place, with interests—is itself made a topic. This behavior of symbolizing is treated in terms of historical conflicts of societal and cultural scale; the problem of illusion is an ideological problem and is represented as such and not an eternal human condition.[63] In the Romantic dramas, reflections on representationality are not primarily philosophical or personal. It is the hierarchical organization of society, under conditions of a revolutionary or reactionary change, that is often represented as earthquake, deluge, or conflagration. That hierarchical organization, however, is also treated in terms of representational illusion. The problem of the fictive and the false escapes the relatively safe condition of a human dilemma in the abstract, and it escapes the even safer condition of playful introversion on the part of the dramatic medium itself.

Of course, the drama was always social and always understood itself in that way. Aristophanes' *The Birds* is in part a play about the bureaucratization of urban life (in the fifth century B.C.); but it was not always the theory of ideology that informed its representations and displacements. It could be said that the role definition of a true prince in Part 1 of *Henry IV* is an ideological construct, and the role reversals in the metadramatic play-within-the-play could be said to exhibit the fictionality of that construct; but it does not follow (and is not the case) that the play represents its own frame of reference as consigned to the mutability of history.

Burwick's fine generalization about metadrama and the problem of illusion in the Romantic drama, which I have already quoted, exhibits two tendencies that differentiate the closural fixity of traditional criticism from the referential frame of the dramas themselves. In traditional usages, "we" are as timeless, as comfortably exempt from troubling difference, as "we" are in *Le Misanthrope* or in the choruses of Sophocles. Like Spenser's *Two Cantos of Mutabilitie*, traditional criticism acknowledges the problem of historical difference only to dissolve it in the timelessness of a universal "we." But the "we" of Molière or Tieck and the "we" of twentieth-century critics are not, in fact, identical; there is no referent that the pronoun can have twice. As Hegel's tortuous narratives of self-objectification have taught "us," even "we," now, are not self-identical. Even when the purveyors of textualized illusion *believe* the textualized illusions, once-eternal constructs (even literary-critical methods and assumptions) crumble and vanish. Attitudes of reverence and redemption are implied by the tones of such rhetorical quests for permanence, but these attitudes grow obsolete. In the planned obsolescence of the academy, new and improved formulas take the place of previously regnant certitudes with an accelerating rapidity. And for these reasons, literary-critical sermons about self, others, and the world—and about "our" access to their truths—lose cogency. Such sermons for eternity become time's cases in point.

The second statement that I have quoted from Burwick, about what the "Romantics endeavored" to do, encloses the project of Romantic drama inside a personalistic frame of specifiable individual intentions. For generations, the theme of Romantic criticism was just this happy if inconsistent conjunction of individualism (the unique personal author) with universalism (the timeless permanence of the philosophical problem). Elsewhere, I have explored that theoretical contradiction in "practical" criticism;[64] here I will cite only one more example of such criticism, this one a description of a play by Shelley:

> According to Shelley's *Defence*, the gaining of heaven is the human mind's release from the "curse which binds us to be subjected to the

accident of surrounding impressions," and because it is poetry that defeats that curse, every poetic unification of thought and thing is also a signal of apoctalyptic redemption.[65]

There is a mismatch between this apotheosis of ideation and the document it tries to explain. Shelley expresses a more wholly dialectical understanding when, in the preface to *Prometheus Unbound*, he observes that "poets, not otherwise than philosophers, painters, sculptors, and musicians, are in one sense the creators, and in another the creations, of their age."[66] In *A Defence of Poetry*, Shelley writes that "The drama at Athens . . . coexisted with the moral and intellectual greatness of the age";[67] and thus clearly Shelley's statement proposes not an attribution of individual genius but an historical hermeneutic.

The Romantic dramas represent the conditions of their own formation, not under the operation of a reflexive cleverness or under the blessing of a mental redemption behind closed eyes, but in a tenacious engagement with their own historicity. In some plays (as in Tieck's *Puss in Boots*), this engagement is thematized with comical excess; in other plays (as in Shelley's *The Cenci*), it generates irresolutions as severe in their way as the ongoing conflicts about which the dramatists write; and sometimes, as in the *Adopted Child*, or Mitford's *Charles the First*, or *DeMonfort*, that engagement with historicity involves an underconsciousness of historical crisis and change.

Notes

1. Important studies of the Romantic drama do, however, include the following: Allardyce Nicoll, *A History of English Drama, 1660–1900*, 6 vols., rev. ed. (Cambridge: Cambridge University Press, 1952–59); George Steiner, *The Death of Tragedy* (New York: Knopf, 1961); Richard M. Fletcher, *English Romantic Drama 1795–1843* (New York: Exposition Press, 1966); Joseph W. Donohue Jr., *Dramatic Character in the English Romantic Age* (Princeton, N.J.: Princeton University Press, 1970); and Terry Otten, *The Deserted Stage: The Search for Dramatic Form in Nineteenth-Century England* (Athens: Ohio University Press, 1972). Dewey Ganzel's essay is informative: "Patent Wrongs and Patent Theatres: Drama and the Laws in the Early Nineteenth Century," *PMLA* 76 (1961): 384–96; and so is L. W. Conolly, *The Censorship of English Drama 1737–1824* (San Marino, Calif.: Huntington Library, 1976).
2. Neil Postman, *Amusing Ourselves to Death* (New York: Viking, 1985), 3–4.
3. Joan Mandell Baum, *The Theatrical Compositions of the Major English Romantic Poets* (Salzburg: Institut fuer Anglistik and Amerikanistic, 1980); Richard Allen Cave, ed., *The Romantic Theatre: An International Symposium* (Gerrards Cross, Buckinghamshire: Colin Smythe, 1986); Jeffrey N. Cox, *In the Shadows of Romance: Romantic Tragic Drama in Germany, England, and France* (Athens: Ohio University Press, 1987): Marilyn Gaull, *English Romanticism: The Human Context* (New York: Norton, 1988), 80–108, including a revised version of Gaull's essay,

"Romantic Theater," *Wordsworth Circle* 14 (1983): 255–63; Erika Gottlieb, *Lost Angels of a Ruined Paradise: Themes of Cosmic Strife in Romantic Tragedy* (Victoria: Sono Nis Press, 1981); Terence Allan Hoagwood and Daniel P. Watkins, eds., "Forum on English Romantic Drama," in *Nineteenth-Century Contexts* 15, no. 2 (1991): 119–80; Alan Richardson, *A Mental Theater: Poetic Drama and Consciousness in the Romantic Age* (University Park: Pennsylvania State University Press, 1988).

4. Stephen Behrendt, *History and Myth: Essays on English Romantic Literature* (Detroit, Mich.: Wayne State University Press, 1990), including Behrendt's "Beatrice Cenci and the Tragic Myth of History"; Julie Carlson, *In the Theatre of Romanticism* (Cambridge: Cambridge University Press, 1994); Jeffrey N. Cox, *Seven Gothic Dramas* (Athens: Ohio University Press, 1992); Terence Allan Hoagwood and Daniel P. Watkins, eds., *Romantic Drama: Historical and Critical essays*, a special issue, *The Wordsworth Circle* 23, no. 2 (spring 1992), including Hoagwood's "Prolegomenon for a Theory of Romantic Drama," 49–64, and Watkins's "Class, Gender, and Social Motion in Joanna Baillie's *DeMonfort*"; Marjean Purinton, *Romantic Ideology Unmasked* (Newark: University of Delaware Press, 1994); and Daniel P. Watkins, *A Materialistic Critique of English Romantic Drama* (Gainesville: University of Florida Press, 1993).

5. Carlson, *In the Theatre of Romanticism*, 6.

6. See, for example, Cox, *Seven Gothic Dramas*, 2; Hoagwood, "Prolegomenon for a Theory of Romantic Drama," 49; Hoagwood, "Foreword" in Marjean D. Purinton's *Romantic Ideology Unmasked*, 9; and Watkins, *Materialist Critique of English Romantic Drama*, 3.

7. *The British Theatre; or, A Collection of Plays, Which Are Acted at the Theatres Royal, Drury Lane, Covent Garden, and Haymarket. . . . with Biographical and Critical Remarks, By Mrs. Inchbald. In Twenty-Five Volumes* (London: Longman, Hurst, Rees and Orme, 1808); and *The Modern Theatre; a Collection of Successful Modern Plays, as Acted at the Theatres Royal, London. Printed from the Prompt Books under the Authority of the Managers. Selected by Mrs. Inchbald*, 10 vols. (London: Longman, Hurst, Rees, Orme, and Brown, 1811). Inchbald's biographical and critical essays from *The British Theatre* are conveniently available in a recent facsimile edition: *Remarks for The British Theatre*, intro. Cecilia Macheski (Delmar, N.Y.: Scholars' Facsimiles, 1990).

8. Inchbald, "Remarks" prefixed to her edition of *Julius Caesar: A Tragedy, in Five Acts; by William Shakespeare. As performed at the Theatre Royal, Covent-Garden. Printed under the Authority of the Managers From the prompt-Book* (London: Printed for Longman, Hurst, Rees, Orme, and Brown, n.d.), 3. This edition appears in the collection entitled *The British Theatre*.

9. For an account of a similarly political history in the appropriation and interpretation on *MacBeth*, see Mary Jacobus, "'That Great Stage Where Senators Perform': *MacBeth* and the Politics of Romantic Theatre," *Studies in Romanticism* 22 (1983): 353–87.

10. [Elizabeth Inchbald], *The Massacre: Taken from the French. A Tragedy, of Three Acts, in Prose* (London: Printed for G. G. J. and J. Robinson, 1792), "Advertisement," sig. A2. The play was never published during Inchbald's lifetime. I quote from the unbound proof copy that is located at the Library of Congress.

11. James Boaden, *Memoirs of Mrs. Inchbald: Including Her Familiar Correspondence with the Most Distinguished Persons of Her Time. To Which Are Added the Massacre, and a Case of Conscience, Now First Published from Her Autograph Copies* (London: Richard Bentley, 1833), 1: 356.

12. On the problem of representation as the central issue in Burke's theatricaliz-

ing response to the French Revolution, see James K. Chandler, "Poetical Liberties: Burke's France and the 'Adequate Representation' of the English," in *The French Revolution and the Creation of Modern Political Culture*, vol. 3 of *The Transformation of Political Culture 1789–1848*, eds. Francois Furet and Mona Ozouf (New York: Pergamon Press, 1990), 45–58.

13. Eliot, "Shakespeare and the Stoicism of Seneca," in *Selected Essays* (New York: Harcourt, Brace and World, 1964), 108–9.

14. Borges's aphorism is quoted by James Wood in a review of George Steiner's *No Passion Spent: Essays 1978–1995*, which in turns quotes it: *New Republic* 215, no. 14 (30 September 1996): 37.

15. Inchbald, "Remarks" prefixed to her play, *Every One Has His Fault: A Comedy* (London: Longman, Hurst, Rees, Orme, and Brown, n.d.), 3. Included in the series entitled *The British Theatre.*

16. See Byron's letter to Lady Byron of 14 September 1821, in *Byron's Letters and Journals*, ed. Leslie A. Marchand (London: John Murray, 1978), 8: 210.

17. Marilyn Gaull cites some facts that attest to the popularity of the drama: for the reading public, in the period 1800–1830, 160 periodicals are devoted to theater; and the popularity of stage performances is indicated by the fact that, in 1794, crowds trampled each other to death in a struggle to get to the pit for a popular performance at Drury Lane. Likewise in 1809, crowds rioted for sixty-four nights when Covent Garden raised admission prices. See Gaull's *English Romanticism: The Human Context* (New York: W. W. Norton, 1988), pp. 81, 83; and Joseph W. Donohue, Jr., *Theatre in the Age of Kean* (Totowa, N.J.: Rowman and Littlefield, 1975), 143–44. Gaull also cites Carl Stratham, *Britain's Theatrical Periodicals, 1720–1967* (1972).

18. Colman is quoted by Richard Findlater, *Banned: A Review of Theatrical Censorship* (London: Macgibbon, 1967), 56. On Mitford's play, see the essay by Kenneth Johnston and Joseph Nicholes in the present volume, "Transitory Actions, Men Betrayed: The French Revolution in the English Revolution in Romantic Drama," below.

19. For an account of how the phrase "mental theatre" refers to "public rather than to private modes of response," see Hoagwood, "Prolegomenon for a Theory of Romantic Drama," 53–54. Purinton explains how the plays of Byron and other Romantic-period playwrights, called "mental theatre," express their "involvement with historical and political material" and "express revolutionary themes": "Byron's reference suggests a mental process, but his reference is national rather than personal" (*Romantic Ideology Unmasked*, 19–22).

20. The removal of *King Lear* from production at the *theatres royal* may suggest one reason for Charles Lamb's famous preference for *reading* plays, as opposed to seeing them. He mentions this preference in his essay, "On the Tragedies of Shakespeare," in which he mentions *King Lear* specifically—a play that he could read but not, in fact, see in a theater. Conolly explains a related reason: "in general, censored passages were included in the printed text of the play" (*The Censorship of English Drama*, 5).

21. Quotations from Shelley's poetry refer to *Shelley's Poetry and Prose*, eds. Donald H. Reiman and Sharon B. Powers (New York: Norton, 1977).

22. Conolly, *Censorship of English Drama 1737–1824*, 86–87.

23. Gaull, *English Romanticism*, 85–86.

24. Bertrand Evans, *Gothic Drama from Walpole to Shelley* (Berkeley and Los Angeles: University of California Press, 1947), 162.

25. *The Robbers. A Tragedy. Translated from the German of Frederick Schiller*

(London: G. G. J. and J. Robinsons, 1792), v. This edition is reprinted in facsimile with an introduction by Jonathan Wordsworth (Oxford: Woodstock, 1989).
26. Wordsworth, unpaginated introduction to *The Robbers*.
27. See Donald G. Priestman, "Godwin, Schiller, and the Polemics of Coleridge's *Osorio*," *Bulletin of Research in the Humanities* 82 (1979): 236–48; and John David Moore, "Coleridge and the 'Modern Jacobinical Drama': *Osorio, Remorse,* and the Development of Coleridge's Critique of the Stage, 1797–1816," *Bulletin of Research in the Humanities* 85 (1982): 443–64.
28. George Watson, *England Preserved; A Tragedy in Five Acts. As Performed at the Theatre-Royal, Covent-Garden,* in *The Modern Theatre: A Collection of Successful Modern Plays,* 8: 309–62. This play was first published as *England Preserved: An Historical Play* (London: Longman, 1795).
29. Watkins, "Class, Gender, and Social Motion in Joanna Baillie's *DeMonfort*," 109–17.
30. Baillie, *Constantine Paleologus; or, The Last of the Caesars: A Tragedy in Five Acts,* in *The Dramatic and Poetical Works of Joanna Baillie* (London: Longman, Brown, Green, and Longmans, 1851), 446.
31. Inchbald, "Remarks" on Baillie's *DeMonfort,* in Inchbald's edition of *DeMonfort* in *The British Theatre* (London: Longman, Hurst, Rees, Orme, and Brown, n.d.), 3.
32. An excellent study of the Romantic dramas' treatment of perspectival relativity, including political and ideological context, is Purinton's *Romantic Ideology Unmasked.*
33. *Analytical Review,* 22 (July–December 1795): 12.
34. Moore, *A View of the Causes and Progress of the French Revolution,* 2 vols. (London: Robinsons, 1795), 1: 194.
35. On this topic, see Hoagwood, "Gillray, Cromwell, and the Problem of Representation," in *Cavaliers and Roundheads First: Romantic and Victorian Recuperations of the English Civil War,* eds. Kenneth Johnston and Joseph Nicholes, 134–38. This collection is a special issue of *The Wordsworth Circle* 25, [no. 3 (summer 1994)].
36. See Gillray, *A Connoisseur examining a Cooper* (London: H. Humphrey, 1792). George III studies anxiously a portrait of Cromwell, seeking to read the meaning of that figure for his own destiny.
37. The best study to date of the Romantic-period dramas' treatments of the English Revolution and the regicide is Kenneth R. Johnston and Joseph Nicholes, "Transitory Actions, Men Betrayed: The French Revolution and the English Revolution in Romantic Drama," *The Wordsworth Circle* 23, no. 2 (spring 1992): 76–97. This essay is reprinted in the present volume.
38. Rousseau, *The Social Contract,* in *"The Social Contract" and Discourses,* trans. G. D. H. Cole (New York: Dutton; London: Dent, 1950), 6.
39. Godwin, *Enquiry Concerning Political Justice and Its Influence on Morals and Happiness,* ed. F. E. L. Priestley (Toronto: University of Toronto Press, 1946), 1: 26.
40. *Analytical Review,* New Series Vol. 1 (January–June 1799): 322.
41. On plays about plays in the period, see Dane Farneworth Smith and M. L. Lawhon, *Plays about the Theatre in England, 1737–1800* (Lewisburg Pa.: Bucknell University Press, 1979). Acknowledging that plays about the theater have been written as long as the theater has been an institution (13), Smith and Lawhon point out that the motif was frequently used in the Romantic period for satires. As an indication of its frequency, they point out that George Colman the Younger wrote nine plays about the theater.

In contrast to the relatively literal understanding of plays about plays that is represented in Smith and Lawhon, Frederick Burwick widens the metaphorical implications of the metadramatic motif: "Illusion, then, becomes for the Romantics more than a fascination with aesthetic experience or with the possibilities of stagecraft. The phenomena of illusion offer insight into the ambiguities of knowledge and the frail and fallible access we have to self, others, and the world. . . . in the dramatic works of Goethe, Hugo, Coleridge, and Tieck, the Romantics endeavored to transform the deliberations of philosophy and critical theory into the very substance and subject matter of dramatic representation" (*Illusion and the Drama* [University Park: Pennsylvania State University Press, 1991], 303).

42. The play was first published as *The Adopted Child: A Musical Drama, in Two Acts* (London: Dilly, 1795). It was published again in a contemporary collection by the managers of Drury Lane, Covent Garden, and the Haymarket. Like Inchbald's collections in multiple volumes, this set of printed plays is a major resource for the study of the drama of the period, and my quotations from *The Adopted Child* refer to this work: *The London Stage: a Collection of the Most Reputed Tragedies, Comedies, Operas, Melo-Dramas, Farces, and Interludes. Accurately printed from Acting Copies, as Performed at the Theatres Royal, and carefully collated and revised*, vol. 1 (London: Published for the proprietors, by Sherwood, Jones, and Co., n.d.).

43. *Analytical Review* 22 (1795): 169.

44. See Oscar Mandel, "Kotzebue's Politics," in his *August von Kotzebue: The Comedy, the Man* (University Park: Pennsylvania State University Press, 1990), 23–29.

45. *Lover's Vows; a Play, in Five Acts, performing at the Theatre Royal, Covent Garden. From the German of Kotzebue. By Mrs Inchbald*, 7th ed. (London: G. G. J. and J. Robinson, 1798), 3.2. I would like to mention again that Jane Austen refers to this play (in *Mansfield Park*), because the popular interest in Jane Austen (and especially the Hollywood movie *Emma*, made by Miramax Films) was recently mentioned by Roger Rosenblatt in the popular TV show, *Newshour*.

46. Kucich, "'A Haunted Ruin': Romantic Drama, Renaissance Tradition, and the Critical Establishment," *The Wordsworth Circle* 23, no. 2 (spring 1992): 64–75.

47. Inchbald, quoted in Conolly, *Censorship of English Drama 1737–1824*, 11.

48. Coleridge, *Biographia Literaria: or Biographical Sketches of My Literary Life and Opinions*, eds. James Engell and W. Jackson Bate, vol. 7 of *The Collected Works of Samuel Taylor Coleridge* (Princeton, N.J.: Princeton University Press, 1983), 2: 233. This one-volume edition uses separate pagination for the two volumes as published in 1817.

49. Baillie, *DeMonfort*, in *A Series of Plays; in which it is attempted to delineate the stronger passions of the Mind; each Passion being the Subject of a Tragedy and a Comedy* (London: Cadell and Davies, 1798), 394. On *DeMonfort*, see two excellent recent studies: Purinton, *Romantic Ideology Unmasked*, 207–67; and Watkins, "Class, Gender, and Social Motion in Joanna Baillie's *Demonfort*."

50. Byron, *Werner; or, The Inheritance: A Tragedy*, in *Byron: Poetical Works*, ed. Frederick Page, new ed. by John Jump (1970; reprint, Oxford: Oxford University Press, 1979), 57.

51. Carlson, "Command Performances: Burke, Coleridge, and Schiller's Dramatic Reflections on the Revolution in France," *The Wordsworth Circle* 23, no. 2 (spring 1992): 117–34.

52. Schleiermacher, *Aphorisms on Hermeneutics*, trans. Roland Haas and Jan Wojcik, in *The Hermeneutic Tradition: From Ast to Ricoeur*, eds. Gayle L. Ormiston and Alan D. Schrift (Albany: State University of New York Press, 1990), 67.

53. Dilthey, *The Rise of Hermeneutics*, trans. Fredric Jameson, in *The Hermeneutic Tradition*, eds. Ormiston and Schrift, 112, 114.
54. Burwick, *Illusion and the Drama*, 290.
55. Schiller, *Ueber naive und sentimentalische Dichtung*, in *Werke: Nationalausgabe*, eds. Julius Petersen, Gerhard Fricke, Lieselotte Blumenthal, and Benno von Wiese (Weimar: Harmann Boehlaus Nachfolger, 1943), 20: 437. For an excellent discussion of Schiller in connection with English Romantic poetry, to which I am indebted, see Lore Metzger, *One Foot in Eden: Modes of Pastoral in Romantic Poetry* (Chapel Hill: University of North Carolina Press, 1986), 7–42.
56. Schiller, *On the Aesthetic Education of Man, in a Series of Letters*, trans. Elizabeth M. Wilkinson and Leonard A. Willoughby (Oxford: Clarendon Press, 1967), 2, 1.
57. Wilkinson and Willoughby, introduction to *On the Aesthetic Education of Man*, lv–lvi.
58. Goethe, *Gedenkausgabe der Werke, Briefe und Gesprache*, ed. Ernst Beutler (Zurich: Artemis Verlag, 1948–71), 9: 650.
59. Schiller, Prospectus for *Die Horne*, in *Werke*, 22: 106–7. I quote here from Metzger's excellent translation of these passages from the Prospectus: 7–8.
60. *Considerations on Lord Grenville's and Mr. Pitt's Bills* (London: Joseph Johnson, 1795); quoted in *Analytical Review* 22 (1795): 543.
61. Hegel, *The Philosophy of History*, trans. J. Sibree (1899; reprint, New York: Dover, 1956), 2.
62. Influential arguments have been made to show that Shakespeare's play *is* a representation of historical conflicts. Its new world setting, for example, its portrayal of patriarchal power, its clear representation of a natural slave class, and its portrayal of anxieties about usurpation are important, and so is the criticism that recognizes them. My point is that it is not the play's project to make a theme of its own status as a subject of historical change.
63. See Watkins, *A Materialist Critique of English Romantic Drama*, e.g. 8, 20.
64. *Politics, Philosophy, and the Production of Romantic Texts* (DeKalb: Northern Illinois University Press, 1996).
65. Hoagwood, *Prophecy and the Philosophy of Mind: Traditions of Blake and Shelley* (University: University of Alabama Press, 1985), 157.
66. Shelley, Preface to *Prometheus Unbound*, in Lawrence John Zillman, *Shelley's "Prometheus Unbound": The Text and the Drafts* (New Haven: Yale University Press, 1968), 41.
67. Shelley, *A Defence of Poetry*, in *The Complete Works of Percy Bysshe Shelley*, eds. Roger Ingpen and Walter E. Peck (London: Ernest Benn; New York: Charles Scribner's Sons, 1926–30), 7: 121.

2
"A Haunted Ruin": Romantic Drama, Renaissance Tradition, and the Critical Establishment

Greg Kucich

> I am convinced the man who is to awaken the drama must be a bold trampling fellow—no creeper into worm-holes—no reviser even—however good. These reanimations are vampire-cold—Such ghosts as Marloe—Webster &c are better dramatists, better poets, I dare say, than any contemporary of ours—but they are ghosts—the worm is in their pages—& we want to see something that our grandsires did not know. With the greatest reverence for all the antiquities of the drama I still think, that we had better beget than revive—attempt to give literature of this age an idiosyncracy & spirit of its own & only raise a ghost to gaze on not to live with—just now the drama is a haunted ruin!
> —Thomas Lovell Beddoes, *The Letters of Thomas Lovell Beddoes*

> ... a great [dramatic] spirit may daily, hourly arise, and the great dread should be, that this critical age doth not mislead or neutralize the talent newly generated.
> —"On the Drama," *Blackwood's Edinburgh Magazine*

Shelley's declaration that "the highest perfection of human society has ever corresponded with the highest dramatic excellence" characterizes the Romantics' tendency to associate their age's electrifying creative and political reforms with their efforts to reconstruct history's most exalted dramatic traditions.[1] Struck by that central convergence of dramatic and cultural aspirations, George Steiner has claimed that "at the origins of the romantic movement lies an explicit attempt to revitalize the major forms of tragedy ... [in] the great traditions of the Elizabethan and baroque theatre.... The thought of such restoration preoccupied the best poets and novelists of the century."[2] Yet ever since the Romantics themselves asserted with gloomy repetition the failure of that project throughout a national culture "deserted" in its own "birth-place" by the "genius of the modern drama,"[3] historians of English literature have been lamenting the utter annihilation of meaningful drama in the Romantic age.[4] An important revaluation of the period's dramatic activity is now underway, however, with numerous critics (Donohue, Otten, Gottlieb, Cox, Richardson, Watkins, Carlson, Purinton) showing that our dismissal of Romantic drama has arisen from conventional and mistaken assumptions about its strategies and principles.[5] By demonstrating how radical shifts in material culture, critical theory, and aesthetic practice were reconfiguring the form and concept of dramatic writing in the early nineteenth century, these critics are teaching us to engage Romantic dramas "on their own terms" (Richardson, 19) and thus develop a more informed appreciation of their aesthetic complexity and cultural relevance. This reconsideration of the drama's significance generally entails a new sensitivity to its increasingly sophisticated evocations of mental conflict, its reconstitution of traditional drama, in Byron's phrase, as experimental "mental theatre."[6]

Yet for all the fresh insights we have gained into the charged interiority of the Romantics' dramatic innovations, their efforts continue to suffer from critical disparagement of what Mary Jacobus calls their "anti-theatrical prejudice."[7] To many, their descents into the theater of the mind still seem like so many retreats from the stage of the world and the inescapable requirements of theatrical action, turning their experiments into a kind of bastard literary form, the "closet drama," which bears little redeeming relation to stage practice, poetic progress, or cultural experience. Even those recent exponents of the aesthetic integrity of Romantic drama find themselves somewhat cornered into the defensive posture of trying to validate the period's "turn from the stage" (Richardson, 2) into a "hopelessly untheatrical" (Cox, 27) form of dramatic exercise. It would seem that at the heart of our ongoing effort to reassess the significance of Romantic drama lies the problem of accounting for the apparent contradiction between the era's passionate dramatic aspirations—its quest through drama for "the highest perfection of human society"—and its seeming abandonment of theatrical activity. Part of our difficulty in resolving that paradox lies in our concentration on a relatively small and sensational body of Romantic theoretical statements about the non-representational nature of dramatic writing, many of which have been read out of context and seriously distorted. A more comprehensive investigation of Romantic dramatic theory, especially as it emerged in the period's influential periodical press, can help us understand the Romantics' profound ambivalence about dramatic production as a complicated outgrowth of their effort to situate themselves in England's dramatic history, a program often haunted by those Renaissance ghosts that Beddoes saw looming before his age.

Our conventional sense of Romantic drama has conditioned us to think of London's nineteenth-century playhouse as a "deserted stage." However, it was, in fact, thriving with a frenetic diversity that was unprecedented in English history,[8] and it was actually the vulgar excessiveness of that teeming stage life that pushed some of the Romantics away from it. The two licensed houses, Drury Lane and Covent Garden, had expanded to such an enormous size, with capacities exceeding three thousand people, that large-scale spectacle had become the most appropriate form of entertainment and the surest guarantee of drawing a sufficiently large audience to compensate for the exorbitant production costs of such cavernous establishments. And though a classical repertory was still maintained at these houses, growing emphasis on star acting and magnificent scenic effects encouraged sensationalism at the expense of intellectual complexity even in their serious dramatic productions. Moreover, as theater audiences became dominated by middle-class spectators governed by bourgeois standards of taste and morality, managers increasingly sought to attract and placate their patrons with sentimental and patriotic melodramas. Opportunities for intellectual or moral controversy on the stage were further curtailed by the severity of the government's Licensers, who were notorious for rejecting the slightest criticism of England's political, religious, and moral establishments.[9]

London's craving for theatrical entertainment created numerous smaller theaters that sprang up to rival the patent houses, but state licensing forced them to serve their audiences a relentless diet of farce, spectacle, burletta, and pantomime. Manuscripts were submitted by the hundreds to service the booming theatrical industry, as Byron complained while serving on the Drury Lane Committee. Popular amusement certainly played a complicated role in the sociopolitical dynamics of English culture, as Gaull and Cox have demonstrated, but such forms threatened to marginalize permanently what the Romantics called "legitimate" drama.[10] In addition, the playgoing audience's increasing notoriety for yelling, brawling, and throwing debris, often resulting in performances being silenced or actually hooted off the stage, left writers as contentious as Byron reluctant to confront the unruliness of a "damnable pit" given to roaring, groaning, hissing, and whistling until the play is "quite inaudible to half the house" (*Letters and Journals* 4: 290). These various inhibiting factors conspired, Matthew Lewis concludes in the preface to the printed version of his *Alfonso, King of Castille,* to make it extremely doubtful "whether even an *excellent* Tragedy . . . would succeed on the Stage at present."[11] Works of substantial intellectual quality, it would seem, had to retire to the closet, to be read before more culturally sophisticated audiences.

That inclination to prioritize the closet over the stage was intensified by the growing emphasis on character and psychodynamics in high Romantic dramatic criticism. Lamb presents the most extreme argument against stage-writing in his claim that the material reality of the theater inhibits the imagination's capacity to explore the depths of mental conflict in Shakespeare's characters. "What we see upon a stage is body and bodily actions," he contends; "what we are conscious of in reading is almost exclusively the mind, and its movements."[12] For that reason, he concludes, "the Lear of Shakespeare cannot be acted" (*Life,* 205). Hazlitt expresses a similar opinion when he writes, "We do not like to see our author's plays [Shakespeare's] acted and least of all *Hamlet.* There is no play that suffers so much in being transferred to the stage. Hamlet himself seems hardly capable of being acted."[13] "Shakespeare's characters," Coleridge concludes, "are never introduced for the sake of his plots." Attention should focus not on the stage action of his plays but on the mental lives of his characters inscribed in his text (quoted in Otten, 7). Given this theoretical orientation toward the imaginatively liberating experience of reading instead of witnessing drama, coupled with the intellectually deadening conditions of the nineteenth-century English theater, it should come as no surprise that Keats seemed most invigorated by Shakespeare when "Sitting Down to *Read* [my italics] *King Lear* Once Again," not when jostling into the theater to *watch* compromised versions of the play. Hardly an obtuse bias against theatrical representation, this preference for the mind's engagement with dramaturgical interiority now seems perfectly consistent with Romanticism's increasing movement toward an interrogative and dialectical poetics of mental action.

However, much as we have been learning to appreciate the historical and intellectual grounds of the Romantics' apparent rejection of the stage, our tendency to make blanket conclusions about their antitheatrical prejudice fails to comprehend the full complexity of their response to dramatic experience. Those conclusions are largely based on a few extreme pronouncements against the stage, like Lamb's, which must be significantly qualified when placed within the broader context of the period's overall debate about the drama. Not only were those statements made partially in response to the debilitating conditions of the English theater, they were also expressed in reaction against the eighteenth-century alterations of Shakespearean texts that continued to provide the basic script for Romantic productions—the "ribald trash" (Lamb, *Life,* p. 202) of Tate and Cibber that both Lamb and Hazlitt deplored. English playgoers had become so accustomed to seeing Shakespeare in these versions that Leigh Hunt could note a consensus that the Fool of *King Lear,* removed from Tate's version of the play, "is now out of date."[14] Moreover, entirely new scenes were often added to Shakespeare's plays to make them more palatable for an audience seeking sentimentality and moral platitudes. Responding in *The Morning Chronicle* to a production of *Richard III* in which Richard is revived after his death in Shakesperae's text to utter a few bromides on ambition, Hazlitt bristles with indignation: "The manner in which Shakespeare's plays have been generally altered, or rather mangled, by modern mechanists, is in our opinion a disgrace to the English Stage."[15] Instead of emphasizing the Romantics' bias against watching Shakespeare performed, therefore, we should recognize that in most cases it was only possible to see or "burn through" the world he actually created, as Keats describes his experience with *King Lear* ("On Sitting Down to Read *King Lear* Once Again," line 7), if one sat down to read the original text.[16]

Such a large part of this debate about stage representation centered on Shakespeare should further qualify our assumptions about the antitheatrical prejudice of Romantic dramatic theory. Although Lamb, Hazlitt, and Coleridge certainly believed that imaginative acts of reading involved a higher exercise of mental activity than observation of stage effects, they often limited this distinction to the special experience of reading Shakespeare's plays. The psychological depth of Shakespeare's writing so far exceeds the range of other playwrights, Lamb concludes, that his plays "are less calculated for performance on a stage than those of almost any other dramatist whatever" (*Life,* 192). That distinction between Shakespeare's non-representational complexity and the more manageable challenge of staging the works of "other dramatists" was echoed by a *Blackwood's* writer who specifically agrees "with Mr. Lamb that Shakespeare's plays read better in the closet than those of any other writer."[17] Making that distinction also helped the Romantics understand that its inversion held true—that is, many of Shakespeare's lesser competitors, unable to survive the rigorous strictures of readers carefully poring over their texts, actually improve through the spectacular and less critically demanding exercise of representation. Thus a *London Magazine* critic argues, "Whoever has entered fully into the spirit of

Shakespeare's plays . . . finds this curious distinction between them and all others . . . that while the latter *gain,* the former *lose* by representation." In the stage productions of inferior dramatists, "the scenery, machinery, decorations, &c. delude the spectator into an expenditure of applause, which the mere reader of these pieces would never sanction."[18] Such a realization grew so prevalent that it eventually became quite common for critics to remark on the manner in which certain plays were "rapturously applauded on the stage" and "severely criticized in the closet."[19] The Romantics were thus so far from assuming that all dramas are best suited to the closet that in many cases, with the notable exception of Shakespeare, they felt playwrights stood better chances of success and popularity on the stage than in print.

The most compelling qualification of Romantic antitheatrical prejudice, however, will arise from our proceeding beyond their specific debate about Shakespeare to their much wider interactions with dramatic experience in general. Those major contributors to the concept of a nonrepresentational Shakespeare were not at all adverse to theatrical activity but instead were all passionately engaged with the life of the stage. Coleridge, as Timothy Webb extensively chronicles ("The Romantic Poet and the Stage, 14–23), was fascinated with the mechanics of stage production and devoted a great amount of his literary planning to various schemes for staging both "legitimate" and popular plays. Not only did he produce the most theatrically successful drama among the major Romantic writers, *Remorse,* but he also composed a melodrama based on *The Winter's Tale,* called *Zapolya;* collaborated with Southey on a historical drama about the French Revolution, *The Fall of Robespierre;* translated Schiller's plays; and concocted a staggering array of potential dramatic projects, which included "a Tragi-comedy, entitled Love and Loyalty. . . . dramatic Romance . . . analogous to the Tempest. . . . The Three Robbers, a mime or speaking Ballet. . . . A scheme at large for a Pantomime."[20] Lamb was an enthusiastic spectator at classical and popular plays, known to laugh with gusto throughout the entirety of farces. Like Coleridge, he also nurtured a variety of dramatic ambitions, producing a serious tragedy, *John Woodvil,* and two farces, *Mr. H.* and *The Pawnbroker's Daughter.* Hazlitt was a regular playgoer throughout his long years as a theater critic for various London newspapers, and the gleeful exuberance of his descriptions of the theater suggests that he may be the most profound lover of the stage, and all the magic of its spectacle, that England has ever known: "The stage is an epitome, a bettered likeness of the world, with the dull part left out: and indeed with this omission, it is nearly big enough to hold the rest. . . . Wherever there is a playhouse, the world will not go amiss. . . . *[P]lay-going* people . . . are among the most sociable, gossiping, good-natured, and humane members of society. . . . We do not much like any person or person who do not like plays."[21]

Such theatrical enthusiasm in the supposed leaders of the high Romantic disdain for the playhouse should lead us to suspect that, in fact, the period was not only intensely receptive to stage action but often suspicious of those who did promote an exclusively closet drama. If we examine the wide range of Romanticism's debate about the theater, we will indeed find a recurrent insistence on stage production as an indispensable component of dramatic writing. The very idea of closet drama seemed a hopelessly tangled contradiction of aims to a number of dramatic critics in the periodical press. "Of all literary productions the most uninteresting, because the most unnatural," explains a writer in the *British Critic,* "is the *closet drama.* It is unnatural, because a drama not designed for action implies a contradiction; the very meaning of the word being an *acted poem.*[22] "[A] play not written for the stage" seemed to many critics "like a ship not built for the water" or a musical composition written "only for the eye" (*RR,* Part B, 1: 306). Summing up this matter about the jarring incongruity of unacted drama, a *Blackwood's* critic concludes, "I presume that it is important to the character of a first-rate tragedy to be capable of exciting popular interest on the stage. A play not fit to be played is an anomaly, and out of calculation."[23]

This privileging of theatrical representation as the only legitimate form of playwriting so dominated Romantic criticism that Lamb's pronouncements against staging Shakespeare seemed more like a glaring aberration from standard critical theory than a representative expression of the period's understanding of the drama. It appeared much more in keeping with the critical spirit of the age for someone like Beddoes to declare that writing for the stage should be "the highest aim of the dramatist, & I should be very desirous to get on it."[24] Thus, reviewers of Lamb's essay could confidently term his thesis a "paradox" that "never can be supported, and which is overthrown by the universal consent of mankind" ("Works of Charles Lamb," 608).

There was a larger paradox in this controversy over stage and closet drama, however, that was not so easy to put by. Although some were calling a universal consensus that drama, by definition, had to be written for the stage, these very objections to nonrepresentational theories came partially in response to an undeniable increase in plays self-designated as "closet" dramas. As part of that contradiction, the very writers who professedly loved the stage and strove for success on it were simultaneously hesitant or defensive about engaging with it. Such a division informs the careers of nearly every major and many minor writers of the period. Wordsworth submitted *The Borderers* to Covent Garden and expressed notable anxiety about its possibilities of being staged, yet he denied that it was calculated for representation.[25] Shelley contemplated numerous theatrical projects, such as his historical fragment *Charles the First* and a projected drama on Tasso. He also attributed the origin of *The Cenci* to his newly awakened "study of dramatic literature" and deliberately designed the play for production at Covent Garden, even selecting the ideal actors, O'Neill and Kean, to represent his principal characters.[26] Yet he harbored an intense "prejudice against theatres," according to Peacock (quoted in Webb, "The Romantic Poet and the Stage," 30), and he attended London playhouses only with great reluctance.[27] Beddoes, as we have seen, was extremely desirous to "get on" the stage, but he also felt serious doubts about the possibilities of success at the contemporary theater (*Works*, 528–29, 624–25). Baillie and Keats expressed similar ambivalence about their eagerness for success on the stage and their reluctance to follow through with their theatrical aspirations.[28]

Byron presents the most intriguing and often bewildering example of this contradictory response to stage writing. His fascination with the drama began as early as his adolescence, when he composed a play he called *Ulric and Ilvina*. His decision to burn that composition is paradigmatic of his lifelong, often torturous ambivalence toward dramatic production. When he first became involved with Drury Lane, he recalled to Thomas Medwin, "I had some idea of writing for the house myself."[29] But his doubts about his native dramatic talent and his increasing awareness of the hostile and unpropitious conditions of the London theater convinced him, so he claimed, to abandon all hope of writing for the stage. Instead, he produced nonrepresentational plays such as *Manfred, Cain,* and *Heaven and Earth*, designed for the theater of the imagination. He even repeatedly insists in the prefaces to his history plays that he had no intention of shaping them for theatrical representation: "I have had no view to the stage . . . not compos[ing] with the most remote view to the stage. . . . I never made the attempt and never will."[30] As most critics of the history plays have recognized, however, they possess numerous stageworthy qualities and seem in many ways to be consciously crafted for representation.[31] *Marino Faliero*, of course, was staged for a limited run at Drury Lane. The melodramatic *Werner*, moreover, continued to hold the London stage well into the nineteenth century. David Erdman has even demonstrated that Byron, believing for a time from the reports he received in Italy that *Marino Faliero* was thriving at Drury Lane, continued on with his series of history plays in eager anticipation of becoming "the Great Playwright" of the nineteenth-century stage.[32]

These contradictions between Byron's ambitions and denials, his gestures toward the theater and strides away from it, provide a striking paradigm of a peculiar kind of ambivalence that runs throughout Romanticism's engagement with the drama. The evidence should compel us to reformulate our basic question of why the Romantics abandoned a form of creative experience they highly valued. Hardly rejecting the stage, they found themselves like Hamlet, to extend Beddoes's metaphor, enthralled by a specter they could neither embrace nor dismiss. We must ask, then, not why they deserted the stage but rather why they simultaneously rushed toward it and pulled themselves back.

That was precisely the question many contemporary observers of the drama asked themselves. The urgent query echoing throughout the period's numerous books, articles, reviews, and lectures on the drama was why a culture so fertile and ambitious in its dramatic talent should be experiencing so much inhibition when it actually came to producing accomplished theater. The "*power* of dramatic writing has [not at all] declined in England during the last half century," insists a *Blackwood's* critic.[33] Numerous examples of great dramatic potential were cited in the plays of Coleridge, Baillie, Maturin, Knowles, Cornwall, and Byron, all of which "held out a promise that the Muse of Tragedy has not quite deserted the English stage" (*RR* Part A, 1: 45). Scott was even more sanguine, arguing that Baillie has "restored the true and manly tone of national tragedy. . . . Besides this gifted person, the names of Coleridge, of Maturin, and other men of talents, throng upon our recollection; and there is one who, to judge from the dramatic sketch he has given us in *Manfred*, must be considered as a match for Aeschylus" (*An Essay on the Drama*, 461). Leaning more toward understatement, Hazlitt agrees that the present age is "not unfruitful in theatrical genius."[34]

Still, many had to admit that all this potential was not reaching fruition. Even the age's most promising dramatic experiments seemed everywhere plagued by signs of restraint and inhibition, both in works for the stage and closet. "The *Remorse* of Coleridge is a noble poem," acknowledges a critic for *Retrospective Review*, but it is weighted down by some "brood[ing] . . . metaphysical cloud."[35] Byron, in particular, seemed plagued by an unnatural constraint in his dramatic writing, with numerous reviewers complaining of "the stiffness and labour of . . . [his] general style . . . the constraint of the poetry."[36] *Marino Faliero* "gives the impression of a thing worked against the grain, and not poured forth from the fullness of the heart or the fancy—the ambitious and elaborate work of a powerful mind engaged with an unsuitable task—not the spontaneous effusion of an exuberant imagination, sporting in the fullness of its strength." This general sense of the constraint holding back the period's talented dramatic artists was so widely felt that one *Monthly Review* critic wonders if there was some kind of a cultural or metaphysical "penal law depress[ing] their efforts and forb[idding] them to rise above a certain station" (*RR* Part A, 2: 720).

More than anything else, that penal restriction was threatening to trap England's dramatic history in a perpetual state of degeneration. Both puzzling and distressing, the problem demanded an immediate answer lest it result in an even more widespread cultural paralysis. "If there be any thing in this footing on which theatrical representations are now placed, that can account for this backwardness," pleads a reviewer of Barry Cornwall's *Mirandola,* "it becomes pressing indeed that the cause, or causes, should be distinctly known, preparatory to being removed."[37] At bottom, then, the Romantics urgently wished to understand and resolve the same dilemma in their playwriting that continues to bother twentieth-century scholars—that is, their tendency, when they turned to dramatic writing, to become labored, awkward, unnatural, quite simply not themselves, as if haunted by something or someone.

This is where Beddoes's vision of Renaissance specters seems particularly intriguing. He was not at all alone in attributing the imprisonments of Romantic dramaturgy to what a *Blackwood's* critic characterizes as the presences of "Shakespeare, Beaumont and Fletcher, Massinger, Ford, and the dramatists in general, of the days of Elizabeth and James . . . held up *in terrorem,* against modern dramatic adventurers."[38] The burden of the past in Romantic drama has not gone unnoticed by twentieth-century scholars, with Bate, Webb, and Richardson all giving it important emphasis.[39] But too often we have accepted this burden as a transhistorical, psychological condition, as if the Romantics passively inherited a preordained, transcendental past and all of its oedipal pressures. If we branch out beyond such Bloomian psychoanalytic readings of the Romantics' anxiety of influence, we may come to understand how the literary tradition confronting them was actually constructed by the very cultural, economic, and sociopolitical dynamics of their own time.

To understand how Beddoes's Renaissance ghosts may have engendered the equivocations of Romantic drama, therefore, we must investigate the ways in which the Romantics formulated their idea of

England's dramatic history. Much of this process was carried out by that powerful engine of cultural identity, the periodical press. It was a process of mapping literary history that was thoroughly implicated in the period's most bitterly contested sociopolitical struggles and that exerted considerable power, as the writer in my second epigraph suspected, to "neutralize" creative energies that were deemed threatening to national institutions.

The Romantics' engagement with Renaissance dramatic tradition was an integral component of their overall effort to create what they often thought of as "a second poetic Renaissance," built up to emulate and ultimately surpass that brightest era of England's poetic history stretching from Elizabeth's reign through Milton's generation. To many of the Romantics, however, it seemed that the second Renaissance was proceeding reasonably well in all poetic categories except the drama. Such a distinction riveted the attention of one perceptive *Quarterly Review* dramatic critic, who describes it as "a phenomenon unparalleled in the history of literature." "While in every department of literature," he explains, "all means have been employed to excite and satiate the appetite for novelty [and progress] . . . the drama still rests her claim on the merit of her earliest productions, and the efforts of competitors or of imitators have only served to establish the triumphs of Shakespeare. . . . To inquire into the causes of this, may not be useless, and certainly cannot be uninteresting."[40] The *Quarterly Review* critic associates those causes with the debilitating influence of Neoclassical dramatic theory in the eighteenth century—a common complaint, we shall find, with significant political implications—but we may arrive at a more comprehensive answer by distinguishing between the different ways Romanticism envisioned the poetic and dramatic legacies of the Renaissance.

A debate continued throughout the period about whether the poetry of Spenser, Milton, and their illustrious peers could ever be matched. Many were confident that such a great poetic tradition was inspiring the present age to do as well, perhaps even better. Contemporary poets "have produced as great a quantity of lasting poetry," declares a critic in *The Annual Review*, "as those who flourished during the reign of Elizabeth, or during any other half century of the British annals."[41] Others were even more sanguine, celebrating their own age's new "heaven of literature" peopled by "a host of genius, which in its amount and activity, is altogether unrivalled in the history of literature." Poetry, flowing out from the great well springs of the Renaissance, thus seemed to be "pouring a thousand streams of inspiration throughout the land."[42]

Comforting as that opinion may have been, it was challenged with many sober reservations about England's poetic progress. "When we look candidly and calmly to the works of . . .those masters of the golden time," Francis Jeffrey argues, "it is impossible . . . to dispute . . . the inferiority of their recent imitators."[43] With a similar concern to "husband enthusiasm" about poetic progress, Hazlitt notes that "in looking back to the great works of genius in former times, we are sometimes disposed to wonder at the little progress which has since been made in poetry."[44]

These doubts were met by counterclaims as the controversy over poetic advancement swayed back and forth to become one of the most engaging points of contention in Romantic literary discourse. Absolute resolutions were never forthcoming, but two points at least were generally agreed upon by both sides of the dispute: the poets of the English Renaissance made up the standard of excellence against which all claims of poetic progress had to be measured; and however one felt about the final achievement of the second Renaissance in relation to the first, there was no question, as Hazlitt and Jeffrey both readily acknowledged, that English poetry was undergoing a laudable rebirth of sorts in the early nineteenth century.

The argument about progress in the drama, however, took on a very different, much more polarized shape, largely because knowledge of England's dramatic tradition lagged considerably behind familiarity with its poetic backgrounds. Cheap, cumulative editions of the British poets appeared regularly from the 1770s throughout the early decades of the nineteenth century, and major figures like Milton and Spenser were elaborately edited and annotated throughout the eighteenth century. Editions of the old English dramatists were not so common, however, with Dodsley's *Selection of Old Plays* (1744) composing the only source of extensive material on the first Renaissance of English drama. John Bell's twenty-one volume *British Theatre* (1776–81) collected numerous English plays, but most of them were from the eighteenth century. Individual editions of the better known Elizabethans, such as Jonson, Beaumont, and Fletcher, had appeared in the eighteenth century, but their texts were generally regarded as unreliable and they never gained a wide readership.

Familiarity with the remaining host of playwrights clustered around Shakespeare was so rare that Lamb's *Specimen's of English Dramatic Poets Who Lived About the Time of Shakespeare* (1808), a collection of dramatic fragments by such writers as Marlowe, Heywood, Webster, Dekker, Middleton, and Ford, was hailed as the first substantial Romantic recovery of its old dramatic tradition. That is exactly the way Lamb promotes the edition in his preface, announcing that "more than a third part of the following specimens are from plays which are to be found only in the British Museum and in some scarce private libraries."[45] Shakespeare was well known, of course, but as we have seen, even he frequently came down to the Romantics in drastically vitiated versions. To those like Lamb, Gifford, Weber, and Hazlitt who set about editing, annotating, and lecturing on the early English dramatists, it therefore appeared that Romantic literary culture was appallingly ignorant of its wealthy dramatic inheritance.[46] Such ignorance, combined with a distaste carried over from the eighteenth century for the perceived vulgarities of Renaissance drama, contributed to a rather smug feeling of superiority pervading many Romantic assessments of the age's dramatic progress.

The intensity of the Romantics' indictments of their contemporary drama has so conditioned us to accept their utter disdain for current dramatic practice that we have generally failed to recognize how those charges came in direct response against this naive optimism. Playbills produced by theater managers were notorious for "puffing" up productions as new milestones in English dramatic history universally greeted with rapturous approbation. And the same was true of dramatic reviews in the London newspapers, many of which were written by individuals connected personally or financially with members of the theater. This facile and compromised celebration of the contemporary stage seemed grossly pernicious to many, such as the *Dramatic Review* critic who complains: "The principal evil which has tended so much to mislead the public, and to deceive the world, is the venality of the reporters who furnish the daily papers with their theatrical accounts. . . . as these persons are for the most part connected with others in the Theatre, impartiality is not to be expected. Falsehood is often substituted for truth, and panegyric for censure."[47]

Whether the periodical reviewers and editors of contemporary drama were liable to the same charge is debatable, but the fact remains that their panegyrics often seemed of a piece with the newspaper enthusiasm. The editor of *The British Drama*, for instance, claims that George Colman the Younger "has produced a variety of excellent comedies . . . that will never be excelled."[48] And Thomas Holcroft, writing in *The Theatrical Recorder*, declares that John Tobin's *The Honey Moon* "may be said to form an epoch in the annals of the drama" through its superlative advances on "the manner of writing which prevailed in the sixteenth century."[49] With this kind of optimism prevailing, many critics felt nothing but scorn for the "wailing and lamentation about . . . [the] imputed dwindling of dramatic intellect,"[50] and they mounted a concerted effort to characterize the present era as the most successful period in the history of

English drama. "So far, therefore, from joining in the cry 'Where is dramatic genius?'" proclaims a reviewer of T. Doubleday's *Babington,* "we aver that it is kindling over the whole land. . . . [Modern plays] may be compared, without obscuration of their power, with the compositions of our best dramatic writers [of the past]. . . . Do they contain less poetry, less passion, less pathos, than the dramas of Ford or Massinger? In our opinion infinitely more."[51]

Such optimism, which seemed to arise from an uninformed contempt for the monuments of the past, outraged those who relished the old English drama and left them determined to extol the ancients in a manner that would thoroughly squash modern pretensions to rivalry. Instead of a thousand magnificent dramas "kindling over the whole land," writes a *Blackwood's* critic in direct response to the *Babington* reviewer, "we have not a *first-rate one,* except within the leaves of Shakespeare."[52] The same provocation made Hazlitt elaborate a similar theme in his lectures on the Elizabethan dramatists. The present age is infected by a "Strange error," of "infatuated self-love," he begins his introductory address, and needs to be cured of its "overweening admiration" of itself and its "unmingled contempt for past time" (*Lectures on the Dramatic Literature of the Age of Elizabeth,* 6–7). Modern critics and dramatists think "that all we have to do to be great, is to despise those who have gone before us as nothing" (*Lectures,* 8). To rid his optimistic contemporaries of their self-complacency and steer them on a more constructive course, Hazlitt launches into an extended portrait of the Elizabethan age as the most spectacularly fertile period for dramatic achievement in human history. The powers of England's early dramatists were "thrown, heaped, massed together without careful polishing or exact method, but poured out in unconcerned profusion from the lap of nature and genius in boundless and unrivalled magnificence. . . . There is no time more populous of intellect, or more prolific of intellectual wealth . . . [and] there was more dramatic excellence in that age than in the whole of the period that has elapsed since" (*Lectures,* 12–14).

Hazlitt's campaign was shared by an increasing group of those who championed the neglected Elizabethans by similarly depicting them as prodigies far beyond the reach of rivalry. Lamenting "the great and injurious change" that beset English drama after the Renaissance, a reviewer of *Marino Faliero* thus eulogizes that great lost era of the drama's apex: "The dramatic writings of the period between Elizabeth and Charles the Second, are confessedly the glory of the literature of this country. They are no where else to be paralleled. They are unique."[53] Due to the current neglect and disparagement of those prodigies, a reviewer of Weber's edition of Ford confesses that he had for some time harbored such attitudes in secret, "long worshipping" England's early dramatists "with a sort of idolatrous veneration." But now, determined to join the new push to bring them forward as "candidates for public applause," he insists that "all true lovers of English poetry" must recognize their unprecedented genius. "The era to which they belong, indeed, has always appeared to us by far the brightest in the history of English literature,—or indeed of human intellect and capacity. There never was, any where, any thing like the sixty or seventy years that elapsed from the middle of Elizabeth's reign to the period of the Restoration."[54]

To put forward such claims to an uninformed and skeptical public required not only this kind of bedrock conclusiveness about the unmatchable achievement of England's early dramatists but also an equally absolute conviction of the inferiority of their modern descendants. As improved and affordable editions of Renaissance dramatists began to roll off the presses with steady regularity and periodicals began featuring regular series of essays on the old playwrights, more critics joined in their defense, and the contrast between Renaissance and contemporary dramatists grew increasingly polarized. Hazlitt even felt the need to be guarded, for instance, about acknowledging that the present age is "not unfruitful in theatrical genius." This situation explains why Romantic dramatic criticism eventually came to proliferate with scathing denunciations of contemporary efforts. "To wage implacable and unrelenting war against the present corruptions of the British stage," according to *The Dramatic Review,* "is the duty of every man who can wield his pen in so laudable a cause" (21). That duty was assumed with the vengeance of a long oppressed multitude who ultimately came to dominate the period's dramatic criticism with endless tirades against "these unimaginative days of ours,"[55] this "lowest state of depression ... [to which] English tragedy ... *has* sunk,"[56] the "poverty indeed of our present dramatic genius."[57] That the battle of the ancients and the moderns was becoming no contest was already evident by 1812, when an irritated defender of Richard Chenevix's modern plays grumbles about "the common doom of mortality which has gone out against all our contemporary dramatists."[58]

The resulting message transmitted to dramatic aspirants was double-edged and highly problematical. On the one hand, it seemed essential to follow the old writers onto the stage if one entertained any serious ambitions of joining the great tradition of English poets; it became common, in fact, for Romantic critics to present stagewriting as the highest form of literary excellence and Renaissance examples as the absolute model for emulation. From Renaissance drama, "if from anything," was the general conclusion, our modern literary enterprise "must be recreated and refreshed."[59] On the other hand, the same advocates of this mission were also insisting that nothing has been or ever will be seen to compare with the gigantic accomplishments of Shakespeare and his illustrious compeers. No one would go so far as to say that everything in Renaissance dramatic literature was superlative, and many weaknesses or excesses were noted; but the consensus remained, as Hazlitt puts it so plangently, that those "giant-sons of genius . . . rose by clusters, and in constellations never so to rise again!" (*Lectures on the English Poets*, 45–46). Follow the old "aera of the drama," thus concludes a writer in the *Critical Review*, but don't expect much success in this "critical age" (*RR* Part A 1: 315).

Our recognition of how that impossibly divided assignment pervaded Romantic critical theory can help us understand a number of contradictions and limitations in the period's drama. It explains why all of Romanticism's major and many of its minor poets attempted stageable dramas self-consciously written in a Shakespearean or Elizabethan mode.[60] It also suggests why so many of these works, constrained by a set of stylistic and thematic restrictions absent from other literary genres and burdened by the haunting presence of inimitable masters, seem labored, artificial, "relentlessly derivative" (Richardson, *Mental Theater*, 154) and smacking of what many twentieth scholars dismiss as "pseudo-Elizabethanism." It further reveals why so many of the Romantics felt simultaneously drawn to the theater and profoundly defensive about engaging with it. And it helps account for their numerous ventures into nonrepresentational drama even when that form was not considered a valid dramatic medium in their age's standard critical theory, for producing closet drama became a way of indirectly maintaining links with England's dramatic tradition while avoiding the severe pressures of confronting the mighty dead on their own terms.

The Romantics' ambivalence about the drama was compounded by the tendency of periodical writers to castigate their repeated failures in directly confronting those "giant-sons of genius." Occasionally successes were noted, as in one review of Barry Cornwall's "quite admirable" endeavor "to write in the style and spirit of the dramatists of the age of Elizabeth."[61] But countless other times, Romantic dramatists were condemned for their inability to "take up the bow" of their predecessors (*RR* Part A, 2: 800), for futilely aspiring toward heights "beyond . . [their] grasp" (*RR* Part B, 1: 314), for only contributing to "the dull line of mediocrity, which connects our living dramatic writers with those of the Elizabethan age."[62] All these attempts, concludes a reviewer directly addressing "the Dramatists of the Day," are "as a zephyr to a hurricane, a wind that bows the reed in the shallows to the blast that shakes the oak of the forest."[63]

We should not underestimate the debilitating impact of these judgments, notwithstanding Byron's surprise that a mere article could have killed Keats or Keats's own assertion that his acts of self-criticism pained him infinitely more than any periodical assault. Many writers on the Elizabethans attributed their prodigal outpouring of riches to the lack of any restraints or strictures from a critical industry, and *The Retrospective Review* seriously warned of the dangerous tendency of the agent's "damnatory criticism" to wipe out youthful poetic promise.[64] Because of modern dramatists' "dread of criticism," Jeffrey concludes, "there is in all their attempts . . . an air of anxiety and labour" that prevents all those writing "in avowed and elaborate imitation of the ancient models" (such as Byron, Coleridge, Maturin, Baillie, Chenevix, Wilson, Cornwall, and Milman) from ever being "ranked with the older worthies."[65] With this anxiety of influence fostered by the same critical establishment that was imposing such divisive conditions for playwrighting, it should not be surprising to find so many of the Romantics turning away from the stage, hovering agonistically between its pressures and the less threatening alternative of the closet or abandoning drama and poetry altogether. The periodical siege on *John Woodvil,* as Hazlitt puts it, made Lamb turn "critic and prose-writer" (*Lectures on the Dramatic Literature of the Age of Elizabeth,* 317).

The complications put upon the Romantics' dramatic experience by their period's critical establishment were further problematized by a significant political factor. Jon Klancher has demonstrated the elaborate ideological conflicts at stake in all Romantic periodical writing, and we have seen how the era's dramatic criticism was particularly implicated in the financial and political dynamics of the theater.[66] In an even more comprehensive way, the period's theatrical activity and criticism participated in and often encapsulated the great social and political upheavals surging out of the French Revolution and drastically reconfiguring the traditional structures of European society. Ever since Burke sparked the controversy over the French Revolution as theatrical spectacle gone out of control, English writers and politicians had come to think of the playhouse itself as an epitome of the revolutionary drama playing itself out on the world stage of Europe. And there was good reason to see all the dislocating forces of that universal drama at work in the London playhouse. It is common for historians of the nineteenth-century English theater to describe the typical audience as a vulgar rabble unfit for the company of respectable personages. In reality, however, the playhouse was becoming a charged site of class contention, still attended by the king and the aristocracy but fast giving ground to rising middle- and working-class people who controlled the smaller houses and increasingly demanded more of place in the patent theaters.

The conventional playhouse division of social classes according to pit, box, and gallery was rapidly dissolving, for instance, with rioters at Covent Garden in 1809 demanding the lowering of entrance prices and the opening up of boxes traditionally reserved for wealthy spectators. When the theater management hired thugs to disperse the angry crowds, the theater literally became a combat zone between the old and new orders. An appalled Leigh Hunt writes in the *Examiner*, "It is impossible that the public should ever forget the time, when to go to the play was to endanger one's liberty and very life. To seizures and skirmishes has now succeeded an unmixed brutality on the part of the retainers."[67] Less violent, but no less disturbing class struggles often broke out over performance practices. *The Times* reported on 7 January 1819 that the removal of a player from a Drury Lane pantomime instigated an uproarious class dispute, with the gentlemen in the boxes throwing orange peels at the common public in the galleries, who "thundered forth their indignation in a very palpable manner" (3). It was this disorienting, often violent reconfiguration of traditional class and social boundaries that made the London theater seem to many all too much like Paris in the 1790s. The destabilizing situation even caused some uneasiness for the liberal Hazlitt, as he states that "we have no fancy for seeing . . . the pit invade the boxes, nor the boxes shake hands with the galleries. We are for a proper distinction of rank at the theatre."[68]

The subversion of social hierarchies was also taking place on the stage itself, notwithstanding the efforts of the government to promote patriotic works and expunge any criticism of the aristocracy in staged performances. Women, radicals, and members of the lower economic orders were getting their plays produced to an extent that seemed far too empowering for conservative critics such as John Lockhart, the infamous author of *Blackwood's* series "On the Cockney School of Poetry," who was outraged by such an apparent breakdown in traditional place that "our very footmen compose tragedies."[69] Another *Blackwood's* writer, obviously distressed by the growing prominence of women, liberal, and working-class playwrights, disparages leftist dramatists as "a pale-faced sallow set, like the Misses of some Cockney boarding school."[70]

The unrest caused by these intrusive presences was exacerbated by the actual content of a number of highly popular contemporary plays that directly or suggestively challenge reigning social and political orders. Although the government licenser could remove expressions of political dissent from spoken plays, similar censorship of pantomimes and spectacles was virtually impossible; and a number of performances emerged, especially in the early days of the French Revolution, that celebrate, as in the case of John Dent's *The Bastille*, the dismantling of traditional state hierarchies. Even more potentially threatening were a group of left-leaning melodramas, such as Pocock's *Miller and His Man*, that escaped the Licenser's pen by presenting elements of class struggle just beneath the surface of their sensational action (see Cox, *In the Shadows of Romance*, 48). Many of these plays were adapted from French and German melodramas that Charles Nodier, friend of the famous French melodramatist René-Charles Guilbert Pixérécourt, characterizes as designed to promulgate "the morality of the Revolution" (quoted in Cox, 48).

August von Kotzebue's plays were easily the most popular and threatening of these revolutionary melodramas: popular because of their sentimental moralism and threatening because of their tendency to champion virtuous citizens forced into desperate, often violent, behavior by an oppressive aristocracy. Their frequent appearances and adaptations on the London stage actually developed into a volatile new context for the Revolutionary debate. Hazlitt thought German tragedies like Kotzebue's are "a good thing," because they disseminate "the extreme opinions which are floating in our time . . . utterly at variance with old opinions, with established rules and existing institutions" (*Lectures on the Dramatic Literature of the Age of Elizabeth*, pp. 346–47). Such productions, as we might expect, appalled defenders of England's sociopolitical establishments, one of whom, writing for the *Anti-Jacobin Review*, feels disgusted by the "violations of all the rules of propriety and decorum" in Kotzebuean plays and in the audiences they attract of "Jacobin cropped head[s]."[71]

It was the transgression of traditional class boundaries and values in these works and their English imitations that so distressed Coleridge, who found such violations in Maturin's *Bertram* a threat to the entire fabric of British social order. "The shocking spirit of jacobinism," he writes in a scathing critique of *Bertram*, "seemed no longer confined to politics. . . . [*Bertram*] poisoned the taste" and "disorganized the moral principles" of the public. The approval of "a British audience" of such violations "pressed as with the weight of lead upon my heart."[72] With the "Body Theatre," as Coleridge puts it, thus reduplicating destabilizations of the "body politic" (*Biographia Literaria,* 257), it became essential for the conservative critical establishment to restrain the growing tide of plays engendered by Cockneys, Jacobins, women, footmen, Germanophiles, and other suspicious types.

One forceful strategy of control was to condemn many contemporary plays as degenerate offspring or total deviations from a national dramatic tradition that honored conventional social, moral, and political hierarchies. This is where Romanticism's construction of its Renaissance dramatic inheritance becomes most intriguing and politically complicated. Much of the enthusiasm for the old English playwrights was openly nationalistic and anti-Gallican, with many writers on English dramatic history presenting the wealth of Renaissance achievement as a great national treasure that had been sacrificed to the corrupt sophistications of French neoclassical theory during the Restoration and the eighteenth century. "One very great merit" of the Elizabethans' plays, nearly everyone agreed, is "that they are national." And in Shakespeare's particularly magnificent example, one could find "the rock upon which English fame . . . [and] her claims to pre-eminent glory . . . must rest."[73] That such preeminence had been seriously compromised by "the taste for rhyming dramas, which, with many other bad things, came over from France at the Restoration" was an equally universal conviction among English writers on dramatic history.[74]

For those eager to wipe Jacobinism off the English stage, this standard contrast between English nationalism and French corruption also entailed a presentation of the old English dramatists as passionate supporters of rank and monarchy. It was common, even for liberals such as Hazlitt, to think of them as "men of classical education" who, with the notable exception of Shakespeare, "came up from Oxford and Cambridge" (*Lectures on the Dramatic Literature of the Age of Elizabeth,* 186). But Hazlitt was less willing to join in with those who insisted on their passionate royalism before and during the disruptions of the Civil War—their devotion to "the cause of loyalty, duty, and honour."[75] "In their political principles," writes Weber of Beaumont and Fletcher, "both poets were evidently royalists. . . . They frequently asserted and inculcated the divine right and inviolability of kings" (*Works of Beaumont and Fletcher,* p. lxii). Shakespeare's history plays, writes a reviewer of *King John,* should "rouse the patriotism of Englishmen . . . [preserve the] SOCIAL ORDER, and the welfare of GREAT BRITAIN."[76]

Gifford was more precise about contrasting the patriotic royalism of England's Renaissance dramatists with the seditious horrors inculcated by contemporary Jacobin playwrights: "It is grateful to notice the noble contrast which the English stage of that day offers to that of Revolutionary France."[77] Such a contrast was frequently applied to liberal English dramatists of the present era as a means of condemning their works on both artistic and political grounds. Byron's self-avowed allegiance to French classical theory in his dramas, for instance, provoked numerous critics to denounce his abandonment of the "good, honest" spirit of old "*English* tragedy" for atheism, sedition, and Jacobinism. "In the name of Jesuitry, Jacobinism, and Gunpowder," cries a reviewer of his tragedies, "look at SARDANAPALUS!"[78] Coleridge went so far as to condemn the overall development of England's contemporary stage, because of its association with "Kotzebuisms" and its rejection of the "rightful dominion" of the Elizabethans (*Biographia Literaria*, 2: 258).

Such a strategic construction of Renaissance tradition may not have seriously retarded England's reform movement, but it did greatly complicate what was already a difficult confrontation between contemporary dramatists and the ghosts of brighter days. Its tendency to deplore current dramatic tendencies as deviations from a superior past made it all the harder to put aside one's anxieties and forget, as Beddoes advised, about those intimidating specters from the golden age of English drama. For many contemporary poets seeking political and dramatic reform, it also posed the troubling paradox of a compelling literary tradition increasingly associated with political reactionism. To follow in the steps of the old dramatists had virtually become a requisite for inscribing oneself, as Keats so memorably puts it, "among the English poets" (*Letters* 1: 394); yet it was also becoming difficult to ignore the manner in which that very act of inscription, essential to one's creative identity, could also constitute a form of political compromise poisonous to one's social conscience.

There were certainly possibilities for escaping this bind—Byron writing historical dramas that follow Shakespearean models yet also align themselves with a French classical theory implicated in republican ideologies;[79] or Shelley claiming an affiliation with Shakespearean interiority in *Prometheus Unbound* while producing a nonrepresentational drama distinctly removed from the standard conventions of Renaissance theater. But even those innovative experiments ran the risk of turning into esoteric or elitist works, written for a privileged audience and unintentionally supporting the very kind of social hierarchies defended by the conservative forces of the critical establishment. Such a set of aesthetic and political contradictions goes far toward explaining why many reform-minded Romantics, such as Shelley, Byron, Beddoes, and Keats, felt uneasy about their dramatic ambitions. And it suggests why so many Romantic dramas, written both for the stage and the closet, directly confront issues of class conflict—as in Byron's history plays—and tyrannical oppression—as in Shelley's *Prometheus Unbound*.[80]

Much as we may thus find the Romantic critical establishment problematizing the experience of dramatic composition in the nineteenth century, we should also recognize how it opened up significant creative opportunities. In complicating the politics of the Renaissance revival, it compelled some of the Romantics to seek other creative outlets, such as Shelley's turn to Aeschylean tragedy in *Prometheus Unbound* or Byron's engagements with French, Italian, and German dramatic traditions. Even more important, its relentless presentation of the contrast between the ancients and the moderns actually provided an energizing theme for much of Romantic drama. Richardson provocatively suggests that the severe contentions of friendship with the spirits of the past—as in Wordsworth's recasting of *Othello* in *The Borderers*, or Byron's engagement with Shakespeare's Roman plays in his own historical works—power the psychic action of many Romantic plays (*A Mental Theater*, 17–19). An important dimension of the period's drama thus emerged, in the terms of Shelley's preface to *Prometheus Unbound*, as a sustained effort to confront and transform the achievements of the mighty dead. The importance of carrying out such a revisionary program was, in fact, stressed by many reviewers of contemporary drama. The "ancient masters are worthy of being imitated," acknowledges one critic, "but not servilely imitated. Their noble and distinguishing qualities are to be adopted, but not transplanted, thought, language, and all, into a modern soil."[81] "It would appear," adds another, "that it is only by striking into some such new tract that dramatic writers can hope to escape from the old exhausted sphere of associations connected with the pieces belonging to the age of Elizabeth; for it is a certain truth, that the same thing can never have been done successfully at two different eras in the same country."[82] The solution, concludes a reviewer of Milman's poetry, is for modern dramatists to "enrich themselves with the spirits, without encumbering themselves with the trammels of antiquity."[83] Thus to stare an enthralling ghost in the face without becoming paralyzed, as Beddoes knew all too well, was no easy task. But if the critical establishment helped situate Romantic dramatists in Hamlet's dilemma, it also drove them, and in some cases ardently encouraged them, to take the action that eventuated in some of their most innovative creative experiments.

Notes

1. Donald H. Reiman, and Sharon B. Powers, eds., *Shelley's Poetry and Prose: Authoritative Texts and Criticism* (New York and London: W. W. Norton & Company, 1977), 492. References to this work are hereafter cited parenthetically in the text as *Shelley's Poetry and Prose.*

There were certainly some Romantic writers who denied the drama any substantial cultural importance. "Plays have, for the most part," wrote one reviewer of Joanna Baillie's plays, "no moral effect at all: they are seen or read for amusement and curiosity only; and the study of them forms so small a part of the occupation of any individual, that it is really altogether fantastical to ascribe to them any sensible effect in the formation of his character" ("Miss Baillie's Plays on the Passions," *Edinburgh Review* 2 [1803]: 275). Such an assertion, however, came in response to a much more widely held conviction of the drama's crucial role in shaping individual and national character. Critics on both the left and right, often thinking of the drama's key role in shaping public opinion during the French Revolution, consistently stressed the tremendous importance of heeding the cultural impact of England's national drama. James Plumptre, for instance, argued that the appearance of numerous liberal antislavery plays in the early nineteenth century "had a very considerable part in inflaming the public mind with respect to the state of the *Negroes,* and the infamous traffic of the *Slave-Trade*" (*Four Discourses on Subjects Relating to the Amusement of the Stage* [Cambridge, 1809], 41). That seemed like no exaggeration to English conservatives, who were acutely concerned about the incendiary power of the stage. John Hugget, author of an anti-Jacobin play, *Count de Villeroi* (1794), claimed that the theater is "most powerfully calculated to influence the public mind. . . . [The French have generated] an astonishing encrease of popularity to the cause" through strategic uses of the stage (quoted in L. W. Conolly, *The Censorship of English Drama, 1737–1824* [San Marino: Huntington Library, 1976], 83). The indefatigable rigor with which the government's Examiner of Plays, John Larpent, expunged political discourse from countless plays throughout his long career is perhaps the best indicator of the state's serious respect for the political and cultural relevance of the theater.

2. George Steiner, *The Death of Tragedy* (New York: Alfred A. Knopf, 1961), 108, 121–22.

3. "Notices of the Acted drama in London, VII," *Blackwood's Edinburgh Magazine* 4 (1818-10): 443–52.

4. Allardyce Nicoll's basic assumption in his important history of the Romantic stage is that no one can be in doubt of "the general debility" of Romantic drama (*A History of English Drama: 1660–1900,* 6 vols. [1930; reprint, Cambridge: University of Cambridge Press, 1966], 4: 58). John W. Ehrstine notes in his useful study of Romantic dramatic theory that "poetic drama collapsed almost entirely in the Romantic period" ("The Drama and Romantic Theory: 'The Cloudy Symbols of High Romance,'" *Research Studies* 34 [1966]: 85). And Timothy Webb provides the most succinct expression of twentieth-century critical attitudes toward Romantic drama in the title of his recent article, "The Romantic Poet and the Stage: A Short, Sad History," in *The Romantic Theatre: An International Symposium,* ed. Richard Allen Cave (Totowa, N.J.: Barnes and Noble, 1986).

5. Joseph W. Donohue Jr., *Dramatic Character in the English Romantic Age* (Princeton: Princeton University Press, 1970); Terry Otten, *The Deserted Stage: The Search for Dramatic Form in Nineteenth-Century England* (Athens: Ohio University Press, 1972); Erika Gottlieb, *Lost Angels of a Ruined Paradise: Themes of Cosmic Strife in Romantic Tragedy* (Victoria: Sono Nis Press, 1981); Jeffrey N. Cox, *In the Shadows of Romance: Romantic Tragic Drama in Germany, England, and France* (Athens: Ohio University Press, 1987); Alan Richardson, *A Mental Theatre: Poetic Drama and Consciousness in the Romantic Age* (University Park, Pa.: Pennsylvania State University Press, 1988); Daniel P. Watkins, *A Materialist Critique of English Romantic Drama* (Gainesville: University Press of Florida, 1993); Marjean Purinton, *Romantic Ideology Unmasked: The Mentally Constructed Tyrannies in Dramas of William Wordsworth, Lord Byron, Percy Shelley, and Joanna Baillie* (Newark: University of Delaware Press, 1994); Julie Carlson, *In the Theatre of Romanticism: Coleridge, Nationalism, Women* (Cambridge and N.Y.: Cambridge University Press, 1994). References to these works are hereafter cited parenthetically in the text.

6. George Gordon, Lord Byron, *Byron's Letters and Journals*, ed. Leslie A. Marchand, 12 vols. (Cambridge: Harvard University Press, 1982), 8: 210.

Otten finds Romantic drama centering in the kind of dialectical interrogations of the self that Peter L. Thorslev and Susan Wolfson locate at the heart of Romantic literary experience (see Peter Thorslev Jr., *Romantic Contraries: Freedom versus Destiny* [New Haven: Yale University Press, 1984]; and Wolfson, *The Questioning Presence: Wordsworth, Keats, and the Interrogative Mode in Romantic Poetry* [Ithaca: Cornell University Press, 1986]). Cox understands the period's drama as a sustained, often anguished, exploration of the gulf between visionary aspirations and the limits of mortality. Richardson sees Romantic drama acting out perilous confrontations, what he calls "border violation" (8), between antagonistic personalities in a torturous field of psychic combat.

7. Mary Jacobus, "'That Great Stage Where Senators Perform': *Macbeth* and the Politics of Romantic Theatre," *Studies in Romanticism* 22 (1983): 353.

8. *The Dramatic Review, and Register of the Fine Arts* (London, 1814), one of the countless pamphlets, journals, and newspapers that sprung up to report exclusively on the bustling stage activity of the period, opened its pages with this celebration of England's theatrical renaissance: "In the present day the Theatre has become a subject of more general interest than it has ever been before; its amusements have excited a more general attention to their excellencies and defects, and at no time have its services been more arduous" (1).

9. Romantic criticism of the London theater regularly focuses on these and other debilitating conditions in the period's effort to account for what was often perceived as its serious dearth of inspired dramatic writing. "The *first* inconvenience" to dramatic excellence, argues Sir Walter Scott in one of the most common complaints, "arises from the great size of the theatres, which has rendered them unfit for the legitimate purposes of the Drama" (*An Essay on the Drama. The Miscellaneous Prose Works of Sir Walter Scott,* 6 vols. [Edinburgh, 1827], 6: 463). Inveighing against the star system that encouraged playgoers to look for Kean, instead of Othello, Mrs. Siddons, instead of Lady Macbeth, a *Blackwood's* critic "attribute[s] the present depressed state of the national drama to the fault of your GREAT ACTORS" ("On the Present State of the Stage," *Blackwood's Edinburgh Magazine* 17 [1825]: 727). The compulsion to write plays suitable for bourgeois taste and fashion appeared to another *Blackwood's* critic as "abhorrent to genius," the obvious reason writers of talent refused to attempt theatrical productions ("Modern Drama and Dramatic Writing," *Blackwood's Edinburgh Magazine* 14 [1823]: 557). Hazlitt found playwrights

hopelessly constricted by government censoring of any references to sedition, social unrest, or political tyranny. Commenting on the censor's removal of such terms as "Tyranny" and "liberty" from James Sheridan Knowles's *Virginius,* he bursts out in exasperation, "Is the name of Liberty to be struck out of the English language, and are we not to hate tyrants even in an old Roman play?" ("The Drama, No. VII," *London Magazine* 2 [1820]: 91). Sensitive to the lethal drawbacks of such restrictions, Elizabeth Inchbald notes the much greater freedom of poets and novelists, who live in a "land of liberty" relatively free of government censorship compared with "the Dramatic Writer [who] exists but under a despotic government" (quoted in Conolly, 11). The poor pay for dramatists, who received much less for their productions than novelists or even periodical critics, and the lack of copyright protection of published plays struck other critics as added factors discouraging authors from attempting to write dramas.

10. See Cox, *In the Shadows of Romance,* and Marilyn Gaull, "Romantic Theater," *Wordsworth Circle* 14 (1983): 255–63.

11. Matthew Lewis, *Alfonso, King of Castille: A Tragedy, in Five Acts* (London, 1802), vi.

12. Charles Lamb, *The Life, Letters, and Writings of Charles Lamb,* Percy Fitzgerald, ed., 6 vols. (1895; reprint, Freeport, N.Y.: Books for Libraries Press, 1971), 4: 207. Hereafter cited parenthetically in the text as *Life.*

13. William Hazlitt, *Characters of Shakespeare's Plays. Liber Amoris and Dramatic Criticism,* ed. Charles Morgan (London: Peter Nevill, 1958), 254.

14. James Henry Leigh Hunt, *Leigh Hunt's Dramatic Criticism: 1808–1831,* eds. Laurence Huston Houtchens and Carolyn Washburn Houtchens (New York: Columbia University Press, 1949), 15.

15. William Hazlitt, *The Complete Works of William Hazlitt,* ed. P. P. Howe, 21 vols. (London: J. M. Dent, 1933), 18: 191.

John I. Ades writes, "In the face of such performances of *Lear* as rearranged by Tate, it is really not to be wondered at that he [Lamb] should conclude, 'the Lear of Shakespeare cannot be acted.'" "Charles Lamb, Shakespeare, and Early Nineteenth-Century Theatre," *PMLA* 85 (1970): 519.

16. John Keats, *The Poems of John Keats,* ed. Jack Stillinger (London: Heinemann, 1978).

17. "Works of Charles Lamb," *Blackwood's Edinburgh Magazine* 3 (1818): 607.

18. "The Drama, November 1823," *London Magazine* 8 (1823): 549–50.

19. Elizabeth Inchbald, "Preface" to *The German Daughter,* in *The British Theatre,* ed. Elizabeth Inchbald, 20 vols. (London: 1823), 18: 3.

20. Samuel Taylor Coleridge, *Collected Letters of Samuel Taylor Coleridge,* ed. Earl Leslie Griggs, 6 vols. (Oxford: Oxford University Press, 1956–71), 4: 606.

21. William Hazlitt, "On Actors and Acting I," in *Characters,* p. 147; and "The Drama, No. 1," *London Magazine* 1 (1820): 65.

22. Quoted in Donald H. Reiman, ed., *The Romantics Reviewed: Contemporary Reviews of British Romantic Writers,* 9 vols. (New York: Garland, 1972), Part B, 1: 344. Hereafter references to this work are cited in the text as *RR.*

23. "The Drama," *Blackwood's Edinburgh Magazine* 18 (1825): 241.

24. Thomas Lovell Beddoes, *The Works of Thomas Lovell Beddoes,* ed. H. W. Donner (London: Oxford University Press, 1935), 640.

25. Webb, "The Romantic Poet and the Stage," 13.

26. Percy Bysshe Shelley, *Shelley: Poetical Works,* ed. Thomas Hutchinson; corrected by G. M. Matthews (1905; reprint; Oxford: Oxford University Press, 1988),

278; and *The Letters of Percy Bysshe Shelley,* ed. Frederick L. Jones, 2 vols. (Oxford: Clarendon Press, 1964), 1: 102–3.

27. The contradictions in Shelley's attitude toward the stage make Donohue wonder why he ignored "his inveterate distaste for the actors and productions of his day" in his desire to see *The Cenci* performed: *Dramatic Character in the English Romantic Age,* 519.

28. Joanna Baillie, *Dramas by Joanna Baillie,* 3 vols. (London, 1836), 1: v, and John Keats, *The Letters of John Keats,* ed. Hyder Edward Rollins, 2 vols. (Cambridge, Mass.: Harvard University Press, 1958), 2: 135, 139, 157, 234.

29. George Gordon, Lord Byron, *Medwin's Conversations of Lord Byron,* ed. Ernest J. Lovell Jr. (Princeton: Princeton University Press, 1966), 93.

30. Byron, *Byron, Poetical Works,* ed. Frederick Page; corrected by John Jump (1904; reprint, London: Oxford University Press, 1970), 408, 453.

31. Richardson argues that "Byron almost certainly wished (contrary to his protestations) to see [his historical plays] produced." *A Mental Theater,* 43.

32. David V. Erdman, "Byron's Stage Fright: The History of His Ambition and Fear of Writing for the Stage," *ELH* 6 (1939): 243.

33. "Modern Drama and Dramatic Writing," *Blackwood's Edinburgh Magazine* 14 (1823): 555.

34. William Hazlitt, *A View of the English Stage. Dramatic Essays: William Hazlitt,* eds. William Archer and Robert W. Lowe (London, 1895), xxxv.

35. "Rhymer on Tragedy," *Retrospective Review,* 1 (1820): 15.

36. "Lord Byron's Dramas," *Quarterly Review* 27 (1822): 490.

37. "Mr. Barry Cornwall's Tragedy," *London Magazine* 3 (1821): 66.

38. "Modern Drama and Dramatic Writing," *Blackwood's Edinburgh Magazine* 14 (1823): 555.

39. Walter Jackson Bate, *The Burden of the Past and the English Poet* (New York: Norton, 1970); Webb, "The Romantic Poet and the Stage"; and Richardson, *Mental Theater.*

40. "The Tragic-Drama—*The Apostate,*" *Quarterly Review* 17 (1817): 250–51.

41. Quoted in Stuart Curran, *Poetic Form and British Romanticism* (Oxford: Oxford University Press, 1986), 14.

42. "English Literature," *Academic Correspondent* 1 (1832): 418–20.

43. Francis Jeffrey, "Lord Byron's Tragedies," *Edinburgh Review* 36 (1922): 416–17.

44. William Hazlitt, *Lectures on the English Poets,* ed. Catherine MacDonald MacLean (1910; reprint, London: Dent, 1967), 44.

45. Charles Lamb, ed., *Specimens of English Dramatic Poets Who Lived about the Time of Shakespeare* (1808; reprint, London, 1813), v.

46. Lamb often complains about how those prolific geniuses of the early English stage are being "slighted" by his contemporaries (*Specimens,* vii). Weber, an industrious early nineteenth-century editor of Elizabethan dramatists, laments that Jonson, Beaumont, and Fletcher "are more frequently talked of and praised than read," that Ford is "almost unknown to any but professed collectors of ancient poetry," and that in general "all our ancient dramas . . . are at present condemned . . . [to] oblivion" (Henry Weber, ed., *The Dramatic Works of John Ford,* 2 vols. [Edinburgh, 1811], 1: vii; and Henry Weber, ed., *The Works of Beaumont and Fletcher,* 14 vols. [Edinburgh, 1812], 1: ci). Gifford presents Massinger as a "much neglected and much ignored writer" (William Gifford, ed., *The Plays of Philip Massinger,* 4 vols. [London, 1813], 1: lxxviii). And Hazlitt, regretting "the long continued neglect of our earlier [dramatic] writers," warns his Surrey Institute audience "that 'there are

more things between heaven and earth, than were ever dreamt of in our philosophy'" (*Lectures on the Dramatic Literature of the Age of Elizabeth* [London, 1821], 8, 10–11).
   47. *The Dramatic Review, and the Register of the Fine Arts* (London, 1814), 22.
   48. *The British Drama*, 2 vols. (London, 1824), 1: 92.
   49. Thomas Holcroft, *The Theatrical Recorder*, 2 vols. (London, 1805), 1: 201.
   50. "On the Alleged Decline of Dramatic Writing," *Blackwood's Edinburgh Magazine* 9 (1821): 279.
   51. "Analytical Essays on the Modern English Drama, No. III," *Blackwood's Edinburgh Magazine* 18 (1825): 119.
   52. "The Drama," *Blackwood's Edinburgh Magazine* 18 (1825): 241.
   53. "Lord Byron's Doge of Venice," *Blackwood's Edinburgh Magazine* 9 (1821): 279.
   54. "Ford's *Dramatic Works*," *Quarterly Review* 6 (1811): 275.
   55. "On the Early English Dramatists," *Blackwood's Edinburgh Magazine* 2 (1817–18): 660.
   56. "The Tragic Drama—*The Apostate*," *Quarterly Review* 17 (1817): 258.
   57. William Hazlitt, "The Drama, No. IV," *London Magazine* 1 (1820): 432.
   58. "Chenevix's Two Plays," *Edinburgh Review* 20 (1812): 206.
   59. Notices of Old English Comedies," *Blackwood's Edinburgh Magazine* 10 (1821): 127.
   60. "[E]very museling," recognizes one reviewer who is highly ambivalent about the whole enterprise, feels compelled "to imitate . . . the old English dramatists" ("On the Drama," *Blackwood's Edinburgh Magazine* 11 [1822]: 447).
   61. "Cornwall's Dramatic Scenes," *Blackwood's Edinburgh Magazine* 5 (1819): 311.
   62. "The Drama, No. 16," *London Magazine* 3 (1821): 560.
   63. "A Letter to the Dramatists of the Day," *London Magazine* 8 (1823): 137.
   64. "John Dennis's Works," *Retrospective Review*, 1 (1820): 317, 319–21.
   65. Francis Jeffrey, "Lord Byron's Tragedies," 416–17.
   66. John Klancher, *The Making of the English Reading Audiences, 1790–1832* (Madison: University of Wisconsin Press, 1987).
   67. Hunt, *Leigh Hunt's Dramatic Criticism*, 32.
   68. William Hazlitt, "The Drama, No. 8," *London Magazine* 2 (1820): 197.
   69. John Lockhart, "On the Cockney School of Poetry, No. IV," *Blackwood's Edinburgh Magazine* 3 (1818): 519.
   70. "Lyndsay's Dramas of the Ancient World," *Blackwood's Edinburgh Magazine* 10 (1821): 732.
   71. "The Theatre," *Anti-Jacobin Review* 1 (1798): 480.
   72. Samuel Taylor Coleridge, *Biographia Literaria*, eds. James Engell and W. Jackson Bate (Princeton: Princeton University Press, 1984), 2: 229.
   Attacking the inversions of traditional class standards in these works, the *Anti-Jacobin Review* critic complains that "none but *noblemen* are guilty of seduction in these *unenlightened* days. . . . The son is the hero of the piece, and being a plebeian, and moreover, a bastard, he, *of course*, possesses every possible accomplishment of mind and body" ("The Theatre," 479).
   73. "The Drama, No. 15," *London Magazine* 3 (1821): 434; "A Fifth Letter to the Dramatists of the Day," *London Magazine* 18 (1811): 538.
   74. "Lord J. Russell—*Don Carlos, a Tragedy*," *Quarterly Review* 29 (1823): 372.
   75. "Ford's *Dramatic Works*," *Quarterly Review* 6 (1811): 376.
   76. "King John," *anti-Jacobin Review* 8 (1801): 413.

77. Gifford, ed., *The Plays of Philip Massinger,* lxxxi.
78. "A Second Letter to the Dramatists of the Day," *London Magazine* 8 (1823): 135–36.
79. Cox demonstrates how classical French dramatic theory and the works of Alfieri, another important model for Byron, were often associated with the French Revolution's ideology of republicanism; *In the Shadows of Romance,* 33–34.
80. For a useful discussion of class conflict in Byron's history plays, see Daniel P. Watkins, "Violence, Class Consciousness, and Ideology in Byron's History Plays," *ELH* 48 (1981): 799–816.
81. "On the Drama," *Blackwood's Edinburgh Magazine* 11 (1822): 447.
82. "Upon the Relation of Music to the Drama," *Blackwood's Edinburgh Magazine* 6 (1819–20): 431.
83. "Milman's *Fall of Jerusalem,*" *Quarterly Review* 23 (1820): 202.

3
Ideology and Genre in the British Antirevolutionary Drama in the 1790s
Jeffrey N. Cox

The bicentennial year of the French Revolution brought a great deal of scholarly energy to bear upon the events surrounding 1789 and upon the literature, usually called Romantic, that grew up in response to it. Little space, however, was found within such studies for the British antirevolutionary literature of the 1790s and none, I daresay, for its antirevolutionary drama. The British plays written against the French Revolution during the 1790s have been completely obscured from critical view by a number of preconceptions about the literary history of the period. Some of these are old prejudices, such as the opinion that the drama of the late eighteenth and early nineteenth centuries is simply not worthy of attention. Others are linked to what Jerome McGann has identified as the "romantic ideology," the tendency to see every work between roughly 1789 and 1832 from the perspective of the self-definitions of the small group of writers we call "Romantic." As Marilyn Butler has also shown, much of the literary work of this period falls outside our definitions, and the antirevolutionary drama offers another example of her point.[1] Our focus on the six major Romantic poets and our interest in the perceived pattern of their response to the Revolution—radical politics giving way to imaginative liberation or escape—renders alternative groups of writers and other patterns of reaction to the events of the day invisible.

The antirevolutionary dramas and the literary history to which they contribute challenge our standard formulations about the period. These plays were not Romantic; they should not even be read as a context for Romantic works—which would subordinate them to models with which they are not engaged—but instead as dramas significant in their own right. These plays are part of a broader reactionary literature and culture as relevant to the literary and political situation of England in the 1790s as the work of Wordsworth, Coleridge, or Blake. Considering the particular contexts that shaped these texts, we will find that these dramas have an important place in the ideological struggles of the day as well as a significant, if subterranean, impact on the development of the English drama and the theater.

I

The antirevolutionary drama of the 1790s—that is, the body of plays directly attacking the French Revolution or Jacobin principles—comprises a surprisingly sizable corpus. These plays can be divided into several groups, if we consider how they choose to dramatize revolutionary history. There are plays that directly present the events transpiring in France, such as William Preston's *Democratic Rage; or, Louis the Unfortunate* (Dublin, 1793), John Bartholomew's *Fall of the French Monarchy; or, Louis XVI* (1794), and Edmund John Eyre's *Maid of Normandy; or, The Death of the Queen of France* (1794). Related to these plays are several others that are placed in France and that deal with central revolutionary moments—the captivity of the king, the September massacres—but that thoroughly fictionalize events. Richard Hey, for example, argues in the advertisement to *The Captive Monarch* (1794) that it is better to offer a drama "which arises from a *general* view of those principles and Proceedings [of the French Revolution], than such as traces the *actual* Events"; and thus he invents a fictitious king and alters history to fit his plot.[2] John Haggit's *Count de Villeroi: or, The Fate of Patriotism* (1794) alludes to actual events but uses only invented characters.

Another group of plays turned from France to treat home-grown Jacobins; these plays are not—as are those in the first two categories—history plays or vaguely historical tragedies but instead are travesties of the Jacobins or celebrations of British virtue and prowess. In this category fall works such as the anonymous *Philistines; or, The Scotch Tocsin Sounders* (1793) and Robert Heron's *St. Kilda in Edinburgh; or, News from Camperdown* (Edinburgh, 1798). These largely satiric plays treat the domestic response to the French Revolution, attacking, for example, the Scotch Jacobins, known for their strong stands and organization and prosecuted at key trials beginning in 1793, the year of *The Philistines*. There were as well plays that sought parallels to the French Revolution in past history, particularly in biblical history, as can be seen in the anonymous *Hezekiah* (1798) and in Henry Boyd's *Royal Message* (1793), which treats the story of Absalom and Achitophel; another source was classical history, as in Boyd's *Helots* (1793) and Arthur Murphy's *Arminius* (1798), the latter taking up the same historical moment as Heinrich von Kleist's anti-Napoleonic play, *Die Hermansschlacht* (1808). Sheridan's last play, his widely successful adaptation of Kotzebue, *Pizarro* (Drury Lane, 1799), also belongs here, offering not-so-veiled attacks on Napoleon and having as its goal—in the words of the theatrical diarist John Genest—"to reprobate the principles of the French Revolution." When we add to these four categories a fifth containing the many plays with negative allusions to the French Revolution, we have a quite large body of antirevolutionary works.[3]

The earliest of these plays was written in 1792 as part of the general reaction to the increasingly violent and aggressive turn of the French Revolution. The political reaction can be seen not only in the war against France but also in the internal war the Pitt government waged against radicals through the Seditious Meetings Act and Treasonable Practices Act, through increasing prosecutions for sedition, through the suspension of habeas corpus, and through the use of spies and conservative vigilante groups. The British government's willingness to use force internally was most clearly revealed in the suppression of the Irish rebellion of 1798, which resulted in at least thirty thousand deaths—more than died at the hands of the Terror in France, as John Brewer reminds us.[4]

When we look to the social and cultural response of the conservatives, it is important to stress the literal meaning of "reactionary." If English Jacobins had formed the Friends of Liberty, the London Corresponding Society, and other associations, then opponents to the Revolution would found, with government backing, so-called "Church and King" clubs such as the Association for Preserving Liberty and Property against Republicans and Levelers, also known as the Crown and Anchor Society for the London tavern where it met. The prorevolutionary productions of medallions and plaques by manufacturers such as Wedgewood were matched by royalist medals and drinking mugs sporting attacks on Paine or popular counterrevolutionary images such as Cruikshank's "The Contrast," which showed the glories of England and the horrors of France. To answer the immense popularity of Paine's *Rights of Man*, the Loyalists began an intense pamphlet war. Conservatives, feeling that too much of the press was in the control of supporters of the Revolution, founded the *Anti-Jacobin; or, Weekly Examiner*, which pointed out in headlined sections the "Lies," "Misrepresentations," and "Mistakes" of the opposition press and provided parodies of suspect literary figures, including imitations of Southey's Sapphics and Erasmus Darwin's didactic poems.

The response in the theatrical realm was equally reactionary, and not just in the sense that the government banned radical plays or censored politically questionable speeches. The antirevolutionary plays are reactionary in a fundamental way, for reaction defines their moment of creation. The antirevolutionary drama is belated; that is, it arises after 1792, three years after prorevolutionary images could be seen on the London stage. The antirevolutionary drama was written as a response to these earlier works. In fact, the conservative drama appears less an attempt to stage revolutionary history than a struggle to rewrite the prorevolutionary drama. It engages not history but Jacobin rhetoric and imagery. In particular, it confronts two forms: the spectacular play on contemporary history and the Gothic drama.

The first category, represented by such works as Dent's *Bastille* (Royal Circus, 1789), John St. John's *Island of St. Marguerite* (Drury Lane, 1789), and Charles Bonnor's *Picture of Paris in the Year 1790* (Covent Garden, 1790), offered London theatergoers an opportunity to cheer the actions of the people of Paris as they liberated the Bastille in Dent's play or freed the Man in the Iron Mask in St. John's. These plays celebrate mass action and trace a movement from the enclosed spaces of the past—the prison, the castle, the convent—to the open spaces of a liberated future, a movement that marks them as parallel to the revolutionary festivals analyzed by Mona Ozouf.[5] In fact, many of these plays themselves end in festivals, not only of public liberation but also of romantic union, an erotic liberation that is seen to arise with political liberty. This turn to the erotic is even clearer in the other potentially radical dramatic form of the day, the Gothic.

The Gothic drama may have its roots in such plays as Horace Walpole's *Mysterious Mother* of 1768, but it did not become a major force on the British stage until after 1789, the year of both the Bastille and the publication of Ann Radcliffe's first novel. I have argued elsewhere that the Gothic was read at the time as an ideologically charged form, a reading revealed powerfully in Coleridge's *Biographia* where he defines the Gothic as the "modern jacobinical drama."[6] For present purposes, it is important to note that the Gothic, when it traces the liberation of its lovers from past restrictions imposed by cruel fathers, lascivious lords, and fanatic monks, moves to the rhythms of the revolutionary spectacular; and when it instead emphasizes the erotic quest of the villain-hero as he pursues pleasure in defiance of any limits, the Gothic portrays a more individual rebellion. The Gothic was seen as embracing either individual or collective revolt, and its celebration of erotic liberation was particularly troubling to the defenders of official morality and culture.

J. C. Cross's *Julia of Louvain; or, Monkish Cruelty*, taken we are told "From a paragraph in a Newspaper during the French Revolution" (99) and staged at the Royal Circus in 1797, offers a kind of compendium of these features of the prorevolutionary drama. It engages both the historical spectacle—drawing upon an actual event and seeming to invoke the patterns of revolutionary festival—and the Gothic. It tells the story of Julia, loved by Clifford but also sought by the noble St. Pierre. When she rejects the libidinous aristocrat, he has her imprisoned in a loathsome convent. The play climaxes when a crowd, led by officers of the Revolution, storms the convent, and Clifford liberates Julia from her dungeon. The final scene recalls the sites of the revolutionary fetes, sharing their open spaces and sporting a pagan altar (the stage directions call for "A Splendid and Picturesque View, with the Altar of Hymen at a distance"); the figures of repressive authority—the nobleman and the churchman—under arrest, the lovers are united as a paean is sung to "Peace and pleasure" (scene 12). The oppressive power of traditional authority, successful popular action, a pagan celebration of the erotic—Cross engages the images of prorevolutionary drama that counterrevolutionary playwrights felt they had to answer.

Arising to counter such plays, the antirevolutionary drama also faced what Ronald Paulson defines as the central problem of all artistic attempts to represent the Revolution.[7] Because the Revolution was seen as an unprecedented event—even Burke called it "the most astonishing that has hitherto happened in the world"—the use of traditional forms and images to present it would misrepresent its uniqueness.[8] What genre does one use for an event that is sui generis? How is one to stage a conservative version of the radically new events of the revolution? The *Anti-Jacobin*, in introducing its poetry section, makes, albeit humorously, an astonishing suggestion—that poetry itself in a revolutionary age might become revolutionary, that there might be no genre for the conservative poet to adopt: "But whether it be that good Morals, or what We should call good Politics, are inconsistent with the spirit of true poetry—whether '*the Muses still with freedom found*' have an aversion to *regular* Governments. . . . We have not been able to find one good and true Poet, of sound principles and sober practice."[9] Of course, as the poetry of the *Anti-Jacobin* itself demonstrates, conservatives did write. One response to this situation, and the one adopted by the *Anti-Jacobin* itself, is to turn to parody, to attempt to undo or revise the forms adopted by one's opponents. It is significant that the greatest antirevolutionary art of the period is created by the caricaturists and that the antirevolutionary dramas that found some stage success tended to be satires on Jacobins. Another course was to react against the new forms arising within the British theaters of the 1790s and to return to traditional tragedy, particularly neoclassical tragedy, as a declaration in formal terms that the Revolution was not new and that history finally spoke of noble individuals and not popular action.

We can discover the two key targets of the conservative drama's revisionary tactics in a satire that appeared in the *Anti-Jacobin* during June 1798. This weekly was founded by a group of Pitt's supporters around George Canning, made undersecretary of foreign affairs in 1796; it included John Hookham Frere, whose adaptation of ottava rima would later inspire Byron, George Ellis, who had earlier proved himself a satirist for the Whigs, and, as editor, William Gifford, who was brought in, Canning's biographer tells us, because he could provide a "thoroughly brutal spirit."[10] Whether or not the journal had financial support from the government, it had the political support of a series of Tory aristocrats, and it is rumored that Pitt himself contributed to the journal's parodies, including its great satire on Jacobin drama entitled *The Rovers; or, The Double Arrangement.*

The play attacks what it calls the German school of drama—what Coleridge later, perhaps recalling this piece, relabels the "modern jacobinical drama (which, and not the German drama, is its appropriate designation)."[11] This school is seen as comprising on the one hand the Gothic and on the other hand the plays literary history identifies as the drama of the *Sturm und Drang,* plays that are seen by the *Anti-Jacobin* as immoral filth preaching "the reciprocal duties of one or more Husbands to one or more Wives" (236). What the play's authors object to are British dramas that imitate foreign models to bring to the stage, first, acts of successful mob violence against the authority of the church and nobility and, second, an ideology of sexual liberation.

The Gothic drama is satirized in the story of one Rogero, who has been imprisoned in an abbey by his father for loving a woman beneath his station. His dungeon provides an opportunity to recite a litany of Gothic clichés:

> SCENE changes to a Subterranean Vault in the Abbey of QUEDLINBURGH; with Coffins, 'Scutcheons, Death's Heads and Cross-bones.—Toads, and other loathsome Reptiles are seen traversing the obscurer parts of the Stage.—ROGERO appears, in chains, in a suit of rusty Armour, with his beard grown, and a Cap of grotesque form upon his head.—Beside him

a Crock, or Pitcher, supposed to contain his daily allowance of sustenance.—A long silence, during which the wind is heard to whistle through the Caverns. (238)

Rogero is liberated from this dungeon in the final scene by a mob action that mimics the Gothic *Julia of Louvain* or *The Island of St. Marguerite* or, for that matter, Dent's *Bastille;* and the play ends with the figures of traditional authority, the prior and Roger's father, the count, being led off in chains. The action of the liberators is undercut, however, as their band—led by a man thought a waiter but revealed to be "No Waiter, but a *Knight Templar*" (245)—is unable to defeat a body of "Choristers and Lay-brothers" until Puddingfield and Beefington, two British barons in exile awaiting the signing of the *Magna Carta,* call for a battering ram and a Roman legion appears to complete the assault.[12] The single scene parodies many central images and ideas of the Jacobins—the appeal to Roman precedent, the admiration for Saxon liberty, not to mention the belief in action by the people. The dramatic image of the people liberating castles and convents is here ridiculed. Clearly only a nobleman, even if he is an exiled nobleman, or a Roman general, even if he is caught in a time warp, could complete such heroic action; no waiter—not even one who is also a Knight Templar—could ever change history.

The other object of the satire—the popularity of such German plays as Schiller's *Robbers* and *Cabal and Love,* Kotzebue's *Stranger,* and Goethe's *Stella*—is announced in the prologue:

> To-night our Bard, who scorns pedantic rules,
> His Plot has borrow'd from the GERMAN Schools;
> —The GERMAN Schools—where no dull maxims bind
> The bold expansion of th' electric mind.
> Fix'd to no period, circled by no space,
> He leaps the flaming bounds of time and place.
> Round the dark confines of the Forest raves,
> With *gentle* ROBBERS stocks his gloomy caves;
> Tells how bad MINISTERS are shocking things,
> How *reigning Dukes* are just like tyrant Kings;
> How to *two* Swains one Nymph her vows may give,
> And how *two* Damsels with *one* Lover live!
>
> (237)

This passage makes an important link between political resistance to authority and the embrace of sexual freedom. This connection is at the heart of the *Anti-Jacobin's* vision, as is made clear in its prospectus, where it identifies its enemy as "JACOBINISM in all its shapes, and in all its degrees, political and moral, public and private, whether as it openly threatens the subversion of States, or gradually saps the foundations of domestic happiness." In the view of Mr. Higgins, the fictitious Jacobin author of *The Rovers,* the German drama calls for a new "SYSTEM comprehending not Politics only, and Religion, but Morals and Manners, and generally whatever goes to the composition or holding together of Human Society; in all of which a total change and Revolution is absolutely necessary" (236). Within the play, this attack on domestic happiness is traced through the relations of Matilda, Rogero's love and mother of his children, who has also borne children by Casimere, who is marred to Cecilia; the cast list includes the children of Matilda by Casimere, the children of Matilda by Rogero, the children of Casimere and Cecilia along with "Several Children; Fathers and Mothers unknown" (237). Political revolution may be abhorrent, but it is the prospect of sexual liberation—particularly the liberation of female sexuality—that is truly terrifying.

The position adopted by the *Anti-Jacobin* was neatly summed up by William Cobbett in a poetic epistle to its editor, Gifford, about his satire the *Baviad.* Cobbett joins Gifford in attacking playwrights who have 'their gothic hands on social quiet laid, / And, as they rave, unmindful of the storm, / Call lust refinement, anarchy reform."[13] This double assault on popular rebellion and sexual liberation defines the project of the antirevolutionary drama. This project, both ideological and generic, seeks to defeat the dangerous erotic power unleashed in both the Gothic and in revolutionary romances through an appeal to domesticity and patriarchal power; in formal terms, there is an attempt to transform the Gothic into the domestic melodrama. And there is also a struggle to replace the image of mass action with conspiracy theories of isolated, ambitious men manipulating the foolish people—in formal terms, the conversion of revolutionary spectaculars such as Dent's *Bastille* into neoclassical tragedies of intrigue.

II

The attack on the French Revolution as the site of sexual excess was established early, in, for example, Burke's *Reflections on the Revolution in France,* as Paulson, among others, has pointed out.[14] Burke first works to establish the French royal family as a model of domestic love and loyalty. Louis XVI, who had difficulty consummating his marriage, hardly made an ideal model for patriarchal potency, but Burke transforms him into an image of manly and kingly prowess. In the figure of Louis confronting the mob at Versailles, Burke offers us a perfect father, husband, and ruler: "As a man, it became him to feel for his wife and his children, and the faithful guards of his person, that were massacred in cold blood about him; as a prince, it became him to feel for the strange and frightful transformation of his civilized subjects, and to be more grieved for them, than solicitous for himself" (488). Marie Antoinette was, if anything, a harder case, known for her flirtatiousness and revealing dress and attacked as an adulteress, lesbian, child abuser, and even incestuous lover. Burke's famous passage on the queen—rising to his complaint "But the age of chivalry is gone"—describes her as not only possessing beauty, "glittering like a morning-star, full of life, and splendor, and joy," but also as embodying "lofty sentiments" and the "dignity of a Roman matron" (488–89). She thus manages to combine physical charm with the ironclad domestic virtue of the Roman wife and mother.

Juxtaposed to the virtuous domesticity of the royal couple are the barbaric and clearly sexual crimes of Burke's "swinish multitude" in their attack on Versailles: "A band of cruel ruffians and assassins, reeking with his [a guard's] blood, rushed into the chamber of the queen, and pierced with an hundred strokes of bayonets and poniards the bed, from whence this persecuted woman had but just time to flee almost naked, and through ways unknown to the murderers had escaped to seek refuge at the feet of a king and husband" (486). Paulson has pointed out that Burke, in his *Letter to a Member of the National Assembly* of 1791, imagined the revolutionaries' sexual licentiousness corrupting all society, as every tutor, valet, or servant, taught by "the false sympathies of this *Nouvelle Eloise*," seeks "to betray his master" by seducing his daughters and destroying "The sanctuary of his house." As Paulson sums up Burke's imagery, we find an opposition of "rootless masculine sexuality, unleashed and irrepressible, against a gentle aristocratic family, patriarchal and based on bonds of love."[15]

We find similar images in popular caricatures and prints.[16] On the one hand, they display the sexuality and bestiality of the revolutionaries—one might think of Gillray's "Representation of the horrid Barbarities practiced upon the Nuns by the Fish-women, on breaking into the Nunneries of France" (1792), where the nuns' backsides are displayed to good effect, or again of the visual puns on the word *sansculotte* that we find in works such as Richard Newton's "The Duke of Brunswick attacking the Rear of the Sans Culottes" (1792). On the other hand, many prints, broadsheets, mugs, and medals celebrate the royal family in such tender scenes as Louis's departure from his family or the queen separated from her children.

The prevalence and consistency of these positive images suggest they serve a serious ideological point; in fact, they sketch the outlines of a standard conservative argument for the monarchy and against the Jacobins. In noting that the images of Louis XVI do *not* use one possible set of associations—those of the French King as Catholic martyr—David Bindman argues that "to accept Louis XVI's claims to martyrdom was also to accept the divine attributes of his kingship. . . . Burke rests his own concept of monarchy upon the Revolution Settlement of 1688, and the British constitutional monarchy. . . . Loyalist claims for monarchy were increasingly constructed in the revolutionary period around such ideas of George III as 'Father of the People.'"[17] These images and ideas seek to answer the radical argument for "natural rights" without depending on an appeal to divine right but instead taking the radical's own ground: nature. The conservatives seem to be saying that if we look to the natural order, we will find not rights but an orderly model for society based in the structure of the family, where, in the words of Hannah More's *Village Politics,* "the woman is below her husband, and the children are below their mother, and the servant is below his master."[18] Patriarchal concepts may have a long history within political discourse, but they take on a new importance and vehemence in the conservative response to the Revolution. Patriarchy becomes sentimental politics, the imposition of an imaginary natural order on a restive social one.

The antirevolutionary drama also adopts this opposition of patriarchal authority and sexual riot. John Bartholomew, in *The Fall of the French Monarchy; or, Louis XVI,* seems at times to have his copy of Burke's *Reflections* at his side as he writes. Louis is the perfect monarch and father. In his scenes with his ministers, we find that Louis is no tyrant but a proponent of constitutional monarchy, that he wants to rule in harmony with the National Assembly, that he promises fiscal reform. Wanting a government like that in England, Louis proclaims himself the "Father of my Country" (1.2). The play also provides wide scope for domestic scenes. We see the love between the royal couple and the tender care Marie Antoinette feels for her children; we are even treated to a scene (2.4) in which the king teaches geography to the royal offspring. Louis's manly fortitude is exemplified in a scene direct from Burke, in which the mob attacks the queen's bedchamber, killing her sentry, only to be driven off heroically by the king himself.

The perverse sexuality of the revolutionaries is also revealed in this scene, for the mob enters dressed in women's apparel, as the author draws upon the hints that the march on Versailles of 5 October 1789 might have involved the kind of political cross-dressing that we are beginning to discover in eighteenth-century mass action.[19] The play again echoes Burke by attacking the sexual principles of the Revolution in a scene in which the royal princesses revile Rousseau and his *New Eloise:* "If Rousseau's maxims shall corrupt the mind, / Farewell to wedded love, uniting souls.—/ Insult to female honour, thro' each page, / Unfolds itself in language most refin'd" (2.2). The play makes it clear that sexual immorality is an essential plank in the revolutionary platform, along with atheism and "this absurd idea Equality, / Which in creation never did exist, / [and which] Destroys subordination" (2.1). The play's position is summed up in the assertion that the "Rights of Man" are in fact the "rights of devils" (2.1)

The pattern of Burke's sexual and domestic imagery is even clearer in Eyre's *Maid of Normandy; or, the Death of the Queen of France.* Set in 1793, the play has a double plot, the first strand of which treats Marie Antoinette, her love for her children, and her suffering as Robespierre plots her death. We often overhear her in prayer, pleading for her country and, more fervently, for her family. We see her forced from her children, in the scene so dear to the artists of the day. We witness her trial, where she demolishes the arguments of her accusers and then pardons them when they condemn her. Throughout she remains devoted to God and to her children and strong in her resistance to Jacobin deviousness. In her final scene, she calls upon God and casts herself as a martyr:

> Oh, thou supreme, who sit'st enthron'd on high! [Kneeling.]
> Who has infus'd within the cup of life,
> The bitt'rest portion for the draught of pride—
> If, in the dispensations of thy pow'r,
> Thou has decreed for some peculiar end,
> That I should suffer for a vicious race,
> With humblest patience I sustain the load.
>   If, in the thoughtless hour of dazzled pomp,
> My heart has been estrang'd from thee, and heav'n,
> In mercy, punish; bless my poor orphans,
> And stretch a ray of pity on their fate!
>
> (4.4)

This strand within the plot establishes the queen as a martyr for order, for true liberty, and perhaps even more importantly, for domesticity.

The second plot offers a stark contrast to the domestic and regal virtues of the queen, as we witness several interviews between Marat and Charlotte Corday, who has vowed to kill Marat—whom she calls "that vile assassin-fiend, the type of Hell" (1.2)—for having killed her beloved Alberto (though Alberto has, in fact, survived, disguised as Theodore and plotting to aid the queen). Marat reveals himself not only to be a vicious power seeker ("Am I the people's friend thro' love of justice? / No, 'tis my int'rest links me to the crowd, / My bold ambition, and my great revenge!" [2.2]) but also a lascivious pleasure seeker. He finds himself strangely aroused by Corday's verbal assaults on him:

> Yet was there something in her aw'd my rage,
> Nay, more, her charms engros'd my am'rous thoughts.
> A happy project, like the dawn of light,
> Bursting thro' chaos, strikes upon my mind—
> Guards shall attend to seize upon her person—
> Her luscious sweets I will enjoy, by force!
> Then, sated with the nauseous banquet, rise,
> And have her apprehended as a rebel—
> Thus shall I glut, at once, my love, and vengeance!
> 'Twill be the feast, the luxury of revenge!

Marat, the plebeian, has taken on the libertine role that the Gothic reserved for the amoral aristocrat. Marat dies on stage in lustful pursuit, not stabbed in his bath as actually occurred. Crying "let me but bask, and riot in thy arms" (3.2), he tries to rape Corday, and she stabs him more to defend herself than to fulfill her planned vengeance. Before she is led off to prison, she is reunited with her betrothed, Alberto/Theodore, to form a portrait of self-sacrificing love in contrast with the lust of Marat. They are allowed to imagine domestic bliss beyond the grave.

The Maid of Normandy offers a simple message: the Jacobins would overturn not only the state but sexual relations; the defenders of monarchy are also the preservers of the family. This attempt to reconfigure the Revolution as a struggle between patriarchal domesticity and rampant sexuality was taken to its logical conclusion in John Haggit's *Count de Villeroi; or, The Fate of Patriotism*, where—despite the fact that the play is set on 3 September 1792 amidst the Paris prison massacres—we are no longer presented with the drama of actual events involving Louis XVI or Robespierre; instead, we are given a family romance. The Count de Villeroi, an aristocrat who has sided with the Revolution only to be appalled by its brutality, is challenged by his son Henry, who has been lured into an alliance with base revolutionaries by Julia, a wealthy but bourgeois widow. Julia wants to marry Henry against his father's wishes, and Henry seeks to rally his father to the cause of extreme democracy, while the older man hopes to reclaim the younger to the duties of family and name. When Henry seeks to engage his father in political debate, the count falls back upon his claim that the king is the "indulgent Father of his people" and reduces Henry's position to "boyish rage" (3.2). To the count, democracy is merely an adolescent tantrum.

In a sense, the debates between Henry and the count center on conflicting readings of the Revolution, which Henry argues is an idealistic attempt to reform society and his father contends is a petty struggle by the young or dispossessed to displace their biological or social fathers. The count's position finally prevails, for even Henry—as he seeks to reject his father's treatment of him as the "peevishness / of aged infirmity"—allows his revolt and his rhetoric to be tinged with the languages of patriarchal authority and oedipal struggle:[20]

> And suits it with the dignity of freedom
> To pay a tame regard to it? to bow to it?
> As well be subject to the Monarch's frown
> As at the beck of an imperious Father.
> What! when we strive to set a nation free,
> Is't fit we truckle to domestic thraldom?
> . . . .
> No, though I find a *Father*, he's my foe;
> More than our Father is our Liberty!
>
> (3.2);

Henry finally lives up to his father's worst expectations, denouncing the count to the Revolution, not as a result of their political differences but because he is pushed to it by the wiles of the beautiful Julia.

Henry almost immediately regrets his stand against his father and returns to him to receive his blessing as the count is dragged off by the officers of the Assembly. Henry, who felt constrained by his father's patriarchal power, now finds that a revolt against it places him under intolerable psychological pressure. The play suggests that once he or any other rebel enters into a struggle with the father—whether familial or political—he cannot escape an oedipal double bind. Henry loses control and rushes from plans to rescue his father to thoughts of suicide to mad schemes for revenge. Julia also begins to go insane with remorse in several scenes that link her to Lady Macbeth. She, too, repents and tries to undo her plots, but the count is executed, and she is then killed by Henry, who himself dies from wounds suffered in murdering one of the Revolution's leaders. This "polluted pair" is contrasted with Henry's sister and her aristocratic lover, who—properly matched by class, appropriately aware of familial duties, and loyal to their royal father—flee France to seek political and domestic order in England (5.11).

It is significant that in this play, which goes further than, say, *The Maid of Normandy* in converting revolutionary politics to a domestic squabble, the source of sexual danger is switched from the male to the female. In *The Maid of Normandy*, the sexual and political are united in Marat, who sees both as fields for the exercise of his will to power. In *The Count de Villeroi*, however, sexual power is isolated from political power and located in Julia, who owes something to Millwood in Lillo's *London Merchant* and to other seductresses in plays on the dangers of sexuality to domestic tranquility; for her, politics is merely the means to get Henry from his father and into her bed. *The Maid of Normandy* offers a parallel between political tyranny and rampant, illicit sexuality and in doing so merely gives a negative twist to the revolutionary drama's own link between eroticism and revolution. *The Count de Villeroi*, however, reduces radical politics to randiness and thereby seeks to domesticate revolt, to redefine the revolutionary as a maladjusted adolescent, someone who has not yet learned how to deal with his father, whether biological or political.

All these plays seek to refute the prorevolutionary drama's celebration of the Revolution as the liberator of Eros. If *Julia of Louvain* and similar works suggested that the Revolution freed lovers and erotic energy from the dead hand of a patriarchal past, the conservative dramatists argue that the Revolution produces only erotic monsters or sexual misfits. The appeal of liberated sexuality is countered with the joys of domesticity, as represented most fully in the royal family itself. These plays insist on the continuity of patriarchal order from father to king, thereby grounding their conservative ideology in "nature" and rendering revolt into an "unnatural" assault on parental power.

In a play such as Haggit's, a move is finally made not just to assert the domestic as a model for the political but to offer it as an alternative to the political, as a refuge from political struggles that should not, it is suggested, concern any of the *people* in the audience. This revisionist and reactionary ideological stand has a formula counterpart, for Haggit's play already points forward to the domestic melodrama that would come to dominate the British stage, shaping all other forms, as the increasing insistence on domestic moralism in comedy, pantomime, and even farce suggests. Gilbert Cross argues that the domestic melodrama thoroughly ruled the British stage by

1820, the year that saw the staging of W. T. Moncrieff's *Lear of the Private Life*, which Cross sees as signaling the melodrama's domination over even traditional tragedy.[21] Although the complex developments within the hierarchy of dramatic genres during this period are not fully susceptible to a brief summary, we do see a movement away from the Gothic of the revolutionary 1790s toward the domestic melodrama, triumphant by the 1820s. Where the Gothic offered the potentially radical pattern of confinement giving way to liberation, of static order of church, lord, and patriarch opening up to the young lovers, the melodrama enacts the restoration of traditional order. The melodrama no longer stages the erotic combat between lovers and a villain-hero. It turns to orphan girls, deaf and disguised fathers, and blind boys; and it stages the discovery of lost domestic bonds, the reunification of families. Its villains are no longer the deeply ambivalent figures of the Gothic but instead clear-cut heavies who thus help to dispel the moral ambiguities the Gothic explored. As Peter Brooks argues, "The melodrama becomes the principal mode for uncovering, demonstrating, and making operative the essential moral universe in a post-sacred era."[22] In different terms, the melodrama reasserts traditional order in a postrevolutionary era, suggesting that the French Revolution was not, after all, an apocalyptic event but a passing challenge to an eternal and interlocked domestic, political, and moral order grounded in patriarchal power.

III

Another major goal of the antirevolutionary drama was to negate the image of the Revolution as a popular uprising founded in actual grievances, created by such plays as Dent's *Bastille*. A considerable amount of counterrevolutionary propaganda was spent in either defaming the "mob" or reducing it to a duped instrument of ambitious schemers. The British caricaturists of the day tended to depict the French crowds as anarchic, barely human grotesques; Gillray's vicious "A Family of Sans-Culotts refreshing after the fatigues of the day" (1792) imagines a revolutionary family devouring the victims of the guillotine, while the mother roasts a child and the Jacobin children devour a bucket of entrails. We find similar images—now to Scottish sympathizers with the Revolution—in the anonymous *Philistines; or, The Scotch Tocsin Sounders* (1793), where Idle appears to echo both Gillray and Burke as he sings:

> Since we are swine,
> On blood we'll dine,
> And rest on desolation;
> Like Sans Culottes
> We'll sharp our snouts,
> And dig up all the nation.
>
> (3)

The play continues to depict the Scots Jacobins as drunks, gluttons, and idlers, easily aroused by a call for blood; but it also engages the other central counterrevolutionary tactic for handling the populace, for it finally argues that the working men who gather in a bar to discuss French politics and ideas are merely the naive pawns of Captain King's Bench, a gentleman, and David Hagabag, a merchant, who, as upper-class sympathizers with the radicals, are seen as the true danger. The play ends as a constable leads these two characters to jail and commiserates with the others:

> Poor misled men! your situations excite sympathy; but what kind of characters are those *gentlemen,* who, to revenge disappointment in unreasonable expectations, have not scrupled to pursue means, which, if God had not prevented them, might have ended in the loss of thousands of lives, and in the utter ruin and destruction of our native country. (28)

Such a speech had an immediate political, even propagandistic purpose. *The Philistines* appeared in the midst of a series of prosecutions in Scotland during 1793 and 1794 that were aimed at intimidating and undermining the strong and radical Scottish popular assemblies. The two most famous convictions were of Thomas Muir and the Reverend T. F. Palmer. Both were accused of the crime of King's Bench and Hagabag, that is, of being educated men who had misled simple common folk by introducing them to radical learning. The lord justice-clerk at Muir's trial accused him of spreading seditious materials to "ignorant country people, and among the lower classes, making them leave off their work." E. P. Thompson notes that Palmer's "'crime' was that of encouraging the reading of Paine, and membership of the Dundee Friends of Liberty—described as a society of 'low weavers and mechanics.'" Both men were transported to Botany Bay, Palmer for seven years and Muir for fourteen. Plays such as *The Philistines* are clearly not innocent works of satiric fun, for they helped to create the ideological climate in which such harsh sentences were tolerated.[23]

Counterrevolutionary tracts find a variety of culprits to blame for such manipulation of the people, from Burke's deluded "men of theory" and their allies the "literary caballers and intriguing philosophers," the "political theologians, and theological politicians" to the illuminati and Freemasons who inhabit the imagination of Abbe Barruel.[24] In the antirevolutionary dramas of the day, the standard tactic is to argue that the Revolution is not so much a popular revolt as the conspiracy of devious malcontents seeking to replace monarchy with their own tyranny.

For example, William Preston's *Democratic Rage; or, Louis the Unfortunate* offers as its villain the duke of Orleans, Philippe Egalite. He enters, like Richard III, for a soliloquy about his plans. He reveals that he detests the "peasant slaves" of Paris and that "the principle / Of new existence" behind the Revolution is really his own pride and ambition (1.2). Orleans clearly believes himself in control of events and of Robespierre and Marat, whom he calls his minions. Robespierre does intend to help him become king, but only because he believes Orleans will provide a purifying dictatorship after which Robespierre will rule. Proclaiming equality rather than nature as his god and concerned about his base background (1.3), Marat depicts himself as a plebeian version of Shakespeare's Edmund; he seems mainly interested in revenge upon his betters and in unleashing the title's democratic rage. The play centers on the machinations of these and other revolutionary leaders, all of whose behavior is contrasted with the conventional calm stoicism of the royal family. But what is most important here is that the fight for control of the Revolution is seen as going on without the people, behind their backs or above their heads. The Revolution is rewritten as a palace intrigue. The Shakespearean echoes align the revolutionaries with older models of dynastic and familial struggle rather than with a new concept of popular or class revolt, and the formal conventions of the palace tragedy erase the role of the populace, the famous Parisian mob. If domestic melodrama offered a generic alternative to the erotically charged Gothic, traditional tragedy—particularly its neoclassical version—provided a formal means for discounting the importance of the mass actions portrayed in revolutionary historical spectaculars.

The antirevolutionary drama, then, gravitates toward two particular dramatic forms and their attendant visions, toward the domestic melodrama on the one hand and neoclassical tragedy on the other. What I am suggesting is that together these forms offered a complete conservative response to the prorevolutionary drama, a resolution in generic terms of the conservatives' ideological project. We might not normally associate melodrama with neoclassical tragedy, but the two are in fact ideological secret sharers during this period. It is no coincidence that when Napoleon reorganized the Paris theaters in

1807, he designated two kinds of drama that could be performed: the melodrama at the boulevard theaters and the neoclassical repertoire at the traditional major houses.[25] Napoleon, seeing himself as the culmination and thus the end of the Revolution, promoted dramatic forms that supported this contention, with neoclassicism offering the upper classes an image of an eternal world immune to historical change, and the melodrama providing the populace with a morality lesson in which violence only leads to the victory of traditional virtue. Together, they present a world that has passed through violence to a final order—that is, they offer a Napoleonic reading of the Revolution.

This link could also be made by sympathizers with the Revolution who wished to question the melodrama and the neoclassical tragedy. Shelley, for example, joins these two forms in his 1821 attack on the current state of the drama in *The Defence of Poetry:* "In periods of the decay of social life, the drama sympathizes with that decay. Tragedy becomes a cold imitation of the form of the great masterpieces of antiquity . . . or a weak attempt to teach certain doctrines, which the writer considers as moral truths; and which are usually no more than specious flatteries of some gross vice or weakness with which the author in common with his auditors are infected. Hence what has been called the classical and the domestic drama." Recalling an earlier Restoration when "hymns to the triumph of kingly power over liberty and virtue" were sung to Charles II, Shelley laments that during the Restoration that followed Napoleon's fall the same two forms that the French ruler supported now serve "the decay of social life" under reactionary governments.[26]

We should not reify dramatic genres or identify them too closely with any single ideological vision. After all, Shelley himself sought to remake tragedy, transforming Aeschylean tragedy into the visionary romance of *Prometheus Unbound* (1820) and revitalizing Elizabethan conventions to fight contemporary ideological battles in *The Cenci* (1820). To see how the Romantics drew upon earlier dramatic conventions only to revise them for new aesthetic and ideological purposes, we need think only of Byron's politically charged use of the conventions of "mystery" plays in *Cain* (1821), of Buchner's turn to Shakespeare and Schiller to dramatize the French Revolution in *Danton's Death (Dantons Tod,* 1835), or of Goethe's reworking of a host of dramatic forms from Greek tragedy to Calderon, from Shakespeare to the melodrama in *Faust.*

Still, within the institution of the British Theatres Royal—where the new drama of the Romantics was not welcome—melodrama and particularly traditional tragedy took on a conservative cast. As we would expect, tragedy was at the forefront of the conservatives' cultural program, while the melodrama continued to be traduced by conservative critics as "illegitimate" drama, a term carrying legal connotations under the Licensing Act but also having aesthetic, moral, and political resonances.[27] Tragedy stood at the summit of dramatic types as the "legitimate" ruler of the theatrical world. Its traditional forms, both neoclassical and Shakespearean, were promoted and preserved by theatrical managers, critics, and star actors; there was an enormous cultural investment in preserving what was seen as the great tradition of the drama against the rising tide of new, popular forms such as the Gothic.

There is surely nothing inherently reactionary about preserving a literary tradition: the particular plays within that tradition represent a wide range of visions and viewpoints. When, however, that tradition was used as a defense against the theatrical innovations of the day—when the project of putting on Shakespeare, Jonson, and Otway can be described by Coleridge as the "redemption of the British stage," the "exterminating" of the German drama, and the restoration of traditional drama to its "rightful dominion over British audiences"—then it becomes clear that this is no innocent exercise in dramatic curatorship but an attempt to keep at bay new forms that were seen as dangerous to the dominion of more than the traditional drama.[28] Within this context, neoclassical and even Shakespearean tragedy could be seen as offering models for presenting history that would serve conservatism. Neoclassical tragedy through the rules of decorum excluded the mass action and violence that had marked the French Revolution as a transforming event. Shakespearean tragedy, as read by audiences and critics of the period, focused on the great, isolated man; it was not the vehicle for portraying historical events shaped by forces or agents other than individuals. Backed by the government-sponsored theaters and revered as the heart of British culture, traditional tragedy offered a prestigious model to imitate, but its very form exerted pressures on content that tended to convert any account of revolutionary events toward a conservative position. That is, even where traditional forms were adopted for largely aesthetic reasons, even where the playwright might have a radical message to convey, traditional tragedy within the context of the theatrical and cultural world of the day carried a conservative ideological charge.

The impact of this generic pressure can be seen in many plays of the period, and not only in expressly antirevolutionary works, which might adopt neoclassical form in a conscious effort to dismiss revolutionary innovations on what appear to be purely stylistic grounds.

The career of Matthew Lewis, a major force in the theater of his day, provides a crucial example of the impact of generic choice upon intention. Lewis was a member of liberal Whig circles, a friend of Lord Holland and Byron, and an admirer of Fox, with strong views on issues such as slavery. A key Gothic playwright, he helped create the rage for a form whose radical potential I have already suggested. In fact, he published his Gothic smash hit *The Castle Spectre* (1798) to combat rumors that his play was "extremely licentious" and "violently democratic"—that is, he was faced with the double charges leveled against the Gothic by the *Anti-Jacobin*.[29] When, however, Lewis sought to write tragedies, his vision altered with his genre. His Gothic plays such as *The Castle Spectre*, or *Venoni* (1808; an adaptation of the revolutionary *Les Victimes Cloitrees* of Monvel) depict figures of authority as oppressors and offer a world denied providential certainties; but his tragedies—*Alfonso, King of Castille* (1801) and *Adelgitha; or, The Fruit of a Single Error* (1806)—offer positive authority figures and evoke the language of divine control. That is, they re-create the hierarchical and providential order that underpinned traditional tragedy and that was subverted in the Gothic. Whatever the liberal Lewis's intentions, the shape of his tragedies leads him to endorse the principle of royal and divine authority.

Perhaps the strongest example of such generic shaping is found in France itself, in Marie Joseph Chenier's *Charles IX*, the most celebrated play of the early days of the Revolution and one that had been blocked by the French royal censor prior to July 1789. Chenier's play on the St. Bartholomew's Day Massacre was read by the censor and its audiences as a commentary on contemporary politics. Chenier wanted to offer a new national, historical tragedy rather than an elite, aristocratic one, the tragedy of a people rather than of a great man. His play, however, never discards the formal limits of the neoclassical palace tragedy; and its generic commitments so shape its vision that the national tragedy at its heart—the massacre itself—cannot be staged, can in fact barely be described within the rules of decorous language Chenier continues to uphold. Chenier wanted to be *the* dramatist of the Revolution, but he remained committed to the culture of the ancien regime. As Jean Starobinski has said, "Such tragedy was doomed to mere repetition."[30]

The generic limits of tragedy, backed by its cultural prestige, at times seemed to radical writers to have the power to enforce a conservative vision. Shelley feared that, under a reactionary government, drama would inevitably be reactionary. Hazlitt went further in his review of *Coriolanus* (which he finds treating the issues at the heart of the French Revolution) written for the *Examiner* of 15 December

1816 during the troubled days following the Spa Fields Riots. He suggests that all poetry is necessarily in sympathy with power: "The language of poetry naturally falls in with the language of power.... The principle of poetry is a very anti-levelling principle.... It is everything by excess. It rises above the ordinary standard of sufferings and crimes.... It has its altars and its victims, sacrifices, human sacrifices. Kings, priests, nobles, are its train-bearers; tyrants and slaves its executioners—'Carnage is its daughter!' Poetry is right royal."[31] Hazlitt makes clear his own sympathies in linking royal power to excess and violence and by including a sharp echo of Wordsworth's "Ode. 1815," he, like Shelley, fears that poetry, at least in their day, is more than half in love with death-dealing power. While the authors of the *Anti-Jacobin* worried that the muse might be a revolutionary, Hazlitt raises the possibility that the imagination itself is an ideological tool of the traditional powers of the monarchy and aristocracy.

IV

There is, however a surprising twist in this tale of dominant forms, which might otherwise suggest that the drama of the day was under the control of a hegemonic conservatism that could impose through the strictures of neoclassical tragedy and domestic melodrama crippling limitations on even the most subversive voices. The twist is that the antirevolutionary plays I have been discussing rarely reached the London stage; in fact, at least one of these plays was blocked by the Examiner of Plays serving the very government these dramatists hoped to support.[32] Given the government's financial backing for the distribution of counterrevolutionary pamphlets and images, its tacit and sometimes direct support for church and king associations, its desire to respond to radical journalism through such vehicles as the *Anti-Jacobin*, it might strike us as surprising that it did not seek to sponsor an antirevolutionary drama within the theaters over which, after all, it had considerable control granted it by the Licensing Act of 1737. This failure certainly surprised a playwright such as Haggit, who protested the government's attitude in the preface to *The Count de Villeroi*. He notes that the drama is "most powerfully calculated to influence the public mind" (vi) and laments that the British government has not followed the members of the French National Assembly, who "by the pieces which they have ordered to be acted, as well as those composed for the purpose ... have gained astonishing increase of popularity to their cause" (viin.).

Far from ordering antirevolutionary plays to be acted, the government seemed to discourage them. It comes as no surprise that as examiner John Larpent censored passages in the prorevolutionary *Island of St. Marguerite* or that he blocked a Covent Garden play on the taking of the Bastille. What is surprising is his decision to prevent performance of *The Maid of Normandy; or, The Death of the Queen of France*—and to do it not once, but twice, in 1794 and 1804. Following the 1794 rejection, the author of the play claimed that the Lord Chamberlain denied a license to the play for "*political* reasons," but he does not spell them out, and we do not have the Examiner's or the Lord Chamberlain's explanation for the action. Larpent often marked objectionable passages for deletion in the licensing manuscripts, but we do not have the 1794 manuscript, and the 1804 copy is merely marked as being "Refused."[33] What we do have is a journal entry made by Anna Margaretta Larpent, the wife of the Examiner, for 14 April 1794.

> Evening worked. Mr. Larpent read loud a MSS tragedy from a Country Theatre The Death of the Queen of France, and the Maid of Normandy. A Strange absurd jumble of C. Corde killing Marat. The Prison of the French Royal family introduced, their sufferings, ridiculous attempts at simplicity in the young Kings conversation. One part perfectly ridiculous. His mother tells him god is his father he alas has no other. The Boy asks if God will take him on his knee & fondle him [.] In short it is devoid of poetry & judgment as it can be & highly improper just now were it otherwise.[34]

Eyre claimed that his play was rejected for "*political* reasons," but Anna Larpent and her husband could not have objected to the play's vision. Anna Larpent's journal reveals her to be a fascinated spectator of events in France, a friend to many emigrés in London, and an avid reader of both pro-and antirevolutionary works. She is in many ways the perfect audience for a play on revolutionary history, and surely one who would have understood the conservative ideology of Eyre's play. A large part of her revulsion at *The Maid of Normandy* is aesthetic: the references to God are found to be indecorous; the simple language is found ridiculous; the play's mixture of styles is found to be a "strange absurd jumble." That is, she simply feels Eyre's play is bad. It was not, however, the job of the censor to keep bad plays off the stage; John Larpent certainly licensed many worse plays than this one. Moreover, Anna Larpent herself signals that there is something more than aesthetic judgment involved here when, in her closing comment, she contends that the play would be "highly improper just now" even if it were aesthetically a better piece of work.

There is a complex link here between the play's aesthetic problems and its ultimate ideological unsuitability. Had the play been aesthetically more accomplished, then perhaps it could have controlled its volatile content within a successful aesthetic form and an acceptable ideological frame. The problem is that the aesthetic ineptitude of the work—its lack of artistic closure and control—frees individual moments within the play, allowing them to work upon the audience. The fear is that the theatrical recreation of particular revolutionary events—even within a play that execrated them—could lead to their reenactment in the streets; a play with such a potential impact was "improper just now" no matter what vision its author espoused or what form he adopted.

We need to remember that if we, as scholars, tend to see works as aesthetic and ideological wholes (despite the prevalence of deconstructive methods and nods to Bakhtinian heteroglossia), audiences and readers often react not to the whole but to a part; a particular scene or speech might move the audience more than its aesthetic architectonics or its ultimate ideological vision. Thus, one of the managers of the Haymarket Theatre wrote to his partner in 1810 of his "utter astonishment" that "over the Water Charley" was to be sung at the end of a play then being performed: "This is putting a lighted match to a barrel of gunpowder.... Surely you must be aware, with all the world, that this is a *rebel* song."[35] The song alone, which had no connection with the harmless play, was felt to be enough to set off a demonstration. The radical textual component could not be controlled by the context of the aesthetic and ideological whole of which it was to be a part. Textual particularities can defeat the ideological and artistic intentions embodied in the complete work, and thus reactionary plays, although trying to stage a conservative pageant, might ignite radical fireworks. Eyre's *Maid of Normandy,* no matter what its intentions, included material that the censor simply could not allow to be put on stage.

Of course, such an argument for Larpent's actions must remain speculation; but we can find a confirming parallel in roughly contemporary France, where the censor, unlike his British counterpart, was required to give a written explanation of his decisions. When Gerard de Nerval offered his play *Leo Burckart,* based on the assassination of the reactionary playwright and polemicist Kotzebue, to the Parisian censor in 1838, his drama was blocked from production for several months. The censor made clear that he had no objection to the final vision of the play: "it is just ... to remember that the trouble with this work is more in the sensual spectacle it unfolds than in the political ideas it excites." The problem was with individual scenes, in particular, the depiction of a secret meeting of a violent student society: all the ceremony of the secret society is "displayed on stage with lively and energetic colors" and thus might seize "the imagination and . . . give birth to dangerous impressions. . . . This spectacle is of a nature to produce very unfortunate effects in certain spirits."[36] From their respective censors' points of view, Eyre's *Maid of Normandy* and Nervals' *Leo Burckart* offer correct ideological visions. But their aesthetic structures render them ideologically dangerous. The power of the spectacle of the conspiracy scenes in Nerval's play may impress its audience independently of the play's total form and vision, and the lack of artistic control in Eyre's play leaves its revolutionary subject matter open to readings contrary to its author's conventional views.

These plays are dangerous because "certain spirits" might misread them and attempt to act out the revolutionary violence they ostensibly attack. We find throughout the period testimonies to the drama's power to shape behavior; such an argument lies behind Haggit's call for government support of conservative dramas, it informs Shelley's links between the drama and politics, and it is expressly stated in Hazlitt's review of *Coriolanus* in which he contends, "What men delight to read in books, they will put in practice in reality."[37] The government was clearly concerned about this power of literary works to provoke action. While Shelley worried about the ability of officially sanctioned genres to limit or even inhibit the author's vision and Hazlitt wondered whether poetry did not always serve power, the British government of the day seemed concerned that neither formal structure nor explicit ideological pronouncement could limit the power of any dramatic representation of the events of the French Revolution to inspire the people to rise up against their oppressors.

The literally reactionary art of the antirevolutionary dramas could not help but evoke the images and motifs of the prorevolutionary drama and behind it the great events of the Revolution itself. It becomes clear that the government did not wish to see revolutionary history put on stage no matter what the form or ideology of the play in question. The Examiner of Plays following Larpent, George Colman, made this quite clear in testifying before Bulwer-Lytton's parliamentary panel in 1832. He advised that the word "reform" not be spoken on stage no matter what the context, because it might provoke a disturbance in the theater. He noted that he banned a play about Charles I, "because it amounted to every thing but cutting off the King's head on stage." In the end, he objected to "anything that may be so allusive to the times as to be applied to the existing moment, and which is likely to be inflammatory."[38]

The government's fear, as Colman suggests, is that the people, hearing the radical speeches of a stage Robespierre, even when that Robespierre is dressed up as a stock villain or transformed into a Gothic villain-hero, will respond to the text of his speech and not to the reactionary context of the play; and even more frightening is the prospect that the people, watching a staging of the successful actions of the Paris crowds, even when the drama insists that those crowds are a lawless, godless, barely human mob, will listen not to the playwright's parable but to that of the people of Paris and go forth and do likewise. And we should not doubt the seriousness of this possibility in a day of major theatrical as well as political riots, when the crowds could close Drury Lane for three months during the Old Price or OP riots of 1809, a struggle over prices and box seating and thus over class distinctions and privileges within the theater. The London theaters, technically under the control of the government, at times appeared instead as a cultural democracy, replete with all the dangers the conservatives had feared from a political democracy. This democratization of the theater perhaps finds its emblem in the often noted absence of the royal family from the theaters of the day. The king and queen did not patronize the Theatres Royal, except for yearly official visits and the unusual attendance of a particularly popular and safe drama, such as Sheridan's *Pizarro*. This retreat from the theater is usually read as an aesthetic matter, a dislike on the part of royalty and the aristocracy for the kind of plays that were in favor with the people; but I would suggest it is also a political sign, a virtual abdication in the theater. Elizabeth Inchbald wrote of the OP riots, "if the public force the managers to reduce their prices, a revolution in England is effected."[39] They did, of course, succeed; and the theater, filled with people, might seem a miniature model of success for the very forces that the power of reaction defeated in the world outside.

We have arrived at what seems to be a contradiction: the intentions of artists, even radical artists, appear to be restricted, even controlled, by the limits imposed by those genres—such as neoclassical tragedy—sanctioned by government and official culture; but the government seems incapable of creating a culture that could carry its own message, as the work of art threatens to escape not only the censor's control but also the author's to become what the people in the theater will make it. On the one hand, we have radical content constrained by conservative form; on the other hand, conservative forms are unable to contain radical content. The contradiction is only an apparent one, however, for both situations reflect the ever varying balances between authorial intentions, generic limitations, institutional controls, and the historical situation. Both radical and conservative playwrights were, of course, unable to escape the limits of dramatic genres, just as—if they wished to have their plays performed—they had to accept the restrictions of the theater, and that meant not just the censorship of the Lord Chamberlain but also the constraints imposed by the entire complex social interaction of writer, manager, actor, audience, and theatrical space that are always part of a dramatic production. Such institutional and generic restrictions were, finally, more problematic for the radical than the conservative playwright; but there were also the constraints of historical context, the interactions of the literary text with its historical situation which posed difficulties for reactionary writers. In particular, the reactionary drama could not overcome the fact that it was belated, that it came after and in reaction to radical plays. The antirevolutionary drama had to incorporate the imagery of the prorevolutionary drama to combat it, but in doing so it re-created for the audience the powerful icons of revolt whose significance had already been established for them by radical literary culture. The rhetoric of reaction was unable to drown out the words of the radicals.

The story does not end there, however; there is at least one more twist. If even counterrevolutionary plays were dangerous, then revolutionary history had to be banned from the theaters. Unable to restage history to meet its vision, the government essentially eliminated history from the stage. After 1793, plays dealing directly with events in France were no longer allowed to reach the London stage; increasingly, any reference to the Revolution was suspect, and certainly prorevolutionary passages were excised by Larpent. As the anonymous author of the rejected *Helvetic Liberty* said of the theater, "In that paradise . . . politics [is] the forbidden fruit, lest the people's eyes should be opened and they become as gods knowing good and evil."[40]

This exclusion—which essentially undid attempts to stage historical plays and tragedies—helped ensure the installment of domestic melodrama as the new central form of serious drama. The ascendancy of the domestic melodrama is both a victory and a defeat for conservative culture. The popularity of this form should not deceive us about its essentially conservative vision; for the conquest of the theatrical world by the melodrama enacts within the hierarchy of genres the victory of domesticity over revolutionary politics that the reactionary drama had sought to depict on stage. The melodrama is often seen as apolitical. Thus, Robertson Davies has said that in the melodrama "poetic justice is preferred to protest."[41] But this displacement of politics and history into domestic morality is not only itself a political act; the continued reliance on the idea of poetic justice is also a reassertion of the hierarchical and providential vision that had been thrown into doubt by the Revolution with its execution of the king and its disestablishment of the church.

But if the rise of the melodrama was an ideological victory for the conservative vision, it was also a generic or cultural defeat; for it meant that the forms embraced by official culture, and particularly neoclassical tragedy, were dead and that the "illegitimate" drama had conquered. Official culture—which on aesthetic grounds wanted to silence the melodrama—comes to speak its ideological message most forcefully through the melodrama. Conservative culture emerged victorious, not by defeating the radical drama's reading of the Revolution but by changing the subject of discussion from foreign and domestic politics to the supposedly apolitical domesticity celebrated in the melodrama. It would not be the last time that conservatism's ideological message would be saved by adopting and co-opting what had been, at an earlier moment, hated popular forms.

Notes

1. Jerome J. McGann, *The Romantic Ideology* (Chicago: University of Chicago Press, 1983); Marilyn Butler, *Romantics, Rebels, and Reactionaries: English Literature and Its Background 1760–1830* (Oxford: Oxford University Press, 1982).

2. Act and scene numbers or, where appropriate, page numbers for the plays under discussion will be given in the text, as well as the play's dates and, for those plays that reached the stage, the place of the first performance: Richard Hey, *The Captive Monarch* (London: Vernor and Wood, 1794); John Dent, *The Bastille* (London: W. More, 1789); John St. John, *The Island of St. Marguerite* (London: J. Debrett, 1789); Charles Bonner, *Airs, Deuetts, and Chorusses, Arrangement of Scenery, and Sketch of the Pantomime, Entitled The Picture of Paris Taken in the Year 1790* (London: T. Cadell, 1790); J. C. Cross, *Julia of Louvain; or, Monkish Cruelty*, in *Circusiana, or a Collection of the Most Favourite Ballets, Melodrames, &c. Performed at the Royal Circus, St. George's Field* (London: Lackington, Allen, and Co., 1809); John Bartholomew, *The Fall of the French Monarchy; or, Louis XVI* (London: n.p., 1794); Edmund John Eyre, *The Maid of Normandy; or, The Death of the Queen of France*, 2d ed. (London: T. N. Longman, 1794); John Haggit, *The Count of Villeroi; or, The Fate of Patriotism* (London: T. Cadell, 1794); *The Philistines; or, The Scotch Tocsin Sounders* (Edinburgh: n.p., 1793); and William Preston, *Democratic Rage; or, Louis the Unfortunate* (Dublin, 1793; London: W. Miller, 1793).

A valuable resource for tracking down plays on the French Revolution is Theodore Grieder's "Annotated Checklist of the British Drama," *Restoration and Eighteenth Century Research* 4 (1965): 21–47; his dissertation, "The French Revolution in the British Drama: A Study in British Popular Literature of the Decade of Revolution" (Stanford University, 1957) is the only full-length examination of such plays. The British drama on the French Revolution has attracted only passing mention (e.g., Allardyce Nicoll, *A History of English Drama 1660–1900*, 6 vols. [Cambridge: Cambridge University Press, 1960], 4: 54–55; Ronald Paulson, *Representations of Revolu-*

tion [1789–1820] [New Haven: Yale University Press, 1983], 141–50; Joseph Donohue, *Theatre in the Age of Kean* [Totowa, N. J.: Rowman and Littlefield, 1975], 34), and hardly any attention has been given to the *anti*revolutionary drama. The French drama of the period has been usefully discussed in Marie-Helene Huet, *Rehearsing the Revolution: The Staging of Marat's Death 1793–1797*, trans. Forbert Hurley (Berkeley and Los Angeles: University of California Press, 1982); Daniel Hamiche, *Le Theatre et la Revolution* (Paris; Union Generale d'Editions, 1973); Louis Emile Dieudonne Moland, *Theatre de la Revolution* (1877; reprint, Geneva: Slatkine Reprints, 1971); and Marvin Carlson, *The Theatre of the French Revolution* (Ithaca: Cornell University Press, 1966). A recent book by Gillian Russell, however, explores the relations between war and theatricality, with a focus on the uses of theater for military and political purposes. See *The Theatres of War: Performance, Politics, and Society 1793–1815* (Oxford: Clarendon Press, 1995).

3. John Genest's comment is found in his *Some Account of the English Stage*, 10 vols. (1832; reprint, New York: Burt Franklin, 1965), 7: 421. On *Pizarro*, see John Loftis, *Sheridan and the Drama of Georgian England* (Oxford: Basil Blackwell, 1976), pp. 124–41; Joseph Donohue, *Dramatic Character in the English Romantic Age* (Princeton: Princeton University Press, 1970), pp. 125–56; and Paulson, *Representations of Revolution*, (note 2), p. 144.

4. John Brewer, "'This Monstrous Tragi-Comic Scene': British Reactions to the French Revolution," in *The Shadow of the Guillotine: Britain and the French Revolution* (London: British Museum Publications, 1989), 18. This is the catalog for the brilliant British Museum exhibit, 12 May to 3 September 1989, by David Bindman, with contributions by Aileen Dawson and Mark Jones. For the political context, particularly that of the political reaction, see E. P. Thompson, *The Making of the English Working Class* (New York: Pantheon, 1963); Albert Goodwin, *The Friends of Liberty: The English Democratic Movement in the Age of the French Revolution* (Cambridge: Cambridge University Press, 1979); Jacques Godechot, *The Counter-Revolution: Doctrine and Action 1789–1804*, trans. Salvator Attanasio (Princeton: Princeton University Press, 1981); Robert R. Dizier, *For King, Constitution, and Country; The English Loyalists and the French Revolution* (Lexington: University of Kentucky Press, 1983); Linda Colley, 'The Apotheosis of George III: Loyalty, Royalty and the British Nation 1760–1820," *Past and Present* 102 (February 1984): 94–129.

5. Mona Ozouf, *Festivals and the French Revolution*, trans. Alan Sheridan (Cambridge: Harvard University Press, 1989), esp. 126–57.

6. Samuel Taylor Coleridge, *Biographia Literaria*, eds. James Engell and W. Jackson Bate (Princeton: Princeton University Press, 1983), 2: 221. On the Gothic drama, see Bertrand Evans, *Gothic Drama from Walpole to Shelley* (Berkeley and Los Angeles: University of California Press 1947); Jeffrey N. Cox, *In the Shadows of Romance: Romantic Tragic Drama in Germany, England, and France* (Athens: Ohio University Press, 1987), 110–26; and "The French Revolution in the English Theatre," in *History and Myth: Essays on English Romantic Literature*, ed. Stephen C. Behrendt (Detroit, Mich.: Wayne State University Press, 1990), 33–52.

7. Paulson, *Representations of Revolution*, esp. 1–10.

8. Edmund Burke, *Reflections on the Revolution in France*, in *The Works of Edmund Burke*, 3 vols. (New York: George Dearborn, 1836), 1: 459. Subsequent page references to the *Reflections* will be to volume 1 and given in the text.

9. *The Anti-Jacobin; or, Weekly Examiner* (1797–98; reprint, New York: AMS, 1968), 7. Subsequent page numbers will be given in the text.

10. Robert Bell, *The Life of the Rt. Hon. George Canning* (London: Chapman and

Hall, 1846), p. 129; quoted in Ray Benjamin Clark, *William Gifford: Tory Satirist, Critic, and Editor* (1930; reprint. New York: Russell and Russell, 1967), 84.

11. Coleridge, *Biographia Literaria,* (note 6), 2: 221.

12. Byron later used the line "No waiter, but a *knight templar*" in the "Addition to the Preface" for *Childe Harold's Pilgrimage,* in *Complete Poetical Works,* ed. Jerome J. McGann, 7 vols. (Oxford: Clarendon Press, 1980), 2: 5–2. Byron defends his Childe against charges of being "unknightly" toward women by suggesting that medieval knights were equally lascivious. He ends by saying, "So much for chivalry. Burke need not have regretted that its days are over, though Marie Antoinette was quite as chaste as most of those in whose honours lances were shivered, and knights unhorsed." The echo of Burke places the quote from *The Rovers* into the context of the debate on the French Revolution and thus suggests that the play and the Gothic conventions it attacked were still read in ideological terms when Byron came to write.

13. In *The Baviad and Maeviad* (New York: n.p., 1799), x; quoted in Barry Sutcliffe, Introduction to *Plays by George Colman the Younger and Thomas Morton* (Cambridge: Cambridge Univ. Press, 1983), 5.

14. Paulson, *Representations of Revolution,* 57–73. See also Isaac Kramnick, *The Rage of Edmund Burke: Portrait of an Ambivalent Conservative* (New York: Basic Books, 1977), esp. 151–77; Steven Blakemore, *Burke and the Fall of Language: The French Revolution as Linguistic Event* (Hanover: University Press of New England, 1988), esp. 31–60; Marilyn Butler, "Telling It Like a Story: The French Revolution as Narrative," *Studies in Romanticism* 28 (1989): esp. 348–55.

15. Paulson, *Representations of Revolution,* 62. Edmund Burke, *A Letter from Mr. Burke to a Member of the National Assembly; in Answer to some Objections to His Book on French Affairs,* in *Works* (note 8), 1: 577, quoted in Paulson, 62.

16. On the political caricatures of the period, see M. Dorothy George, *English Political Caricature,* 2 vols. (Oxford: Clarendon Press, 1959); Paulson, *Representations of Revolution,* 111–214.

17. Bindman, Introduction, *The Shadow of the Guillotine* (note 4), 48.

18. Hannah More, *Village Politics. Addressed to All the Mechanics, Journeymen, and Day Labourers in Great Britain,* in *Burke, Paine, Godwin, and The Revolution Controversy,* ed. Marilyn Butler (Cambridge: Cambridge University Press, 1984), p. 181.

19. See Natalie Z. Davis, *Society and Culture in Early Modern France* (Stanford: Stanford University Press, 1975), esp. 147–50. For the literary uses of cross-dressing, see Jill Campbell, "'When Men Women Turn': Gender Reversals in Fielding's plays," in *The New Eighteenth Century,* eds., Felicity Nussbaum and Laura Brown (New York: Methuen, 1987), 62–83; and Terry Castle, *Masquerade and Civilization; The Carnivalesque in Eighteenth-Century English Culture and Fiction* (Stanford: Stanford University Press, 1986).

20. Paulson in *Representations of Revolution* argues that there are "two basic interpretations to the phenomenon of revolution in this period. . . . One is Oedipal and the other is oral-anal. In one the son kills, devours, and internalizes the father, becoming himself the authority figure, producing a rational sequence of events, although a sequence that might be regarded unsympathetically as prerational. In the other the revolution is seen . . . merely as regression to earlier stages of being, an ingestion that produces narcissism rather than an internalized paternal authority" (8). Even the "positive" version of revolution here—the oedipal destruction of the father—essentially dooms the revolutionary project, turning it into a guilt-ridden murder that results in the revolutionary himself becoming the parental authority

figure he has attacked. As the use of the oedipal struggle in reactionary plays suggests, the attempts to align the revolution with the family romance and its psychological tensions is perhaps necessarily conservative; it renders revolution into a domestic drama in which the rebellious son cannot win. Sex and revolt are clearly linked, in the Revolution and in the dramatic response to it. But this oedipal pattern (or the alternative oral-anal one) is inadequate to the historical reality or its representation, as both sought alternative constructions of sexuality outside this oedipal configuration. Under Robespierre and St. Just, the Revolution turned toward an ideology of puritanism. Sympathetic portrayals of revolt in England turned to the erotic outside normal configurations (i.e., an incest or androgyny) as a means of imaging human freedom, as the case of Shelley in, say, *The Revolt of Islam* (1818) suggests.

21. Gilbert Cross, *Next-Week—"East Lynne": Domestic Drama in Performance 1820–1874* (Lewisburg, Pa.: Bucknell University Press, 1977). See also Michael Booth, *English Melodrama* (London: Herbert Jenkins, 1965); Peter Brooks, *The Melodramatic Imagination* (New Haven: Yale University Press, 1976); Cox, *In the Shadows of Romance,* 45–51; Alexis Pitou, "Les Origines du melodrama francais a la fin du XVIII siècle," *Revue d'histoire litterarie de la France* 18 (1911): 256–96; and Frank Rahill, *The World of Melodrama* (University Park: Pennsylvania State University Press, 1967).

22. Brooks, *Melodramatic Imagination,* 15.

23. Thompson, *Making of the English Working Class,* 124–25. See also Malcolm I. Thomis and Peter Holt, *Threats of Revolution in Britain 1789–1848* (London: Macmillan, 1977), 8–11; Goodwin, *The Friends of Liberty,* 282–89.

24. Burke, *Reflections,* 472, 459. The Abbe Barruel, *Memoirs, Illustrating the History of Jacobinism,* 4 vols. (Hartford, Conn.: Cornelius Davis, 1799).

25. The proclamation was made in the *Bulletin of Laws,* July 1807. See Marvin Carlson, *The French Stage in the Nineteenth Century* (Metuchen, N.J.: Scarecrow Press, 1972), 12–16.

26. Percy Bysshe Shelley, *Defence of Poetry,* in *Shelley's Poetry and Prose,* eds. Donald H. Reiman and Sharon Powers (New York: Norton, 1977), 491.

27. See Sutcliffe, *Plays by George Colman,* 1–7; L. W. Connoly, *The Censorship of the English Drama 1737–1824* (San Marino, Calif.: Huntington Library, 1976); and Watson Nicholson, *The Struggle for a Free Stage in London* (1906; reprint, New York; Benjamin Blom, 1966).

28. Coleridge, *Biographia Literaria,* 2: 208.

29. Matthew Lewis, "To The Reader," in *The Castle Spectre* (London: J. Bell, 1798), p. 100. The play was marked for censorship; see Larpent's copy of the play in the Huntington Library, LA 1137.

30. Jean Starobinski, *1789: The Emblems of Reason,* trans. Elizabeth Bray (Charlottesville: University of Virginia Press, 1982), 122.

31. William Hazlitt, *"Coriolanus,"* in *Hazlitt on Theatre,* eds. William Archer and Robert Lowe (New York: Hill and Wang, n.d.), pp. 113–14. See Jonathan Bate, *Shakespearean Constitutions: Politics, Theatre, Criticism 1730–1830* (Oxford: Clarendon, 1989), p. 163–73.

32. Of the antirevolutionary plays under discussion, *The Philistines,* Bartholomew's *Fall of the French Monarchy,* and Haggit's *Count de Villeroi* were never performed. Preston's *Democratic Rage* received a few performances in Dublin in 1793 and later appeared as *Louis XVI* in Charleston, South Carolina, in 1795 and in Boston in 1797. Eyre's *Maid of Normandy* was twice denied a license, once for Bath and once for Norwich; but the published text claims performances in Dublin, Chelten-

ham, Worcester, Wolverhampton, and Shrewsbury. Other antirevolutionary plays such as Hey's *Captive Monarch,* any of Boyd's plays, or Murphy's *Arminius* failed to achieve performance; Heron's *St. Kilda in Edinburgh* was offered in Edinburgh in 1798. None of these plays was performed in London.

33. The 1794 published text of *The Maid of Normandy* indicates that "the present Drama was preparing for the representation at the Theatre-Royal Bath. . . . The Lord Chamberlain, however, influenced by *political* reasons, refused to sanction the performance, by the necessary license" (2). There is no licensing manuscript for this proposed performance. There is an 1804 licensing manuscript (Huntington Library, LA 1413), which is marked for the Theatre Royal Norwich and tagged with the word "Refused"; it is also marked "refused" in Larpent's account book, "Lord Chamberlain, List of Plays Licensed by John Larpent," 2 vols. (1801–24), Huntington Library, HM 19926, but this list obviously does not include an entry for 1794.

34. *The Diary of Anna Margaretta Larpent,* 16 vols., Huntington Library, HM 31201. This entry is in volume 2.

35. George Colman, letter to James Winston, quoted in Sutcliffe, *Plays of George Colman, 6,* from the Broadley Collection (Little Haymarket Theatre, fo. 93), Westminster Public Libraries.

36. The complete report is included in Jean Richer's edition of *Leo Burckart,* in *Oeuvres complementaires de Gerard de Nerval,* 8 vols. (Paris: Minard, 1981), 4: xxxv–xxxxix.

37. Hazlitt, *On Theatre,* p. 117.

38. George Colman, testimony in *Report from the Select Committee Appointed to Inquire into the laws Affecting Dramatic Literature* (1832), Irish University Press Series of British Parliamentary Papers, Stage and Theatre, vol. 1 (Shannon: Irish University Press, 1968), 66.

39. Quoted in James Boaden, *Memoirs of Mrs Inchbald,* 2 vols. (London: R. Bentley, 1833), 2: 143. There are many comparisons between theatrical politics and politics in general during the period. See, for example, Dent's use of planetary images and the idea of "revolution" in his dedication to *The Bastille* (p. vii), where he calls his play a "new & grand EPOCHA in the history of the stage," for the Royal Circus, a "mere *satellite*" revolving around the planets of Drury Lane and Covent Garden, had now become—as everyone flocked to see his play—the center of the theatrical universe. Again, there is Coleridge's remark on Samuel Whitbread's management of Drury Lane in his letter to the editor of *The Courier* on Maturin's *Bertram* (29 August 1816), reprinted in Engell's and Bate's edition of the *Biographia:* "Mr. Whitbread . . . proposed to the assembled Subscribers of Drury-Lane Theatre, that the concern should be farmed to some responsible individual. . . . whether he admitted, with regard to the Body Theatric, what the ardent spirit of party . . . had prevented him from seeing in the body politic, namely: that the right of suffrage may be too widely diffused, and the representatives in consequence too promiscuous, we have not the means of ascertaining" (2: 257).

40. Postscript in *Helvetic Liberty, An Opera in Three Acts by a Kentish Bowman* (London: Wayland, 1792), vi.

41. Robertson Davies, *The Revels History of Drama in English,* 8 vols. (London: Methuen, 1975) 6: 224.

4

Transitory Actions, Men Betrayed: The French Revolution in the English Revolution in Romantic Drama

KENNETH R. JOHNSTON AND JOSEPH NICHOLES

SITTING NEXT TO WILLIAM WORDSWORTH AND ACROSS FROM ROBERT BROWNING at a dinner party celebrating the premier of Thomas Noon Talfourd's play *Ion* on 26 May 1836, William Macready quoted a passage to Wordsworth from his starring performance that evening. The actor had evidently suggested the lines to Talfourd as a revision. "Wordsworth seemed pleased when I pointed out the passage in *Ion*, of a 'devious fancy,' etc.," Macready wrote in his diary, "as having been suggested by the lines *he* had once quoted to me from a MS. tragedy of his; he smiled and said, 'Yes, I noticed them' and then he went on—

> 'Action is transitory—a step—a blow,
> The motion of a muscle—this way or that—
> 'Tis done; and in the after vacancy
> We wonder at ourselves like men betrayed.'"[1]

Later Macready pleaded in jest: "Write a play, Browning, and keep me from going to America." To which Browning replied: "Shall it be historical and English: what do you say to a drama on Strafford?"[2] Macready approved, and the transitory action that resulted was the last effort by a major British writer to invigorate Romantic drama. Browning's *Strafford* and Wordsworth's *The Borderers* serve well as bookends on the shelf of the period's dramatic literature, particularly that section in which volatile contemporary themes are represented in the displaced terms of another era's political discourse.

One might imagine Coleridge or Southey addressing Wordsworth in the late 1790s with words similar to Macready's: "Write a play, Wordsworth, and keep us from going to America." And Wordsworth replying, "Shall it be historical and English: what do you say to a drama of the border wars." "As to the scene and period of action," Wordsworth did comment in 1843, when the play was finally to be published, "little more was required for my purpose than the absence of established Law and Government; so that the agents might be at liberty to act on their impulses."[3]

He might have written on Robespierre and the French terrors, the subject really on his mind, as Coleridge and Southey had already done in *The Fall of Robespierre* of 1794.[4] But scholars agree that in spite of his later denials, Wordsworth was genuinely hopeful that his play would be successful on the stage, and subjects with contemporary political implications were guaranteed immediate rejection by the government censor. Considering these circumstances, it is not difficult to see *The Borderers* as the dramatized form of Wordsworth's continuing reflections on the revolution in France. "During my long residence in France," Wordsworth recalled, "while the revolution was rapidly advancing to its extreme of wickedness, I had frequent opportunities of being an eye-witness of this process, and it was while that knowledge was fresh upon my memory, that the Tragedy of 'The Borderers' was composed." The play was written "to preserve in my distinct remembrance what I had observed of transition in character, and the reflections I had been led to make during the time I was a witness of the changes through which the French Revolution passed" (*Works*, 1: 342). Though late in life Wordsworth emphatically described the work as a character study rather than political allegory, modern critics, familiar with the poet's habit of sublimating his post-revolutionary political concerns, find in it rich political significance.[5]

A similar sublimation of contemporary political concerns occurs in other Romantic dramas set in circumstances of civil conflict and upheaval. In this essay, we will examine plays by writers of the Romantic era depicting scenes of political crisis and demonstrate their relevance to British politics after the French Revolution—a relevance easily obscured by the shifting, treacherous fogs of a reactionary political climate. As the special case of greatest significance, we will focus on the "historical and English" setting chosen by Browning and a number of other Romantic writers, a time particularly well suited for analogies to contemporary political turmoil in France and Britain: the Civil War era of seventeenth-century England.[6] Romantic dramas of the English Revolution had the potential to be as important in the cultural history of their time as Shakespeare's history plays about the fall of the Plantagenets and the rise of the Tudor dynasty were in the reign of Elizabeth I. They concerned fundamental political questions about who had the right to rule in the commonwealth, and they were set in a time approximately the same distance in the past, far enough away from the present not to engage immediate political rivalries, yet close enough that all parties interested and intelligent enough to recognize the issues could easily see them beneath the trappings of popular dramatic spectacle. But, besides lacking a dramatic genius akin to Shakespeare's—though the Romantics were the first generation with the critical genius to recognize Shakespeare's full stature—most of the best Romantic writers who tried their hand on the subject were on the "wrong" (i.e., republican) side. And the times were so much more threatening to the nation than even the 1590s had been, that even those writers on the "right," Royalist side of the question had difficulty getting a fair showing for their works.

From the late eighteenth century through the 1830s, when Romantic verse drama had run its course, a significant number of important authors wrote or attempted to write plays set in seventeenth-century England. These include such major figures as William Godwin, Charles Lamb, Percy Bysshe Shelley, and Robert Browning; lesser figures widely known at the time such as Douglas Jerrold, William Moncrief, James Sheridan Knowles, Mary Russell Mitford, and Edward Bulwer-Lytton; and in France, Honoré de Balzac and Victor Hugo.[7] Add to this list a host of popular adaptations of Walter Scott's Waverly novels by such hack writers as Isaac Pocock, rare examples of permanent worth like Vincenzo Bellini's opera *I Puritani* (1835), and numerous obscure melodramas based on seventeenth-century themes, and the profile of a significant popular phenomenon emerges.[8] Although hardly revolutionary in aesthetic terms, this phenomenon provides modern readers with insight into how the revolutionary "Spirit of the Age" was adapted to the predominantly conservative stages of British theater and thought. Although politically heterogeneous, Romantic Civil War dramas consistently examine, to use Wordsworth's phrase, the "transition in character" that occurs when civil strife tests the stress points of political sensibility within exemplary individuals.

When the French executed Louis XVI in 1793, the parallel to the fate of Charles I rendered analogies between the French and English Revolutions virtually unavoidable to Romantic writers.[9] In 1795 Coleridge announced his intention to give six lectures on "A Comparative View of the English Rebellion under Charles the First, and the French Revolution," including a discussion of the "Characters of Charles Ist and Louis the XVIth" (the evidence is mixed as to whether or not he actually gave them).[10] As the Revolution produced its own series of tyrants, comparisons and contrasts with Cromwell became equally fruitful. In *The Fall of Robespierre* (1794), an opponent of Robespierre refers to him as "This worse than Cromwell" (from act 3, written by Southey); and the prospectus to Coleridge's 1795 political lectures on the Civil War promises a comparison of "Oliver Cromwell, and Robespierre" (*Lectures 1795*, 256).

Observers in England later replaced Robespierre with Napoleon in their comparisons with Cromwell. Lamb suggested such a comparison to Coleridge in a letter, 23 October 1802, the same year Lamb's *John Woodvil: A Tragedy,* also set in the seventeenth century, was published: "Have you anticipated it, or could not you give a Parallel of Bonaparte with Cromwell, particularly as the contrast in their deeds affecting *foreign* states: Cromwell's interference for the Albigenses, B's against the Swiss. Then Religion would come in; &. Milton & you could rant about OUR COUNTRYMEN of the period."[11] Cromwell had interfered *"for"* the oppressed Swiss, Napoleon *"against,"* so Lamb here considers Cromwell a noble foil to modern tyranny.

Lamb did some ranting of his own about his seventeenth-century countrymen in "What Is Jacobinism?," an 1801 essay that Winifred Courtney has identified as his in the short-lived radical newspaper *The Albion, and Evening Advertiser.* After defending Godwin and other liberals from vague and inconsistent incrimination as Jacobins by bellicose reactionary journalists, Lamb concludes:

> Not content with *living* names, they persecute and spoil the *dead,* with whom man should *not war;* and pass sentence of *Jacobinism backwards* upon such men as Milton, Sidney, Harrington, and Locke. It is sufficient, that these benefactors to mankind sought the happiness of their species in *ways* which *they* cannot *understand.* We have heard of *general lovers,* though we dislike the character: but these men are a sort of *general haters,* and discredit and cry down, at random, all that is *new,* and *good,* and *useful.*[12]

Lamb refers here to Algernon Sidney (1622–83), venerated martyr to the cause of constitutional liberties, whose *Discourses Concerning Government* (1698) became a chapbook of revolutionary politics at the end of the eighteenth century; to James Harrington (1611–77), the influential republican political philosopher who wrote the utopian treatise *Oceana* (1656); and to the philosopher John Locke (1632–1704), whose writings attacked the central Royalist doctrine of the divine right of kings. Lamb's complaint illustrates the contemporary tendency for political writers to make such associations.

The idea that Lamb was one of the least politically minded of Romantic writers has been, since Lamb's own day, a prominent fea-

4: TRANSITORY ACTIONS, MEN BETRAYED

ture of his literary reputation. Burton Pollin and Winifred Courtney have shown, however, that Lamb was more concerned with politics than either he or his friends and biographers have been prepared to admit.[13] "That Lamb was not apolitical can no longer be in doubt," Courtney writes in her critical biography of Lamb, "nor did he just stop being political after a certain age" (p. 186). Lamb began *John Woodvil* within a month of being lampooned as a Jacobin in James Gillray's famous "New Morality" cartoon and a poem by George Canning, John Frere, and George Ellis in the *Anti-Jacobin Review and Magazine* for July 1798. The historical setting of *John Woodvil*, just after the Restoration of 1660, when examined in light of the late eighteenth-and nineteenth-century practice of drawing analogies between contemporary politics and the constitutional crises of the seventeenth century, invites a reading of the play as a veiled response to the *Anti-Jacobin*'s attack and its aftermath in the author's private and public affairs. In the tale of a political renegade of seventeenth-century England, Lamb found a vehicle for indirect comment on the volatile politics of his own day.[14]

In 1800, John Kemble rejected *John Woodvil* for production at Drury Lane, and Coleridge and Southey advised Lamb against publication—though Coleridge told Godwin in December 1800 that his "love and admiration" for the work increased every time he read it (McKenna, 63). In January 1801, Lamb was annoyed by Wordsworth's delayed and subdued "liking" of the play (*Works*, 5: 354). In spite of these mixed responses, Lamb had *John Woodvil* published in 1802, at a personal cost of twenty-five pounds, and reprinted in his *Works* of 1818. Although critics have dismissed the play as a failed imitation of Shakespeare (McKenna, 55–63), the work was important to Lamb, and he cared that it reach an audience.

Lamb gives the setting of *John Woodvil* as "soon after the Restoration" (131). In the first scene, a drunken servant sings that traditional anthem of Charles II's return, "When the King Enjoys His Own Again," and with his companions toasts their improved access to spirits since that day (131, 134). The drink provokes loose talk of betraying the whereabouts of their former master, Sir Walter Woodvil, a Parliamentarian who has been hiding since the king's return (135–36). The loyal steward, Sandford, overhears the men and rebukes them for disloyalty. Then Margaret, John Woodvil's sweetheart since childhood, enters "as in a fright, pursued by a Gentleman" (137), one of the Cavalier courtiers John Woodvil has befriended in his father's absence. Sandford laments the "debauch and mis-timed riotings" (137) the courtiers have introduced to the Woodvil household. Unable to endure the "atheist riot, . . . profane excess, / . . . And free discourses, of the dissolute men" (138) retained by Woodvil, Margaret resolves to leave the estate where she has been reared as Sir Walter's ward. The elder Woodvil has been too honor-bound to the Parliamentarian cause to ask the king's pardon (135, 147) and now has a price on his head of two hundred pounds (135). Consequently, the son's association with Cavalier courtiers represents a blatant rejection of the family's politics and, combined with his neglect, his self-betrayal of a character "That was by nature noble" (139). "'Tis these court-plagues, that swarm about our house," says Sandford, "have done the mischief, making his fancy giddy / With images of state, preferment, place / Tainting his generous spirits with ambition" (139). Woodvil confirms this assessment with an introspective soliloquy:

> Now Universal England getteth drunk
> For joy that Charles, her monarch, is restored: . . .
>   Fools do sing,
> Where good men yield God thanks; but politic spirits,
> Who live by observation, note these changes
> Of the popular mind, and thereby serve their ends.
> Then why not I? What's Charles to me, or Oliver,
> But as my own advancement hangs on one of them?
> I would be great, for greatness hath great *power,*
> And that's the fruit I reach at.—
>   (145–46)

This key passage, reminiscent of Rivers's temptation of Marmaduke in *The Borderers,* strongly intimates that Woodvil has assumed the role of Cavalier courtier purely to gain personal advancement, or, vaguely, to gain power for unspecified "good" ends, and that if the Parliamentarians were still in power he would be one. Lamb gives no indication of how long Woodvil has been associated with the king's party, and it is only through this association that Lamb establishes Woodvil's identity as a Cavalier—an identity that seems "affected" at best. Sandford, Sir Walter Woodvil, and John Woodvil himself each assert that he "affects" the "favours," "manners," and "fashions" of the Cavalier court (139, 146). A moment before Woodvil's pragmatic soliloquy on his "own advancement," he offers to show his Cavalier friend Lovel a recently purchased Van Dyke depicting a favorite scene of Royalist iconography, "The late King taking leave of his children" (145). Among his Cavalier drinking mates, he proclaims the king's birthday and suggests another round of drinks "for the better manifesting our loyalty this day" (156–57); and he contributes to jokes about persecuting Puritans (157). But, feeling guilty immediately after getting drunk and telling Lovel the secret of his father's hiding place, he mocks his friend by keenly satirizing Cavalier pretensions (164). In sum, Woodvil never displays genuine loyalty to the Cavalier cause.

The kind of political opportunities exemplified by Woodvil's behavior was particularly distasteful to Lamb, because it betrayed a fundamental moral insincerity, self-interested pragmatism, and even cowardice. The best illustration of this sentiment appears in an epigram, "To Sir James Mackintosh," from the *Albion,* for which Lamb wrote extensively in the summer of 1801—a few months before the final revisions and publication of *John Woodvil:*

> Though thou'rt like Judas, an apostate black,
> In the resemblance one thing thou dost lack:
> When he had gotten his ill-purchased pelf,
> He went away, and wisely hanged himself.
> This thou may'st do at last; yet much I doubt
> If thou has any *bowels* to gush out!
>
> (*Works,* 5: 102)

Mackintosh (1765–1832), the author of *Vindiciae Gallicae* (1791), an important rebuttal to Edmund Burke's *Reflections of the Revolution in France* (1790), had repudiated his former radical opinions.[15] At the time of Lamb's epigram, Mackintosh was seeking government employment, which he attained in 1803—hence the imputation that he had sold his ideals for personal advancement. The *Albion* folded shortly after the epigram appeared; Lamb blamed its demise on the withdrawal of support by a wealthy patron offended by the severity of his ridicule of Mackintosh.

Lamb already had in mind this kind of abrupt reversal in politics while he was at work on his play in 1798 and 1799. His close friend Charles Lloyd, with whom he had published *Blank Verse* in early 1798, and with whom he was satirized as a frog croaking over that volume in Gillray's cartoon, had embarked on a public campaign to absolve himself of the charge of Jacobinism, and he constantly drew Lamb's name into the controversy. The details of this episode suggest that Lamb may have initially acquiesced in this process, only to regret it soon thereafter (Pollin, 640–43; Courtney, *Young Charles Lamb,* 197–200). In *Lines Suggested by the Fast Appointed on Wednesday, February 27, 1799,* one of several pamphlets Lloyd issued to prove his political respectability, he cites, "undoubtedly with [Lamb's] full permission" (Pollin, 643), an extract from Lamb's poem "Living Without God in the World" (ca. 1798, pub. 1799, *Works,* 5:17–18, 290) introduced by Lloyd as "a satire on the Godwinian jargon." After meeting Godwin in February 1800, however, Lamb confirmed his political consistency by developing a warm friendship with this godfather of English radicalism and by his writings for the *Albion* the following year—it was Godwin who introduced Lamb to John Fenwick, editor of the paper. Courtney argues that the acerbity of Lamb's attack on Mackintosh in the *Albion* was motivated largely by the fact that Mackintosh had been Godwin's friend and was now publicly attacking him ("New Lamb Text," 2).

In spite of Lloyd's protest, the proprietors of the *Anti-Jacobin* repeatedly thrust their labeling of Lamb and Lloyd as Jacobins before the public eye. The satirical poem "New Morality," an excerpt of which appeared as caption to Gillray's cartoon, specified with the names of more notorious "Jacobins" John Thelwall and Godwin, "C——DGE and S——TH——Y, L——D, and L——B and Co." The poem was originally published in the 9 July 1798 *Anti-Jacobin, or Weekly Examiner* (the predecessor of the monthly *Anti-Jacobin Review and Magazine*, of which the July 1798 issue, with Gillray's cartoon, was the first). The grouping of Coleridge, Southey, Lloyd, and Lamb occurs again in a poem entitled "The Anarchists" in the September 1798 issue, with Thelwall and Godwin again mentioned in close proximity. "New Morality" was reprinted in *Poetry of the Anti-Jacobean* (1799) and *Beauties of the Anti-Jacobin, or Weekly Examiner* (1799). The latter includes a note on the poem that slanders Coleridge as unpatriotic, irreligious, and an abandoner of wife and children, and refers to Lamb and Southey as "his associates." "Some of these youths," the note asserts, "were early corrupted in the *metropolis* . . . when scholars at that excellent seminary, CHRIST'S HOSPITAL" (306). In "What Is Jacobinism?" Lamb defended Godwin and other liberals from those who use "the uncivil language of party" to "brand better men than themselves with Jacobinism"—a defense he surely intended for himself as well (Courtney, "New Lamb Texts," 7).

The characterization of John Woodvil probably owes much to Lamb's contemplation of his own political status after the *Anti-Jacobin*'s assault and to concern over Lloyd's public abdication of his liberalism. "The character of Woodvil," observes Courtney, "with his abrupt shifts, is reminiscent of both Coleridge and Lloyd" (*Young Charles Lamb*, 218). Lloyd's political retreat entangled Lamb in the controversy over "renegadism," a divisive concern of two generations of Romantic writers in an era of extreme conservative entrenchment. Lamb's epigraph on Mackintosh is reminiscent of Wordsworth's unpublished criticism of Richard Watson, Bishop of Llandaff, who revised his liberal views after the execution of Louis XVI. Lamb needed a subtle method for exploring the sensitive issue of political and personal betrayal, and he chose a setting for his play that offered ideal subject matter for indirect political discourse.

John Woodvil's opportunistic fraternization with the Cavaliers had clear potential for analogy with the "betrayal" of the liberal community by Mackintosh, Lloyd, and others, perhaps including, at the back of Lamb's mind, Wordsworth and Coleridge. That is, it is a play about the unpalatable behavior of a young man from the "good" side after the "bad" side has won—about the difficulty of maintaining principles in the face of defeat.

The first three acts of Lamb's play take place on 29 May, the birthday of Charles II and anniversary of his triumphant return to London in 1660. The day became a national holiday observed well into the nineteenth century, commonly referred to as "Royal Oak" or "Oak-Apple Day" and commemorated by the wearing of oak leaves as a token of the storied hiding of Charles in the Boscobel oak tree after the Battle of Worcester in 1651. Lamb establishes the 29 May date with the well-known song in the opening scene and two references to celebration of the King's birthday (144 and 156). Because Sir Walter Woodvil has been in hiding since the king's return (134–36), and the setting is "soon after the Restoration" (131), the implied date of the plays' opening is 29 May 1661, the "first" Oak-Apple Day. This chronology is reinforced by a servant's comment that the elder Woodvil "has been excepted by name in the late Act of Oblivion" (136), which was passed in August 1660. In opening his play on the primarily Tory holiday, Oak-Apple Day, and featuring drunken servants and dissolute Cavaliers, Lamb unmistakably expresses his political bias. His negative depiction of England after the Restoration of Charles II and his Cavalier court provides, through analogy, a satiric comment on the conservative ascendancy in England at the turn of the nineteenth century, as the public reaction against France began to solidify.

In a manuscript of the play, Lovel and Gray, the two false friends who reveal Sir Walter's hiding place, are identified as "two Court spies" (*Works*, 5: 356; see also 362). The parallel to the notorious government spy system of Lamb's day is telling, as further illustrated by Lamb's vitriolic epigram of 1820 in which he compares three contemporary government spies to Bedloe and Oates, two disreputable seventeenth-century characters of the same profession employed by Charles II:

> Close by the ever-burning brimstone beds
> Where Bedloe, Oates and Judas, hide their heads,
> I saw great Satan like a Sexton stand

With his intolerable spade in hand,
Digging three graves....
"These graves," quoth he, "when life's brief oil is spent,
When the dark night comes, and they're sinking bedwards,
—I mean for Castle, Oliver, and Edwards."

(*Works*, 5:105)

In *John Woodvil*, Lamb introduces motifs similar to several Walter Scott used in his Civil War novel, *Woodstock, or the Cavalier, a Tale of the Year 1651* (1826), which subsequently appear in works by writers influenced by Scott. Probably because of the accumulated lore of "Priest's holes" and Cavaliers disguised as servants fleeing roundheads, including a future king hiding in an oak tree, refugees in forests became a common figure in the genre. *Woodstock* features a fictional sequestering of Charles Stuart on the secluded, well-forested royal Woodstock estate. Frederick Marryat's *Children of the New Forest* (1847), as the title suggests, recounts the adventures of orphaned children of a Cavalier officer who have sought refuge in a forest. Lamb's noble Parliamentarian hiding in Sherwood Forest anticipates this pattern with its own characteristic inversion.

Lamb also pioneered a more significant motif: two lovers from opposite sides of the political conflict who are reconciled at the end of the story as an image of national reconciliation. At the end of both *Woodstock* and *Children of the New Forest,* lovers with familial loyalties in political opposition are shown blissfully united in overt association with the king's return on 29 May 1660. Scott's 29 May tableau at the end of *Woodstock* features the same song that begins *John Woodvil:* "O, the twenty-ninth of May, / It was a glorious day, / When the King did enjoy his own again." Both Scott and Marryat use the marriage of Puritan and Cavalier lovers on 29 May to represent the Tory myth of national peace and reconciliation brought about by the Restoration.

After Woodvil betrays his father under the corrupting influence of Cavalier courtiers and their free-flowing holiday wine, he eventually comes to his senses, and, following a painful repentance, he is reconciled with Margaret. Lamb makes it clear that Margaret has remained loyal to her Puritan sensibilities. She is a "true protestant" (174), thus making possible the tensions produced by Woodvil's role as a Cavalier. But in Lamb's play the celebration of 29 May contributes directly to the alienation of the two lovers, and they can only set things right when Woodvil repudiates his dishonorable behavior as a Cavalier courtier. Furthermore, this reconciliation is entirely a private matter. In significant contrast to the endings of *Woodstock* and *Chil-*

dren of the New Forest, the prospect of domestic joy for the lovers in *John Woodvil* seems but an isolated compensation for life in a time characterized by misguided political prejudice and persecution—a political climate much like that of Britain at the beginning of the nineteenth century. Particularly exemplified in the figuration of the division and reconciliation of the lovers, Lamb's play turns upon Whig/Liberal versions of motifs supposedly invented years later by Scott. Whether Scott was at all influenced by *John Woodvil* must remain a matter of conjecture, but Lamb's work should be given its place in the development of an important theme in nineteenth-century political and historical iconography.[16]

In *Politics and English Romantic Poetry,* Carl Woodring makes an important observation about Lamb's tendency "to exaggerate his distaste for politics": he "practiced in all his essays, and even in his letters, the devices of understatement, covert allusion, self-refuting exaggeration, and the inversion of fact that he called 'matter-of-life.' Aided by these devices, he gradually reduced first the appearance and then the reality of his political anxieties."[17] The political meaning of *John Woodvil* was disguised by a strategy of indirection perfectly suited to relieve "political anxieties" without risk of offending friend or foe with an overt expression of partisan views. Recalling work at the *Albion* in his essay "Newspapers Thirty-Five Years Ago," Lamb wrote facetiously that his editor, Fenwick, was "resolutely determined upon pulling down the Government in the first instance, and making both our fortunes by way of corollary" (*Works,* 2: 225). "Our occupation . . . was to write treason," Lamb continues in this vein: "Blocks, axes, Whitehall tribunals, were covered with flowers of so cunning a periphrasis, . . . never naming the *thing* directly—that the keen eye of an Attorney General was insufficient to detect the lurking snake among them." Perhaps Fenwick's strategy inspired Lamb to couch his own political sentiments in an essentially psychological tale of a confused young man in an earlier time of violent and perplexing political change.

In correspondence with William Godwin, September 1802, the year *John Woodvil* appeared, Lamb advised him extensively on his play, *Faulkener,* a tragedy also set shortly after the Restoration and based on an episode in Defoe's *Roxana* (1742; *Letters* 2: 17–20, 23–25). This included advice on how Godwin should handle a detail upon which the drama hinges: that the hero's mother was briefly a mistress of Charles II during his exile in France (64, 71). The play was produced with Henry and Sarah Siddons playing leading roles at Drury Lane in 1807 and published with a prologue by Lamb the same year. Godwin had begun writing a history of the Commonwealth period in

1798, having in common with other figures of his circle, including, eventually, Shelley, "a feeling of kinship with the Puritan revolutionaries."[18] But the completed history would not appear for another thirty years.

Godwin set *Faulkener* in Florence, 1669, where the English Captain Faulkener, recent hero of the battle of Candia against the Turks, has come in search of his mother, mysteriously lost to him in childhood sixteen years earlier. Faulkener's father "fell gloriously, fighting for his country and his king, in the battle of Worcester" (2), and shortly thereafter his mother disappeared. The boy was denied any explanation of her absence by the grandfather who reared him. Receiving financial assistance from an unknown benefactor, Faulkener has been contacted by a secretive Italian gentleman, Benedetto Marsigli, who has enigmatically promised to reveal the identity and whereabouts of his mother. The mother, Arabella, remarried as the Countess Orsini, confesses to Faulkener's friend and fellow English officer, Colonel Stanley, that she has kept her identity secret from her son to protect his honor because her own life has become "a shameful" and "disgraceful tale to relate" (14). However, Arabella depicts Charles II with considerable kindness. He "was then just twenty-one years of age," and his "figure was prepossessing; his mind was sober; and his thoughts were guileless. It was the mutual innocence of our hearts, aided by unrestrained occasions and familiarity, that led to what followed" (15). Nevertheless, it was an "ignominious condition" into which she "had fallen" and "a moment of guilt and horror." Consequently, Charles "swore never more to attempt to mislead me," and they "parted forever."

The key word here is "mislead," for the real subject of the play is purity of emotions, not of politics. Instead of investigating the moral consequences of the future monarch's ruining the reputation of a loyal officer's widow, Godwin's drama swerves widely around the evident political issue to enter an obscure avenue of ideological communication, the various moral implications of highly romanticized states of feeling. Indeed, given Godwin's former reputation as the author of *Political Justice*, what is most remarkable about *Faulkener* is the radical evacuation of political discourse in it, and the substitution of an apparently entirely private emotional discourse. There is in fact no particular reason for this play to be set with characters from the English Civil War era, because in its bare essentials it is a sentimental tale of how true feeling will out. But for that very reason, Godwin's choice of a Civil War milieu is all the more interesting, interpretatively. It would be too much to claim that we see here the return of the political repressed under the sign of emotional excess, but that is at least the intriguing possibility raised by Godwin's flawed melodrama.

Lamb discouraged Godwin's original intention to have Arabella "turn whore to one of the Lords of [Charles's] bedchamber," arguing that her having "been mistress to King Charles, is sufficient to all the purposes of the story" (*Letters*, 2: 23). So Godwin painted his picture of royal corruption with a more delicate brush, though he allows other characters to describe Charles's behavior in cruder terms than Arabella's. One of the villains, Benedetto, asks Faulkener provocatively, "You have heard of the well-furnished seraglio of Charles Stuart?" (39). Stanley, a noble officer presently in Charles II's service, temporarily deceived by the machinations of Benedetto and Lauretta Delmonte, the former mistress of Count Orsini who seeks revenge for his marriage to Arabella, provides the harshest indictment of Charles's and Arabella's behavior: "mistress to the libertine Charles Stuart, one of the jewels of his wanton court—the eye of drunken license surveyed her beauties, and laughed" (64). And in the play's final scene, Arabella finally confesses to her son that she has been "the unhappy victim of an exiled monarch" (71). As in *John Woodvil,* corrupt Cavalier morals mirror liberal disapproval of Stuart politics, and the fate of Arabella and her husband symbolizes the plight of the English nation in the seventeenth century, that is, betrayed and victimized by its royal patriarchs.

But Godwin's conception is altogether simpler than Lamb's. Insofar as there is a political question at issue in the play, it is, How can a person be (or have been) *legitimately* on both sides of such fundamental political and moral issues? John Woodvil's rationalized ambivalence of feeling has much richer possibilities when applied to the issue of radical retrenchment or "renegadism" in the late 1790s and after. By contrast, the character of Arabella, who is certainly represented as emotionally unstable, would seem to represent merely the possibility that even seduced royalists can have fine human feelings. In this light, her emotional reunion with her son, who is touted as "the bulwark of the Christian world," could be read as a healing reunion between those who suffered through loyalty to both Charles I and his young heir during the Civil Wars and those now loyally serving the restored monarch Charles II.

But this does not make much sense, even if it were interesting. Rather, it is more interesting to speculate why Godwin, who held strongly critical views of the Stuarts, should have followed Lamb's advice to present Charles II so benignly in *Faulkener,* where he appears as little more than a handsome youth unable to resist beauty in tempting circumstances. Of course, Godwin's willingness to compromise himself in his long and unsuccessful effort to recoup his lost public reputation should not be discounted. With both the Siddons in lead roles, and not one but two epilogues spoken by Mrs. Siddons, desperately if jocularly pleading for the audience's approval (they are invited to buy shares in the play's production), we are evidently dealing here with a stage "vehicle" aiming for success at all costs. As such, it represents an extreme instance of the tendency of "the Romantic ideology" to displace political concerns to the level of the merely private and emotional—and commercial.

In terms of political drama, Lamb's advice was all wrong: if we understood that Arabella had been cruelly seduced and abandoned by Charles—or even better, really corrupted into one of his decadent mistresses—there would be much more point to her agonies at being discovered by her son. As it is, these emotions come out in a very wrong and surprising place: the mysterious passion of mother and son for each other. In the opening scene, Faulkener describes his successful but obsessionally driven life in the astonishing words, "I made a mistress of my never-to-be-approached mother"; and he anticipates recovering her with an infantile eagerness, noteworthy, to say the least, in a man fresh from triumph on the battlefield:

> Oh, I shall babble,
> Like prattling infancy; say o'er and o'er
> Speak and forget; be very, very eager,
> And nothing known but that I am most happy!
>
> (7)

When he says in act IV, as the plot of the vicious Italians progressively ensnares all the excessively virtuous English, "The passion of my life has been to find my mother; . . . I have led the life of a fanatic, and shall die the death of an idiot" (58), we may feel that he and his creator speak more truly than they realize. And when mother and son are finally, though briefly, reunited at the end, he acknowledges her in terms that are perhaps too dear: "The wondrous woman I own my mother. Countess, or dearer name, Arabella!—your errors I weep for—but your virtues, radiant, exalted and angelic, my heart acknowledges, my soul adores!" (73).

The mother is every bit as obsessive as her son, first about the secret of her past reputation, and subsequently about the net of misunderstanding and intrigue it has coiled around her. Confession has been good for her soul, but just when she feels redeemed in every way—"I have done what a British matron ought" (75)—she learns that her Italian husband has been killed defending her honor against the slander of Stanley. Having once again gained a son, and lost a husband almost in the same instant, she can no more "retire to our native country" (as Faulkener proposes) than she could have after the royalist defeat at the Battle of Worcester, and the play ends with her suicide, rendering her son an orphan once more: "Never!— The loss of you, my son,—that was the first issue of my fall!—And now, this, this, is mine!—Earth will no more support, and nature sickens at me" (76). In "a tone of unutterable anguish" (Godwin's stage direction), she falls and the play ends.

Something indeed is left "unuttered" in the play, but it is difficult to say what, unless it is that the full emotional freight of political intensity has been transposed, consciously or unconsciously, into a domestic drama that skirts near to incest-tragedy, or the family romance cast into the tropes of civil war. That the political emotions are, however, anything but simple is suggested by Godwin's other work on the Civil War period. Here again it appears that his interest is elicited not solely by the republican cause, but, as in the case of Arabella, by good people who find themselves for one reason or another enlisted in an evil cause. This may suggest, in turn, that the bedrock of Romantic interest in the seventeenth-century republicans is less admiration for their cause (for that might go without saying) than feelings of guilty implication in their defeat, presumably reflecting the Romantic authors' ambivalence about their own various changes of heart regarding the hopes for English reform contained in the example of the French Revolution.

In an unpublished essay written around 1809, entitled "Interview of Charles the First and Sir William Davenant in the Scottish Camp before Newark Considered," Godwin explicitly recorded his opinions of the elder Charles and of monarchy:

> Much pains has [sic] lately been taken to varnish the character of King Charles the First. The years of his reign are a momentous period to the friends & the enemies of the liberties of mankind, & the latter are deeply interested in having him painted as the most innocent & unoffending of his species. Hume, I should hope, has a soul superior to the base desire of paying court to the men in power of his time; but he was influenced . . . partly by the feeling that the tragic fate of his hero afforded the materials of an elegant & pathetic tale.
>
> Charles was of a character weak, narrow & frigid. . . .
>
> Monarchy, hereditary monarchy, may, for aught that is necessary to be said in this place, be the wisest & most beneficent mode of government; but, even upon that supposition, it is only a mask played for the benefit of mankind, & when the performance is over, the actors lay aside the

dresses they wore on the stage, & are to be considered only for their intrinsic merits. (*Shelley and His Circle*, 1: 450–52)

However, the interest of this unpublished essay (which Godwin did not incorporate in his later history of the Commonwealth) is Godwin's focus on the character of Davenant at the moment he was called on by Charles's advisers in France to counsel a negotiated compromise with the rebels. As Cameron says, it "was something of a turning point" in the fortunes of the rebellion (*Shelley and His Circle*, 1: 454). But Charles refused to compromise, banished Davenant for his presumption, and eventually lost his head for his stubbornness. Remarkable, at least to modern readers, is Godwin's finely nuanced attention to Davenant's strength of character in standing up to the king's anger and in stoically accepting his disgrace. Godwin finds the source of this strength in Davenant's genius: "To say all in a word, Sir William Davenant was a poet" (451).

Even more remarkable is Godwin's fantasy of what Davenant could or should have done:

> He would not have said a word about himself; he would have forgotten his own individuality in the magnitude of the cause he had to plead, & he would have clothed that pleading in all the eloquence which his genius so well knew how to furnish. He would have said, "Awake, oh king, from the dream of majesty, & think for this time of your duties only. . . . Think that no man, however wise, turns a deaf ear to information & advice. . . . Awake at length from the dream of royalty. . . . Know that these are new times, & that he who is intrusted with a considerable part in them, must not content himself with merely repeating what has been said & done before. . . . The muse of history is ready, accordingly as you shall now conduct yourself, to close your story here, or to turn another & more honorable page." (457–58)

The calm rationalism of this "Davenant's" advice, sweetened with all the confidence of hindsight, strongly suggests that these are words such as Godwin himself would have addressed to Charles, had he had the chance—or to George III, or the Prince Regent. But, he ruefully notes, "Davenant however did not thus far trample upon the mummery of established forms; the door of the royal apartment was shut upon him; & Charles ended his life upon a scaffold" (458)

Godwin's draft essay had its own historical moment, as a projected contribution to a controversy that arose in 1808–11 over the posthumous publication of Charles James Fox's *History of the Early part of the Reign of James the Second*, in which Fox not only attacked Charles's character but also defended his execution. But Godwin's attention to Davenant's character is more important for our present purposes. Like surprisingly many of the Romantic dramas on the Civil War written by liberals, Godwin finds his hero not on the republican but on the royalist side and at a moment when the hero must recognize that royalty is wrong. (Faulkener and Arabella may be said to have felt this truth on their romantic pulses, without benefit of any political illumination.) And for such a character at such a moment, Godwin creates the outlines of a poet-philosopher-genius, the kind of single-minded hero that both Wordsworth and Byron, to cite two Romantic polarities, often imagined saving (or losing) the whole world by sheer force of personal genius. It is Godwin's imagination of what Davenant *might have done* at such a moment that engages his own creative energy, for he admits that Davenant, though "an honest man & a witty," was "in all respects inferior to such a trust." But, though Davenant failed to deliver such words as Godwin puts in his mouth, his defeat and disgrace become almost as noble in Godwin's eyes as his political failure—a correlation highly relevant to the hidden dialectics of the buried genre of Romantic republican drama. For Davenant, like almost all the young, intellectual generation of the 1790s that had lionized Godwin, was forced into retirement: "He ceased to think of himself as a courtier; his occupation was gone. . . . He felt himself a free man." In the passage of twenty years, Godwin could well imagine the same words applying to himself.

Davenant turned from politics to poetry, and in a "solemn and erected spirit," Godwin says, turned himself to the composition of *Gondibert,* published with a preface resonant with the similar dialectics of Wordsworth's Preface to *Lyrical Ballads.* Davenant says that "that grave Mistress of the World, Experience . . . hath taught me, . . . that when the ancient poets were valued as prophets, they were long & painful in watching the correspondence of causes, ere they presumed to foretell effects; & that it is a high presumption, to entertain a nation (who are a poet's standing guests, & require monarchical respect) with hasty provisions" (459). The salient points here are the need for caution in predicting causes and effects, especially in politics, and the figural substitution of the nation for the monarch as the proper object of a poet's respectful concern. Godwin, like Davenant, had learned the first lesson beyond recall, but the second lesson he, like Wordsworth, Coleridge, and (later) Shelley, felt he might still profit from. *Faulkener* is "hasty provisions" concocted from a bad recipe: too bland in politics, too spicy in emotions. But his *History of the Commonwealth,* published another fifteen years later (1824–28), indicates the more considered and appropriate bent of his genius, and might be read as his final, displaced commentary on his own revolutionary era.

This, however, would take us well beyond drama. Nevertheless, the imaginative substitution of philosophical poet for political activist or essayist is underwritten in the draft essay on Davenant by Godwin's detailed tracing of the provenance of Davenant's arrest and subsequent pardon—by Milton, to whom he subsequently returned the favor, when "a set of the greatest geniuses for government the world ever saw" (462; quoting Bishop Warburton) were condemned to be "put to death with every circumstance of horror." This preservation of genius becomes for Godwin the final test of moral integrity: "I understand [Davenant] as the author of Gondibert," but "I love [him] as the preserver of Milton" (463). Far better to be the savior of Milton than the instructor of Charles I. He cites with strong approval Waller's encomium to Davenant in exile, lines that we may well feel Godwin applied to himself:

> you let your country know,
> they have impoverished themselves, not you,
> Who, with the Muses' help, can mock those Fates,
> Which threaten kingdoms, & disorder states.
> To Banish those who with such art can sing,
> Is a rude crime, which its own curse doth bring.
>
> (460)

In both *Faulkener* and the essay on Davenant, Godwin's attention is on persons who are or have been partly in both camps, or who, at a moment of decisive change, must forge a new option. Shelley's *Charles the First* shows a similarly ambivalent focus, with the moral cruxes of the drama distributed alternatively between Charles, the republicans (especially Hampden), Strafford, the queen and Archbishop Laud, and Archy, the court fool. There can be little doubt that Godwin's views on Charles I and the Civil War epoch had influenced Shelley when he began writing *Charles the First* in 1820, though he asserted to Thomas Medwin, 20 July, that it would be written "without prejudice or passion."[19] In 1818, Godwin had written to Shelley in Italy of his desire to resume a history of the Commonwealth period, though he expressed a lack of confidence that he could complete it and suggested that Mary Shelley might try the project. Evidently, Mary did begin work on a Civil War play shortly thereafter but soon left off because of a scarcity of source material at hand.[20] From 1820, Shelley's play is "continually referred to in his letters," Joan Mandell Baum summarizes, "as his great task" until a few months before his death.[21] His trouble completing the project has been well rehearsed by Baum and others, with considerable critical energy devoted to speculation about why he did not finish it and whether he would have, and to detective work on his probable seventeenth-century sources.²² Yet a fully demonstrable but overlooked truth is that, even in this fragment, Shelley left a remarkably complete and vivid picture of the Civil War crisis and a strong interpretation of its applicability to his own times.

Charles the First is a tragedy of royal downfall that depends for its effects not only on knowledge of the events of 1640, but—to a greater degree than any of the plays we are considering—on recognizing their similarity to the events of 1789 and after. These parallels are further underscored by strong signatures of Shelley's views on the "Spirit of the Age" and the state of England in 1819, which are apparent to modern readers with access to the full range of Shelley's unpublished or posthumously published works. Shelley sets his play in a moment of crisis similar to that in Godwin's essay on Davenant but some years earlier, when Charles is still in control of the government, though the country is just beginning to slip out of his grasp. The main political issue in the play is the need to keep raising revenues without the danger of calling a Parliament to endorse new tax measures: in short, a paradigm of the situation of Louis XVI in 1789, which, by 1821, had become the schoolboy truism it remains today. Shelley reinforces this parallel with several creative anachronisms, such as the king's reference to "the terrors of the time" (2.457) and Strafford's pointed warning that England should not become the "sole pattern of extinguished monarchy" to "the world to come" (2.185–86).²³ Shelley could anticipate his audience's thinking that England *had* provided that pattern—until 1793. And because Louis's France had become a second, more famous pattern by 1821, Strafford's catalog of Charles's "brother Kings" (173) has, except for its first item, equal applicability to the mid-seventeenth or the late-eighteenth century:

> Such popular storms
> Philip the Second of Spain, this Lewis of France,
> And the elate German head of many bodies,
> And every petty lord of Italy,
> Quelled or by arts or arms. Is England poorer
> Or feebler?
>
> (177–82)

Strafford's concept of a "pattern" is very similar to Shelley's statement on the Civil War in his 1819 essay, *A Philosophical View of Reform:* "By rapid graduation the nation was conducted to the temporary abolition of aristocracy and episcopacy, and to *the mighty example* which, 'in teaching nations how to live,' England afforded to the world—of bringing to public justice one of those chiefs of a conspiracy of privileged murderers and robbers whose impunity has been the consecration of crime."[24] Moreover, in these references and others, Shelley was thinking of both 1642 and 1789 in terms of the potentially revolutionary situation in England following the Peterloo Massacre, particularly on the issue of quelling popular dissent by force of arms.

It is a fair supposition that while Shelley worked on his play he had access to Godwin's essay on Davenant and Charles I, and he would have noted that "the tragic fate" of Hume's hero indeed "afforded the materials of an elegant & pathetic tale." The first scene of Shelley's play may have been inspired by Godwin's ironic metaphor of monarchy as a "mask played for the benefit of mankind." In this scene, the opinions of four spectators observing a masque at the Inns of Court illustrate the wide range of views held by the citizenry of London, who here literally and figuratively observe the pomp and circumstance of Charles I's court. A "First Citizen" benignly comments that this "quaint masque," in its depiction of Charles as the rising sun, an oblique reference in the iconographic tradition of the "Sun King" of Versailles, transforms "night to day, and London to place / Of peace and joy" (1.2–5).[25] This citizen expresses a hope persistently held by many parliamentarians for reconciliation with the king:

> I will not think but that our country's wounds
> May yet be healed. The king is just and gracious,
> Though wicked counsels now pervert his will:
> These once cast—
>
> (1.124–27)

But the vitriolic opinions of the "Second Citizen," combined with the even more extreme views of a third, drown out the voice of compromise. Nevertheless, this view of Charles comes close to summarizing Shelley's relatively sympathetic depiction of him as a man who was led to betray his better nature and his people through acquiescence to advice from Royalists and Churchmen as fanatical as the harshest Puritan, embodied in the characters of Archbishop Laud and Queen Henrietta.

The Puritan commentary in this scene includes a prophecy of the king's downfall that develops the "Sun King" imagery:

> This Charles the First
> Rose like the equinoctial sun, . . . [MS break]
> By vapours, through whose threatening ominous veil
> Darting his altered influence he has gained
> This height of noon—from which he must decline
> Amid the darkness of conflicting storms,
> To rank extinction and to latest night. . . .
>
> (1.46–53)

The "Third Citizen" rails against this procession of "papists, atheists, tyrants, and apostates" (1.75)—the final epithet carrying the most contemporary political significance for Shelley, as we see in the frequency of changes he rings on it. The citizens estimate that the "apostate Strafford" (1.54) was even bolder and more brazen than Judas (1.55–57), and when Strafford rebukes Archy, the fool retorts, "If all turncoats were whipped out of palaces, poor Archy would be disgraced in good company" (2.55–56). "Turncoat" was Byron's and Shelley's synonym for "renegade" in alleging that Wordsworth, Coleridge, Southey, and others had forsaken the republican spirit of their youth and were now enjoying the patronage of the Royal government. Among Shelley's notes on Hume's *History of England* is this entry: "Sir T. Wentworth, Lord Strafford the apostate—Charles resolved to confer offices on the popular leaders—but their leaders were considered as traitors."[26] Too late, Shelley's Strafford tries to give "back the wealth thou gavest" (2.299), but this "perfect, just, and honourable man" (2.310), as Charles styles him, is no match for Laud and the Queen. Although Shelley's Strafford is, like Browning's, apparently motivated by personal devotion to Charles, he displays throughout the most unmitigated royalism and has little of the potential for reconciling Crown and Commons that Browning will later explore through his character.

Moral ambivalence rather than political correctness is Shelley's center of attention throughout, extending even to the republican heroes themselves—a complexity of treatment that has puzzled later commentators looking for a direct reflection of Shelley's politics in the play, and that, no doubt, contributed significantly to Shelley's difficulty in completing it. As befits the title character of a tragedy, Charles is the most consistently sympathetic character in the play as we have it. Even his weakness of character does not tell much against him, insofar as we appreciate his evident desire to do good when torn between wolfish advisers like Laud and Henrietta Maria on the one hand, and Romantic idealists like the republicans on the other. When Laud "walks / As if he trod upon the heads of men," looking "elate, drunken with blood and gold" (1.60–61), we feel we are watching Sidmouth and Castlereagh parading in *The Mask of Anarchy*. And in his Queen Henrietta Maria, Shelley may be said to have combined the "best" characteristics of Lady Macbeth and Marie Antoinette. She betrays no understanding of the English people, their grievances, or the danger to her husband in her counsel when she says, "I see the new-born courage in your eye / Armed to strike dead the Spirit of the Time" (2.114–15). The capital letters mark one of Shelley's capital concepts. For the Shelley of *A Defense of Poetry*, this is much worse than telling starving people to eat cake, for the "Spirit of the Age" is the life force of an era, its specific genius, and any one who would presume to kill it will certainly be killed by it. When the queen admonishes her husband to "banish weak-eyed Mercy to the weak" (2.125), in preparing for war against his own ancestral kingdom of Scotland, *Macbeth* comes strongly to mind (White, p. 436; Wright, p. 44). Macbeth, we should remember, is a victim of regicide as well as its instigator, and the violations that Laud urges upon the *bodies* of Charles's state make the allusion contextually appropriate, further supporting Mary Jacobus's thesis that regicide in *Macbeth* was associated in Romantic theater with the French Revolution.[27] Shelley spares no invective in making Laud's advice sound like state treason coming from the very mouth of the state:

> To death, imprisonment, and confiscation,
> Add torture, add the ruin of the kindred
> Of the offender, add the brand of infamy,
> Add mutilation: and if this suffice not,
> Unleash the sword and fire, that in their thirst
> They may lick up that scum of schismatics.
> I laugh at those weak rebels who, desiring
> What we possess, still prate of Christian peace. . . .
>
> (2.227–34)

But the villains are not the only characters given strong rhetoric in *Charles the First*, as we have seen in the opening scene's chorus of street invective. Indeed, the Second Citizen's diatribe upon the passing masque sounds like nothing so much as a reprise of Shelley's extremely bitter apocalyptic sonnet, "England in 1819," with undertones also of his "Song to the Men of England":

> Here is the pomp that strips the houseless orphan,
> Here is the pride that breaks the desolate heart.
> These are the lilies glorious as Solomon,

> Who toil not, neither do they spin,—unless
> It be the webs they catch poor rogues withal.
> Here is the surfeit which to them who earn
> The niggard wages of the earth, scarce leaves
> The tithe that will support them till they crawl
> Back to her cold hard bosom. Here is health
> Followed by grim disease, glory by shame,
> Waste by lame famine, wealth by squalid want,
> And England's sin by England's punishment.
>
> (1.150–65)

And to Archy the fool is given Shelley's vein of urbane sarcasm. When he says to Charles, "Hell is the pattern of all commonwealths: / Lucifer was the first republican" (2.364–65), we not only hear the satiric voice of *Peter Bell the Third* ("Hell is a city much like London," 1.148), but we also sense the ambiguity of Shelley's political stance in the play. He had promised Charles Ollier, his publisher, that it would not be "coloured by the party spirit of the author" (11 January 1822; *Letters,* 2: 372). Of course, a fool may say anything, and because Archy mostly speaks out against the corruption of the court, we might let this slap at the republicans pass by as an anomaly permitted to court jesters. Yet the terms of his joke are so directly connected with Shelley's satires against Wordsworth and the Lakers that they cannot be discounted as a mere generic effect of fool's talk. Building on an apocryphal tradition that the Puritan leaders were about to embark for America like the pilgrims before Charles's severe measures provoked them into civil war (see Cameron, 206–7, for probable sources), Shelley has Archy taunt, "they think to found / A commonwealth like Gonzalo's in the play, / Gynaecocoenic and pantisocratic" (2.360–62; see *The Tempest,* 2.1.144–70). There will be "No marrying" in Gonzalo's "commonwealth" (2.147, 166), so "Gynaecocoenic," to have women in common, is attributed to the communal nature of the "Pantisocracy" Coleridge and Southey planned in 1794–95 to form in Pennsylvania. We, and Shelley's audience if he had had one, might well echo the king's surprised reply "What's that, sirrah?" for the allusion wonderfully links the excesses of republican and/or Puritan idealism with Southey's and Coleridge's Pantisocratic project. The humor of this jibe at the older Romantics should not obscure the satiric seriousness of Shelley's implied comparison between the heroes of England's republican past and the elder statesmen of Romanticism. Both despaired of England's future, and thought of transferring their hopes and talents to more congenial soil. Both were forced by circumstances to remain, but whereas the Puritans made a political revolution that succeeded and then failed, the Romantics failed to make a political revolution and made a successful literary one instead.

Not knowing what to make of such multifaceted "voicing" (in the Bakhtinian sense) in the play, Woodings was led to the conclusion that Shelley's creation of Charles as a tragic figure required doubting the poet's approval of the Parliamentarians, because he "could not afford, even if this reaction came easily to him, to denounce the rebels or, by implication, the King" ("Shelley's *Charles the First*," 231). Woodings's unlikely assumption that denouncing the rebels should come "easily" to Shelley is based on an older, rigid model of source study; that is, because Shelley relied heavily on Hume and because he presents Charles sympathetically, it must follow that he agreed with Hume's defense of Charles and vilification of Cromwell. Although this is clearly wrong, Woodings nonetheless responds to ambiguities in the play that are everywhere endorsed by an immediately recognizable and effective Shelleyan rhetoric. One of the most poignant examples of this is the "Youth" who watches the opening procession with the vitriolic Citizens. Although on the immediate level of staging we are to see that the Youth is a naive idealist, the beauty of his visions, when contrasted with the extreme spitefulness of the Citizens, makes us aware (if we have read our Shelley well) that the Youth is also one of Shelley's favorite *personae*, the visionary crushed by sordid realities of the present. This is quite clear in his first description of the masque procession: "'tis like the bright procession / Of skiey visions in a solemn dream / From which men wake as from a paradise, / And draw new strength to tread the thorns of life" (1.17–20). Although the Citizens repeatedly smash his visions, the Youth seems never to hear or to be affected by them, and always insists on putting the most beautiful construction on the king's display:

> how glorious! See those thronging chariots
> Rolling, like painted clouds before the wind,
> Behind their painted steeds; how some are shaped
> Like curved sea-shells dyed by the azure depths
> Of Indian seas, some like the new-born moon;
> And some like cars in which the Romans climbed
> (Canopied by Victory's eagle-wings outspread)
> The Capitolian!
>
> (1.137–44)

Even though this speech is followed immediately by the Second Citizen's diatribe against "Nobles, and sons of nobles," the youth never learns. The repeated power of his visions, counterpointing the satiric invective of the Citizens, and coupled with Charles's sweet (if weak) reasonableness, and Shelley's anachronistic jibes at the republicans *via* the Romantic Pantisocrats—all these tend toward the conclusion that *Charles the First* had the potential of becoming the most complex and searching of all Romantic dramatic analyses of the "Spirit of the Age."

This is not to say that Shelley's politics are muddled or "incorrect" but that his drama would have been a true and excellent tragedy, as we would expect of the author of *The Cenci*. Although he admitted he could not "seize the conception of the subject as a whole" (*Letters,* 2: 388), his own sentiments are not in doubt, as we see in almost the last words of the manuscript, the magnificent speech (composed first [Woodings, 24]), given to Hampden, whom Shelley chooses to represent as leader of the republicans. (Cromwell is mentioned only once in the play, at the end of the standard catalog of republicans, Hampden, Pym, and Vane, along with "other rebels of less note" [1.157].) True, this speech is a farewell speech, as the republicans ostensibly set sail for America, yet its idealism turns sharply (like the 1819 sonnet's) from visionary escape to apocalyptic retribution:

> This glorious clime, this firmament . . .
> . . . .
> Presses upon me like a dungeon's grate. . . .
> The boundless universe
> Becomes a cell too narrow for the soul
> That owns no master. . . .
> . . . the eagle spirits of the free,
> . . . scorn the storm
> Of time, and gaze upon the light of truth. . . .
> Like eaglets floating in the heaven of time,
> They soar above their quarry, and shall stoop
> Through palaces and temples thunderproof.
> (2.37–39, 44–58)

At such a moment, we feel that the idealism of the Youth has joined the political force of the republicans and that we are hearing the very voice of "the Spirit of the Time," which Henrietta Maria urged Charles to "kill," thus forecasting his coming catastrophe. Shelley had hoped his play would represent the "birth of severe and high feelings" and be worthy of comparison to his openly acknowledged Elizabethan models.[28] Hampden's speech illustrates his success in both ambitions. But how this apocalyptic image of execution could have correlated with the tragic stages of Charles's fall may have been beyond Shelley's interest. In her note to the poems, Mary Shelley opined that "he could not bend his mind away from the broodings and wanderings of thought divested from human interest which he loved best . . . and he threw [*Charles the First*] aside for one of the most mystical of his poems, *The Triumph of Life*" (453). Yet if we are to call the *Triumph* "mystical" in its grand representations of the cycles of human history, we must also reflect that the political or "human" interest of *Charles the First* is equally informed by a mystic or visionary imagination inseparable from Shelley's reflections on the greatest political subject—and tragedy—of his times, as Shelley claimed the French Revolution was, in his *Philosophical View of Reform*. With his professed distaste for the minutiae of history (historical realism being virtually the opposite of his accustomed styles), Shelley may have had trouble proceeding simply because, having done the requisite research, he had already portrayed the essence of his characters, thus saying all he had to say about the subject. Yet as extraordinary efforts by virtually all the Romantic writers show, it is a great miscalculation to equate "fragment" with "failure" in this literature. Although *Charles the First* is incomplete, its perspective is full enough to prevent its lightly being labeled a failure, except in form. It has the necessary ingredients of thematic roundness, dramatic adequacy, and poetic eloquence and could well stand the test of production, with a little cutting and pasting, as a potent political "interlude."

Considering Shelley's trouble with the censor over *The Cenci* (1819) and his efforts to soften his rendition of Charles, it is interesting that a play with the same subject, Mary Russell Mitford's *Charles the First*, was banned at London's licensed theaters in 1825. Charles Kemble, considering it for production, found the play "admirable though somewhat dangerous," and unfortunately for Mitford so did George Colman, the Examiner of Plays.[29] "The very mention of regicide made the censor pale," writes Richard Findlater, "and Colman felt that he was 'unable to take the responsibility of sanctioning its performance,' although Miss Mitford was a devout Royalist."[30] "The fact is that the subject of this play and the incidents it embraces are fatal in themselves," Findlater further quotes Colman; "they are an inherent and incurable disease; the morbid matter lies in the very bones and marrow of the historical facts, and defies eradication. . . . I give Miss Mitford full credit for the harmlessness of her intentions, but mischief may be unconsciously done, as a house may be set on fire by a little innocent in the nursery." The edifice Colman was empowered to protect from conflagration was the English state, and he passed the play on to the Lord Chamberlain, the duke of Montrose, who affirmed his judgment. After being rejected by a second Lord

Chamberlain, the duke of Devonshire, in 1831, *Charles the First* was finally produced in 1834 at the Victoria Theater (later the Old Vic) "without incident of any kind" (Findlater, p. 57).

Mitford is justly remembered for her sketches and stories of rural England, *Our Village* ([1832]; a new edition was recently issued by Penguin Books), and for her extensive correspondence with more prominent writers, including Coleridge, Lamb, and Elizabeth Barrett Browning. In her own day, she was a prominent dramatist. In 1823, Macready starred in a successful Covent Garden production of her drama *Julian,* and greater successes followed, with Charles Kemble presenting *Foscari* in 1826 at Covent Garden and *Rienzi* in 1828 at Drury Lane.[31] Forced by the improvidence of her father to live on earnings from her writing, Mitford was justifiably upset at the rejection of her play. In a letter to her friend Talfourd she reports testing the play's offensiveness on a Church of England cleric, who did "not say a word about Cromwell's cant, and if he, the clergyman, does not mind it, I should hope that George Colman would not, especially as it is now a high tory play."[32] But in 1834, in an unlicensed theater and with less-heralded actors, *Charles the First* was a success with both reviewers and audiences (Watson, 207; Astin, 37).

To understand why the death of Charles I was considered by the British government to be such an incendiary topic, one must remember that from 1825 to 1831, the years just preceding passage of the Reform Bill, fears of popular revolt steadily increased. Not only had the crown fallen from public favor because of the profligate lifestyle of George IV, including his notorious attempt to divorce his wife, but the constitutional crisis threatened by the divisive debate over reform kept the French Revolution and its English precedent prominent in the national consciousness. Thomas Babington Macaulay's famous speech to the House of Commons in March of 1831 illustrates this consciousness. Macaulay called the Bill "our best security against a revolution," citing and rebutting arguments based on seventeenth-century precedents.[33] When William IV showed reluctance to approve the measure the following year, Macaulay wrote to his sister: "I fear—I fear—that he has entered on the path of Charles and Louis" (8 June 1834; 447). Macaulay wrote his *History of England from the Accession of James II* (1848–55) in an attempt to demonstrate the parallels and contrasts he saw between England at the constitutional resolution of the Civil War in 1688 and the England of 1832.

The text of Mitford's *Charles the First* is of interest primarily as a "high tory" treatment of the Civil War theme. Nonetheless, Mitford's politics were not so simplistically one-sided as generally thought, and the evidence suggests that she was interested in exploring the political and personal complexities of Cromwell's conflict with the Monarch. "I am an inconsistent politician, I confess it," Mitford wrote in 1842 to her lifelong confidante Elizabeth Barrett Browning, "with my aristocratic prejudices and my radical opinions."³⁴ Mitford's spirited characterization of the Roman republican Rienzi, who rises as a friend of the people but threatens to become a tyrant, achieves a high level of political objectivity and sophistication, as summarized by Fletcher:

> His final speeches reveal insights that pierce to the heart of the issues of liberalism, freedom, and liberty which the dramatists of the 1820's from Knowles to Mitford were raising and attempting to resolve. Basically the problem is not the form of liberty but its essence.... Too late Rienzi realizes that he has become as evil and despicable as any of his enemies and with him, as with the enlightened liberals of Miss Mitford's time, the question has not arisen: what next? what can be done?" (*English Romantic Drama*, 158)

In the political treatment of her historical subjects, Mitford appears to have been an "enlightened" conservative.

As with Rienzi, Mitford saw in Cromwell the dramatic possibilities of a democrat tempted by power, a theme with considerable topical force in post–Napoleonic Europe. In the letter to Talfourd already quoted, Mitford asserts that "in spite of my having written Charles *up* as much as possible, Oliver is the life of the piece." And in a preface to the play published in 1846, she writes:

> In attempting to delineate the characters of Charles and Cromwell, especially Cromwell, on the success or failure of which the Play must stand or fall, I have to entreat the reader to bear in mind—or I shall seem unjust to the memory of a great man—that the point of time which this tragedy embraces was precisely that in which the King appeared to the most advantage.... Never throughout his splendid history were the chequered motives and impulses of Cromwell so decidedly evil; never was he so fierce, so cruel, so crafty, so deceitful, so borne along by a lower personal ambition, a mere lust of rule, as at that moment.... but if I had undertaken to portray these remarkable men at any other part of their career, it is certain that my drawing of Charles would have been much less amiable, and that of Cromwell much more so.³⁵

This double-edged apology for an overly negative portrait of Cromwell and overly positive one of Charles may be accounted for by Mitford's mixed political sympathies and by the fact that many of her literary friends were liberals. In any case, Mitford's statement provides a good summary of the presentation of both Cromwell and Charles in the play.

Cromwell is everywhere in his "great aims justified" by the "high and holy purpose" of the Puritan and Parliamentary cause—for him one and the same thing (654). Whereas Shelley distances freedom-loving Parliamentarians such as Hampden and the younger Vane from the Puritan zealots, and associates Cromwell with this group, Mitford makes no such distinction. The only middle ground in her play is occupied by General Fairfax, who opposes the king's execution but is no match for Cromwell's deceptive maneuverings; the latter acknowledges the general's value in time of war, but calls him, behind his back, a "weak / Wife-ridden faintling" (654). Charles, meanwhile, makes historically suspect protestations about his unwillingness to "forfeit that great bond / Of honour, a King's word" by escaping England (655), as well as a profusely noble and self-sacrificing show of holding firm in protecting the sacred prerogatives of the crown. Mitford intended to portray the Royal Martyrdom, and at this she certainly succeeded.

This portrayal includes the required elements of Royalist hagiography, including, most notably, Charles as Christ figure, and the poignant separation of the king from his wife and children before his death. To his judges, Charles quotes Christ's parables of the sower and of the wise and foolish virgins. The farewell scene was no doubt exploited for its full sentimental impact on the stage (667–68), but the most dramatically interesting moment occurs with Mitford's presentation of a supposedly historical episode from the trial—the head of the king's walking stick, fashioned in the form of a crown, portentously falls to the floor and "rolls across the stage," coming to rest directly before Cromwell (661–62).

To his credit, Cromwell acknowledges that responsibility for the king's execution lies ultimately at his feet. In refusing the titles and hollow preferment the queen desperately offers if he will spare her husband, Cromwell sternly but admirably promises that she will "learn faith in one man's honesty" through his actions (660). The play ends with a bald exemplification of that honesty, Cromwell saying simply, "The deed / Is mine" (672). The question of honesty occurs ubiquitously in traditional detractions from the characters of both Cromwell and Charles: Cromwell the self-serving hypocrite; Charles the untrustworthy monarch. Ironically, in Mitford's "high tory" play, Cromwell passes this crucial test better than Charles, the latter straining credulity by protesting his honesty too strenuously. Facing impending execution, the king betrays his troubled conscience in a telling allusion to that loyal supporter he once abandoned to the same doom: "Oh, Strafford! Strafford! / This is a retribution!" (664).

The play is reasonably effective until it takes the obligatory turn toward the end, and Charles rises up the royal Martyr while Cromwell descends almost to the status of a comic villain. In this regard, Mitford was right to apologize in her preface for being historically unfair to Cromwell. It is noteworthy that Mitford focuses on Cromwell as the hinge of dramatic action, whereas Shelley, like Godwin, had focused on the tragic flaws of Charles. If Shelley's problem was to make his hero sympathetic, Mitford's was to keep her villain from becoming too unsympathetic.

The dramatic moment is also interesting to compare to Godwin's essay and Shelley's play. Charles has *almost* agreed with the commissioners, so Cromwell and his associates must find a way to tip the balance against him: Who will accuse, and who will judge? Who can Cromwell trust to *usurp* these functions? This question is linked to a highly ambivalent sense of who should speak for the people. We hear of "the tyrant many" (664), and elsewhere the people are called "lubbard" and "smug," but the king's speech as the "voice of all England" (662) is not much more reassuring. The queen (as in Shelley) speaks as a Fury of Revenge, threatening retribution from the Allies in ways that suggest the beleaguered situation of the French revolutionaries in 1793-94: the moment before *their* descent into Terror, which is essentially the "moment" of Mitford's play. Apparently, in Mitford's drama, "we" are to see peace and tranquility just slipping out of England's reach—and to feel relief that "we" have survived the lesson of history that France has just relearned, at great risk to a world that should be grateful for its new Restoration, of 1815. When the Queen refers to Cromwell as "the master-spirit of the time," Mitford is pushing her character beyond personal ambition into a figure of history, such as Robespierre or Napoleon.

As in Shelley's play, and as in Romantic Civil War dramas generally, the allusions to Shakespeare's plays are important in establishing the backward perspective of cultural history. Mitford's Charles reads *As You Like It* in his sequestration in Carsbrooke Castle (655). But more important are echoes of Richard II speaking to Bolingbroke in Charles's speeches to Cromwell, with overtones of Macbeth added to Cromwell. And when Cromwell is called "a great bad man" (664), we hear Clarendon's famous Satanic tag line ("a bold bad man") applied against him as well.

The play reaches its dramatic climax at the end of 4.3, when the king and Cromwell stand over against each other, each representing, in humanly attractive terms, his own ideology: the king, as God's anointed; Cromwell, as the representative of Freedom. With liberal reformers like Henry Brougham already on the stump (whose demagoguery even Byron could not stomach), Mitford was challenging her audience to recognize that the voice of "progress" (or of the future) might not necessarily be attractive. But after this effective tableau, in act 5 the play rapidly degenerates into predictable hagiography. All in all, it is not too surprising that Mitford's play was censored until well after the passage of the Reform Bill, because any audience would have had to wait until this final act to see the play's considerable dramatic tension resolved in a politically acceptable denouement.

Before seeking out the young and little-known Robert Browning after the Talfourd dinner party, Charles Macready turned to a well-established playwright at the table and off-handedly asked her if she planned to write another drama. "Will you act in it?" Miss Mitford replied. But already wounded by well-deserved criticism for his brutish revisions of Mitford's *Julian,* Macready was taken aback and did not answer (Watson, 216–17). Macready had been predictably critical of the acting in the Victoria Theater production of Mitford's *Charles the First.* Before long, however, Browning gave him an opportunity to interpret the same subject in *Strafford: An Historical Tragedy,* produced at Covent Garden in 1837.[36]

Browning's choice of that subject provokes a persistent question about the play. The two great influences of his formative years had been his mother's nonconformist religion and the Romantic poets, Shelley and Byron—his delicate, dandyish appearance at Talfourd's reflecting an outward emulation of the latter. Mitford recalled, probably with mild exaggeration, that he "resembled a girl dressed in boy's clothes," featuring a head of "long ringlets."[37] These two major influences on the young Browning combined to form the basis of his liberal and reformist political orientation, and his choice of the second most prominent Royalist martyr of the seventeenth century as the hero of his tragedy appears in retrospect profoundly contradictory. Yet choosing his hero from the "wrong" side is entirely consistent with analogous choices by Lamb, Godwin, Shelley, and Mitford. An important clue to help explain this choice in Browning's case is found in his poem "The Lost Leader" (1843), which William DeVane characterizes as perhaps "the finest expression of his liberalism":[38] "Just for a handful of silver he left us, / Just for a riband to stick in his coat—."[39] Asked frequently in later years to account for the poem in an 1875 letter Browning made an apologetic

> confession, on my part that I *did* in my hasty youth presume to use the great and venerable personality of Wordsworth as a sort of painter's

model; one from which this or the other particular feature may be selected and turned to account: had I intended more, above all, such a boldness as portraying the entire man, I should not have talked about "handfuls of silver and bits of ribbon." These never influenced the change of politics in the great poet; whose defection, nevertheless, accompanied as it was by a regular face-about of his special party, was to my juvenile apprehension, and even mature consideration, an event to deplore.[40]

At Talfourd's "the company was toasting the author of *Paracelsus* as one of the 'Poets of England,'" writes DeVane; "Wordsworth leaned across the table and said, 'I am proud to drink to your health, Mr. Browning!'" (146). Understandably, Browning had difficulty sustaining the harsh tone of his poem, and it ends with imagining the "lost leader" resuming his rightful place in an enlightened afterlife: "Then let him receive the new knowledge and wait us, / Pardoned in heaven, the first by the throne!" DeVane's trenchant commentary includes a brief mention of a possible connection with Browning's first play: "The phrase which Browning uses concerning Wordsworth, 'Pardoned in Heaven, the first by the throne,' and indeed his whole attitude of lofty charity towards a political apostate, seems to be an echo of the great speech of forgiveness to Strafford, another 'apostate,' which Browning had put into Pym's mouth in his drama, *Strafford*" (145).

DeVane's insightful connection between *Strafford* and "The Lost Leader" is missing from most criticism focusing on the play.[41] In fact, examining Strafford as a political apostate is the key to understanding the work not as "an early Victorian tragedy," as it has usually been treated, but as the last Romantic tragedy—produced and published in the year Victoria took the throne. "The occasion, and perhaps the composition" of "The Lost Leader," DeVane continues, "seems to have risen upon Wordsworth's acceptance of the laureateship on April 4, 1843." Perhaps Wordsworth's pension was "the culmination of the 'apostasy' of which Browning had learned from Shelley, Byron, Hazlitt, and possibly by word of mouth from Leigh Hunt" (144).

Browning sets his play at roughly the same juncture of Civil War history as Shelley's, when, with the approach of rebellion in Scotland, Charles loses an opportunity, here urged on him by Strafford, to gain popular support for his policies and chooses instead the confrontation with Parliament that will lead to disaster. From the play's opening, Browning establishes the identity of Strafford primarily as a not entirely converted political renegade, and thus there is another work in which the central dramatic conflict rests in the transitional nature of the hero's political being. In the first scene a group of Parliamentary leaders, including Hampden, the younger Vane, Nathaniel Fiennes, and representatives of the Scots, discuss Strafford's return from his post as governor of Ireland after being summoned by King Charles, now desperate for competent help in dealing with rebellious Scotland. It has been ten years since the last English Parliament, and "when the last sat," exclaims Fiennes, "Wentworth sat with us!" (1.1.23).[42] Vane laments that he cannot help thinking "on all that's past / Since that man left us; how his single arm / Rolled the advancing good of England back / And set the woeful past up in its place" (30–33; cf. 49–59). Discussion of fears that such a formidable opponent will gain full confidence of the king and thereby power "to rule" England provokes frustrated, angry cries of "Renegade!" (61, 89). Vane recounts the apocryphal story of friendship between Pym and Strafford that Browning includes and deliberately exaggerates to play up Strafford's political defection as fully as possible: "You must have heard—ere Wentworth dropped our cause . . . [that] Pym and he were sworn, 'tis said, / To live and die together" (105, 110–11). The two supposedly parted ways with Pym vowing, "You leave us, Wentworth!" but "while your head is on, / I'll not leave you" (119–20). The rest of the act depicts Pym's effort to keep this promise by restoring an alliance with Strafford, who he knows will be angered and discouraged when he learns that the king has dissolved the Scottish Parliament and approved civil war in the north without consulting him.

Pym enters expressing a desire that his compatriots "believe, / Spite of the past, Wentworth rejoins you, friends!" (188–89). But Vane and the others react with exclamatory skepticism: "Wentworth? Apostate! Judas! Double-dyed / A traitor!" (190–91). Pym then reminds Vane that he too "loved that man," and "used to stroll with him, arm locked in arm, / Along the streets to see the people pass, / And read in every island-countenance / Fresh argument for God against the King" (192–96). Vane acknowledges that their former ally framed "the choicest clause / In the Petition of Right," but points out that only a month later he accepted advancement from Charles (201–5). Pym concedes the truth of this rejoinder, but wistfully replies, "I have had friends—. . . / But I shall never quite forget that friend" (207–8).

In scene 2 Strafford arrives at court still uninformed of its decisions, asking his confidante Lady Carlisle, "Why does the King distrust me?" (31). She blames "the party / That poisons the queen's ear, Savile and Holland" and "old Vane" (34–36). When he inquires about the activities of "Pym and the people," she derisively refers to them as "the faction" and wishfully dismisses them as "of no account," asserting "there'll never be / Another Parliament" (62–64).

Strafford neither believes nor wants this. Caught in a double bind of mistrust from both sides because of his political past, he reveals how seriously he is considering giving up the royalist cause in disillusionment and disgust: "in my earliest life / I was not . . . much that I am now" and "I'll not be their tool / Who might be Pym's friend yet" (66–67, 71–72; cf. 145–48). The king's persistent lack of trust and appreciation wounds most deeply, but Strafford's conscience also troubles him because of the "rash" and violent repression being planned without his consultation, in which he will certainly be called on to participate and which he will even be asked to supervise (75–83). Nonetheless, in spite of anger and frustration, he hopes that matters can still be put right if he wins the king's full confidence and corrects his own appearance of neglecting the rights and welfare of the English populace.

When Strafford admits to Pym that he is "discontented with the King" (148), Pym charges him with selling former principles for personal achievement: "you sold your soul for [a title]" (155). Strafford is deeply stung that Pym has had access to his supposedly private petitions to the King, another sign of the monarch's duplicity. Pym anticipates this and pleads that his former ally "wake" himself, "your true / And proper self, our Leader, England's chief, / And Hampden's friend!" (177–79). But at this critical moment, Charles enters, and the stage direction reads, "Wentworth lets fall Pym's hand."

Strafford's personal devotion to King Charles overpowers his doubts and Pym's arguments. The latter leaves, and the kneeling Strafford pathetically begs, "Sir, trust me! but for this once, trust me, Sir!" (195). Informed that the Scots are negotiating an unlawful alliance with France, Strafford suggests that popular support and funds for war in Scotland could be gained if the king does what his opposition least expects: "The People for us—were the people for us! / . . . Summon a Parliament! In Ireland first, / Then, here" (227, 229–30). Charles acquiesces and conveniently grants the long-awaited earldom. Strafford departs "grown young again" (248), and Henrietta Maria enters to castigate her husband for his decision to call the Parliament. "Were I in France again to see / A king" (285–86), she taunts in her Lady Macbeth persona, and Charles responds by promising, "I have schemes, such schemes," including bribing the leaders of Parliament and looking for an "excuse for breaking it for ever" (291, 294). Browning's Charles is disingenuous, easily manipulated, and shows little sense of any good but his own advantage. He is unworthy of the devotion of the far stronger and nobler Strafford, who genuinely believes he can still serve England's people by saving its lawful king from bad advice and from his refusal to recognize the constitutional validity and practical inevitability of representative government. The historical Strafford was by most accounts less sensitive to democratic concerns in carrying out the policies of Charles, and that reality brings into sharper relief the ideological profile of Browning's hero.[43]

Strafford's devotion to Charles and his shift in political loyalties are historical realities; his friendship with Pym, however, is a myth Browning embellished to emphasize his protagonist's role in the play as renegade. As a member of Parliament, Strafford had been imprisoned by Charles in 1626 for refusing to support his attempt to force unwilling subjects to lend him money. In the Parliament of 1628, he appeared as a leader of Parliamentary opposition to the administration of Buckingham. During this period, he was a colleague and ally of those he later opposed as the king's minister, but no hard evidence was available to Browning that Strafford and Pym had been close friends. The apocryphal friendship is favorably implied in the *Life of Strafford,* on which Browning collaborated with his friend John Forster. Pym's supposed comment, "You leave us, Wentworth! while your head is on, / I'll not leave you," derives from an obscure early eighteenth-century source and occurs in both the *Life* and the play.[44]

Curiously, a passage from the *Life* that Bruce Busby ascribes to Browning decries the tradition of historical character assassination through simplistic application of the dire label "apostate": "I have always considered that much good wrath is thrown away upon what is usually called 'apostasy.' In the majority of cases, if the circumstances are thoroughly examined, it will be found that there has been 'no such thing'" (61).[45] Those "who carry their researches into the moral nature of mankind" should "expect no monsters," and against "all such conclusions I earnestly protest in the case of the remarkable personage whose ill-fated career we are now retracing" (62). If this statement is Browning's, "The Lost Leader" is a blatant deviation from the principle espoused; and the constant highlighting of Strafford's alleged apostasy in Browning's play also requires explanation. Busby points out that Forster unambiguously labels Strafford a political turncoat in his other writings on the period and criticizes Browning for an overly sympathetic characterization in the play: "where the author places the popular cause in the very front of all our sympathies, the criminality of *Strafford* [sic] should have been made equally prominent with this grandeur" (46–47).[46] But clearly Browning "expect[ed] no monster" in his examination of Strafford and found on the contrary a heroic *victim* of an untrustworthy king and a number of genuinely monstrous characters who advised and supported him. "Strafford, loyal to Charles, fighting for his sake a war not in the public interest," writes D. M. de Silva, "is tragic because he still thinks to serve that interest" (15). Browning's play is the portrait of a political renegade, but it is also an apology for what he thought of as the sincerely misguided renegadism he had diagnosed in Wordsworth. The youthful Browning considered the "loss" of both acknowledged and unacknowledged legislators of democratic reform authentically tragic.

Throughout *Strafford*, Browning persists in employing his hero's renegadism as the crux of dramatic tension both internally, in terms of Strafford's motivations and development, and externally, in his interactions with the Parliamentarians and the king. Act 2 opens with young Vane, Hampden, and others blaming Strafford for the exorbitant demand of the twelve subsidies and for the war in Scotland: "We all believed that Strafford meant us well / In summoning the Parliament. . . . / Clear me from having, from the first, hoped, dreamed, / Better of Strafford!" (14–15, 18–19; see also 1–7). But Pym says he is sure that "Strafford is wholly ours," because Charles has just dissolved the Parliament: "no Parliament for us, / No Strafford for the King! . . . / Strafford, our comrade now. The next will be / Indeed a Parliament!" (100, 105–6, 109–10). Pym cannot believe that Strafford will continue to support a monarch who reverses himself so suddenly and shows so little respect for the institution of political representation. Pym rightly anticipates Strafford's reaction in the next scene when the king informs him of this drastic action as a fait accompli, but the zealous Parliamentarian badly underestimates Strafford's personal devotion to the "man with the mild voice and mournful eyes" (2.2.293).

In a revealing passage Strafford refers to lost Parliamentary support as "one last hope" to "cure / All bitterness one day, be proud again / And young again, care for the sunshine too" (2.2.82–85). Strafford has held out that he might someday be reconciled with the Parliamentarians and has felt ashamed of appearing to be an opportunistic turncoat. Now he will be forever unable to "think of Eliot any more"—the noble specter of his egalitarian past.

In private, Strafford confronts Charles with his "perfidy" (121), but when the angry Pym, Hampden, and Vane enter, he shields the king with a self-sacrificing claim "Of counselling the measure" (142). This is Strafford's point of no return, determined to save his weak master though it means his own destruction—Pym equally resigned to destroying the monarch's most capable supporter and punishing him for his perceived treachery. As in Lamb and Godwin, the focus is on the character who may, or may not, shift *legitimately* from one side to the other.

Strafford defends himself so capably at his impeachment that young Vane pleads that Pym and Hampden show mercy (4.2.142–45). But Pym admits that revenge motivates him more strongly than political necessity:

> can we come
> To the real charge at all? There he is safe
> In tyranny's stronghold. Apostasy
> Is not a crime, treachery not a crime. . . .
>
> (167–70)

So Pym presents Charles with a choice between personal danger and signing Strafford's death warrant, and though the king is remorseful (4.3.1–8, 37–49), he predictably agrees to the latter (82–83). When Strafford's son and daughter lament the slurs against him heard among an angry populace, he exclaims with philosophical resignation: "Forsook them! What, the common songs will run / That I forsook the people? Nothing more? / Ay, Fame, the busy scribe, will pause, no doubt, . . . / Beside that plain inscription of The Name—/ the Patriot Pym, or the Apostate Strafford!" (5.2.50–52, 57–58). Summoned to the scaffold, Strafford poignantly quotes the Psalmist, "Put not your trust / In princes, . . . / In whom is no salvation!" (153–55), even as he protects Charles a final time by insisting that the king's pathetic last-minute attempts to save him are kept a secret.

As in Godwin's portrait of Davenant, Strafford's principled and self-sacrificing *failure* to save Charles is elevated to heroic proportions, thus clarifying Browning's choice of protagonist. While the issue of political apostasy remains foregrounded throughout the play, the progressive dynamic is a move in emphasis from politics to feeling, from political imperative to emotional value. The political tragedy of Strafford's apostasy is gradually subsumed by the personal tragedy; his courageous pursuit of individual idealism to the brink of self-negation, however politically misguided, transcends Browning's disapproval. But this movement in the play occurs not so much as a displacement of politics as a compensation for the political error, as demonstrated by the imagined reconciliation of Strafford and Pym, that parallels Browning's lament over Wordsworth's magnificent lifetime of poetic achievement lost to the service of liberal reform. The play ends with a high-toned exchange between Strafford and Pym, Pym's speech echoing much of "The Lost Leader," especially the final lines where Browning envisioned Wordsworth "Pardoned in heaven, the first by the throne!":

> Have I done well? Speak, England! Whose sole sake
> I still have laboured for, with disregard
> To my own heart,—for whom my youth was made
> Barren, my manhood waste, to offer up
> Her sacrifice—this friend, this Wentworth here—
> Who walked in youth with me, loved me, it may be.
> . . . .
> Ay, here I know I talk—I dare and must,
> Of England, and her great reward, as all
> I look for there: but in my inmost heart,
> Believe, I think of stealing quite away
> To walk once more with Wentworth—my youth's friend
> *Purged from all error, gloriously renewed.* . . .

In discussing Browning in the context of "The Liberal 1830's," Richard Fletcher asserts that he "is a typical Romantic playwright," though supposedly showing "indifference" in *Strafford* and later plays to "the guiding key word of Romantic drama, 'remorse'" (*English Romantic Drama*, 198). But remorse results from guilt, and guilt usually originates in Romantic drama from the deeper problem of personal and political betrayal. *Strafford*'s most fundamental qualification as a Romantic tragedy lies in its portrayal of a great man betraying himself, his friends, and "the people" for a flawed ideal, and being, in turn, betrayed by that ideal.

It is uncanny how closely the same characterization fits *The Borderers*. In a historical English setting analogous to the apparently anarchic conditions in contemporary France, through Oswald's Godwinian corruption and betrayal of Marmaduke, Wordsworth dramatized his belief that the French Revolution had betrayed his idealistic expectations for it—especially because of the changes of *character* that he said he saw in it. Lamb, Godwin, Shelley, Mitford, and Browning, setting their plays in a period of English history with inescapable parallels to the Revolution in France, dramatized their view that the cause of freedom and liberty had been forsaken by some who should have been among its most influential proponents. Deeply political as these plays are, in ways that understanding of Romanticism current until very recently could not appreciate, they are political in very Romantic ways, with most emphasis falling finally on the personal, whether of sincere emotion or faithful love and friendship. Each play demonstrates a conviction that the transitory actions of individuals are seldom private or without far-reaching consequences and that unless they are governed by trustworthy principles the result can be, to continue Wordsworth's passage from *The Borderers,* "Suffering" that "is permanent, obscure and dark, / And shares the nature of infinity." As political dramas, they focus inordinately on the personal agonies of characters caught *in transition* from one view of their political obligation to a fundamentally different one. The English Romantic Civil war dramas show how readily and deeply the experience of the French Revolution could be encoded in England's national character.

Notes

1. *The Diaries of William Charles Macready, 1831–1851,* ed. William Toynbee, 2 vols. (London: Chapman and Hall, 1912), 1: 319. Richard Fletcher gives an account of this evening in *English Romantic Drama: 1795–1843; A Critical History* (New York: Exposition Press, 1966), 164–69.
2. Mrs. [Alexandra] Sutherland Orr, *The Life and Letters of Robert Browning,* rev. Frederic G. Kenyon (1891; reprint, Westport, Conn.: Greenwood Press, 1973), 125.
3. *The Poetical Works of William Wordsworth,* ed. Ernest de Selincourt, 2d ed., rev. Helen Darbishire, 5 vols. (Oxford: Oxford University Press, 1952–59), 1: 342 (hereafter cited as *Works*).
4. No other play by a major English Romantic writer is set in Revolutionary France; see Nicholas Roe, "Imagining Robespierre," *Coleridge's Imagination: Essays in Memory of Pete Lever,* eds. Richard Gravil, Lucy Newlyn, and Nicholas Roe (Cambridge: Cambridge University Press, 1985), 161–78.
5. For recent articles that discuss political implications in the play, see the special issue of *Studies in Romanticism* devoted to it, especially Reeve Parker's essay "'In Some Sort Seeing with My Proper Eyes': Wordsworth and the Spectacles of Paris," 27 (1988): 369–90.
6. For other analogues, see Arnold B. Fox, "Political and Biographical Background of Coleridge's *Osorio,*" *JEGP* 61 (1962): 258–67; John David Moore, "Coleridge and the 'Modern Jacobinical Drama': *Osorio, Remorse,* and the Development of Coleridge's Critique of the Stage, 1797–1816," *Bulletin of Research in the Humanities* 85 (1982): 443–65; and Thomas L. Ashton, "*Marino Faliero:* Byron's 'Poetry' of Politics,'" *Studies in Romanticism* 13 (1974): 1–13.
7. Plays by Godwin, Lamb, Shelley, Browning, and Mitford will be discussed in this essay; those by others mentioned here are Jerrold's *Nell Gwynne* (Covent Garden, 1833); Moncrieff's *Rochester; or, King Charles the Second's Merry Days* (Olympic, 1818); Knowles's *Woman's Wit* (Covent Garden, 1838); Balzac's *Cromwell* (1819); and Hugo's *Cromwell* (1827; with its famous preface). See Allardyce Nicoll, *A History of English Drama, 1660–1900* (Cambridge: Cambridge University Press, 1940–60), 4: 16–17. Macready records in his diary (on the same page he first mentions Browning's intention to write *Strafford*) that he read with disappointment the manuscript of a play by Bulwer-Lytton entitled *Cromwell* (p. 340; see also 342). Macready's judgment was evidently taken to heart by the author, because the play was never produced or published.
8. For a long list of dramatic adaptations of Scott's novels, see Nicoll, 4: 91–95. Bellini's opera, derived from *Old Mortality,* premiered in Paris in 1835, and was

"Englished," notes Nicholl, as *Cavaliers and Roundheads* by Pocock for the Drury Lane Theatre in the same year (4: 93 n). Bellini's version was produced regularly throughout the nineteenth century at the Royal Opera House in Covent Garden (see Jerome Mitchell, *The Walter Scott Operas* [University: University of Alabama Press, 1977], 57–63).

9. For discussion of analogies in nineteenth-century literature between seventeenth-century English history and the French Revolution, and nineteenth-century views of the English Civil War, see Joseph Nicholes, "Revolutions Compared: The English Civil War as Political Touchstone in Romantic Literature," in *Revolution and English Romanticism: Politics and Rhetoric,* eds. Keith Hanley and Raman Selden (Hartfordshire: Harvester Wheatsheaf; New York: St. Martin's Press, 1990), 261–76; Roy Strong, *Recreating the Past: British History and the Victorian Painter* (New York: Thames and Hudson, 1978), 40, and 139–40; and Martin Meisel, *Realizations: Narrative, Pictorial, and Theatrical Arts in Nineteenth-Century England* (Princeton: Princeton University Press, 1983), 232. See also David Rogers, *"For King or Parliament?": Attitudes of 19th Century painters to the Civil War,* the catalog to an exhibition mounted in 1978–79 by the Wolverhampton and the Mappin Art Galleries; J. W. Burrow, *A Liberal Descent: Victorian Historians and the English Past* (Cambridge and New York: Cambridge University Press, 1981), 12–17; and Ian Fletcher, "The White Rose Rebudded: Neo-Jacobitism in the 1890s," in *W. B. Yeats and His Contemporaries* (Brighton: Harvester, 1987), 83–123. We use the term "English Revolution" somewhat loosely in this essay to cover the entire period, 1642–88, following a common nineteenth-century perception, especially among liberals, that the Revolution of 1688 was the culminating constitutional resolution of the Civil Wars. Thus, Burrow notes that Thomas Babington Macaulay, the most influential historiographer of the century, asserted the "essential continuity" of the Glorious Revolution, "which no Tory would be disposed to allow, with the Parliamentarians in the Civil War and even the regicides" (16–17).

10. *Lectures 1795: On Politics and Religion,* eds. Peter Mann and Lewis Patton (Princeton: Princeton University press, 1969), 255; xl, 254. For Coleridge's preoccupation with seventeenth-century political history, see *Coleridge on the Seventeenth-Century,* ed. Roberta Florence Brinkley (1955; reprint, New York: Greenwood Press, 1968), esp. 3–36. For Wordsworth's, see Z. S. Fink's "Wordsworth and the English Republican Tradition," *JEGP* 47 (1948): 107–26.

11. *The Letters of Charles and Mary Anne Lamb,* ed. Edwin W. Marrs Jr. (Ithaca: Cornell University Press, 1975–78), 2: 82.

12. "New Lamb Texts from *The Albion?* I: 'What is Jacobinism?'" *Charles Lamb Bulletin* 17 (1977): 9. Lamb's essay appeared 30 June 1801 and is reprinted in its entirety in Courtney's article. She identifies Lamb's allusion to *"general lovers"* as a passage in *John Woodvil* that he had published separately from the play in November 1800 (11), and she cites other references in Lamb's writings to Sidney, Harrington, and Locke (10). Material in the present essay on Lamb's *John Woodvil* appeared originally in Joseph Nicholes, "Politics by Indirection: Charles Lamb's Seventeenth-Century Renegade, John Woodvil," *The Wordsworth Circle* 19 (1988): 49–55.

13. Burton Ralph Pollin, "Charles Lamb and Charles Lloyd as Jacobins and Anti-Jacobins," *Studies in Romanticism* 12 (1973): 633–47; Winifred Courtney, *Young Charles Lamb, 1785–1802* (New York: New York University Press, 1982).

14. For an account of the composition, publication, and reception of the play, see the notes of E. V. Lucas, ed., *The Works of Charles and Mary Lamb,* 7 vols. (1903–5; reprint; St. Clair Shores, Mich.: Scholarly Press, 1971), 5: 350–68 (hereafter cited as *Works*). Lamb first called his play "Pride's Cure," completing a first draft

4: TRANSITORY ACTIONS, MEN BETRAYED 155

between August 1798 and May 1799; the present title dates from revisions completed around November 1801 in preparation for the play's publication (see *Works*, 5:350, 353–56; and Lamb to John Rickman, 24 November 1801 [Marrs, ed., *Letters*, 2: 37–41]). Wayne McKenna summarizes contemporary reviews of the play, mostly negative, in *Charles Lamb and the Theatre* (New York: Barnes & Noble Books, 1978), pp. 58–59, 63. The Gillray cartoon is reproduced in both Pollin and Courtney. Pollin discusses the *Anti-Jacobin*'s attack on Lamb in detail, as does Courtney in a chapter entitled "Political Lamb"; see also her article "Lamb, Gillray and the Ghost of Edmund Burke," *Charles Lamb Bulletin* 12 (1975): 77–82. Lucas and Courtney cite satirical verses of 1820 by Lamb aimed at Canning as evidence of a prolonged grudge (*Works*, 5: 106–6, 334; *Young Charles Lamb*, 199–200).

15. For further background on Mackintosh and Lamb's epigram, see Lucas's note (*Works*, 5:333); Pollin, 644; and Courtney's "New Lamb Texts," 2 (important information on Lamb's politics continues through two issues of the *Charles Lamb Bulletin* 18 [1977]: 28–40, and 20 [1977]: 73–92).

16. Lamb and Scott met briefly in 1821. In 1822, Lamb wrote to Scott petitioning financial aid for Godwin, and Scott sent £10 but asked to remain anonymous. With his reply, Scott evidently asked Lamb to his home in Scotland, and an invitation "as early as 1818" has also been reported (E. V. Lucas, *The Life of Charles Lamb* [1921; reprint, London: Methuen & Co., 1968], 610). It is likely that Scott had read *John Woodvil* by the time he wrote *Old Mortality*.

17. Carl Woodring, *Politics in English Romantic Poetry* (New York: Columbia University Press, 1970), 74.

18. Kenneth Neill Cameron, ed., *Shelley and His Circle: 1773–1822*, vol. 1 (Cambridge: Harvard University Press, 1961–   ), 464 (hereafter cited as *Shelley and His Circle*); see 448–67 for material on Godwin and seventeenth-century history. For an account of the composition and production of *Faulkener*, see C. Kegan Paul, *William Godwin: His Friends and Contemporaries*, 2 vols. (Boston: Roberts Brothers, 1876), 2: 122–23, 162–63. Paul also provides information on Godwin's composition of his *History of the Commonwealth of England* (2: 130, 143–44, 291–95), regarded by Godwin and his friends as a corrective to David Hume (2: 143–44) who defended the Stuarts and was hostile to Cromwell in his *The History of England from the Invasion of Julius Caesar to the Revolution in 1688* (1763–83; reprint, Indianapolis, Ind.: Library Classics, 1983–85). Paul expresses particular admiration for the originality of Godwin's positive portrait of Cromwell, "which deserves to stand by the side of that which Mr. Carlyle has painted for the world" (2: 291). See Godwin's comments on Charles I and Hume in his essay, "Interviews of Charles I," cited below.

19. *The Letters of Percy Bysshe Shelley*, ed. Frederick L. Jones, 2 vols. (Oxford: Clarendon Press, 1964), 2: 219–20 (hereafter cited as *Letters*). Shelley evidently felt a need to reassure his friend that he would not let his bias in favor of the Parliamentarians overwhelm the play, a need rendered understandable by the opposite bias revealed in Medwin's suspect comments on *Charles the First* in his biography of Shelley: "Shelley could not reconcile his mind to the beheading of Charles . . . much less could he make a hero of that arch hypocrite Cromwell, or forgive him for aiming at the royal sceptre" (*The Life of Percy Bysshe Shelley* [1847], ed. H. Buxton Forman [1913; reprint, St. Clair Shores, Mich.: Scholarly Press, 1971, 1971], 340–41). Cameron writes, "Medwin's picture of Shelley's admiration for Charles and hatred of the Puritans is clearly part of his attempt to make his hero respectable; but he is certainly right in saying that Shelley 'abominated' Cromwell's Irish massacres and disliked the general intolerance of Puritan fanaticism; but these Shelley considered as minor factors overshadowed by the great political advance of the Commonwealth"

("Shelley's Use of Source Material in *Charles I*," *Modern Language Quarterly* 6 [1945]: 198 n).

20. For an account of this exchange and the relevant portion of Godwin's letter, see *Shelley and His Circle*, 1: 464. In reference to Mary's intention to write a play, Cameron cites Mrs. Julian Marshall, *The Life and Letters of Mary Wollstonecraft Shelley* (1889) and mentions that Mary refers to this intention in her note to *Charles the First* in the 1832 edition of Shelley's poems (*Shelley and His Circle*, 1: 198–99). Mary's Civil War expertise is evident from a passage in *Frankenstein* (1818) in which her hero's visit to Civil War sites in and around Oxford clearly reflects his republican sympathies (chap. 19 of the novel; see Nicholes, "Revolutions Compared," 268–70).

21. Baum, *The Theatrical Compositions of the Major English Romantic Poets* (Austria: Institut fur Anglistik und Amerikanistik, Universitat Salzburg, 1980), 204. Baum provides a detailed account of the play's origins and the most trustworthy and substantial commentary to date.

22. See Cameron's "Shelley's Use of the Source Material"; Newman I. White, "Shelley's *Charles the First*," *JEGP* 21 (1922): 431–41; Walter Francis Wright, "Shelley's Failure in *Charles I*," *ELH* 8 (1941): 41–46; and two articles by R. B. Woodings, "Shelley's Sources for 'Charles the First,'" *Modern Language Review* 64 (1969): 267–75, and "'A Devil of a Nut to Crack': Shelley's *Charles the First*," *Studia Neophilologica* 40 (1968): 216–37.

23. *Poetical Works: Shelley*, ed. Thomas Hutchinson, corrected by G. M. Mathews, 2d ed. (London: Oxford University Press, 1970).

24. *The Complete Works of Percy Bysshe Shelley*, eds. Roger Ingpen and Walter E. Peck, 10 vols. (1926–30; reprint, New York: Gordon Press, 1965), 7: 7 (emphasis added; hereafter cited as *Works*).

25. Shelley also employs traditional Royalist iconography of Charles as a Christ figure: Charles's use of Christ's phrase the "uttermost farthing" (Matt. 5: 26); his metaphor "the sharp thorns that deck the English crown" (456); Archy's characterization of Charles as a shepherd (463); and the queen's description of a Correggio Christ child as a "cradled miniature" of the infant Charles (464). The way Shelley employed these images might simultaneously have appealed to Royalists in his audience and appeared ironic to liberals. For a history of this iconography, see Roy Strong, *Van Dyck: Charles I on Horseback* (London: Allen Lange, 1972).

26. Bodleian MS Shelley adds. e. 7, 255–58, as quoted in Woodings, "Shelley's Sources," 269. Woodings writes that a manuscript "outline of the second act suggests that Strafford, with his impeachment and execution, was to dominate a considerable part of the play" (272; he reproduces this outline in "Shelley's *Charles the First*," 234–35; see also Cameron, 208).

27. Jacobus, "'That Great Stage Where Senators Perform': *Macbeth* and the Politics of Romantic Theater," *Studies in Romanticism* 22 (1983): 353–87.

28. Letter to Charles Ollier, 22 February 1821; *Letters*, 2: 269. Woodings cites two of Shelley's statements recalled by Edward Trelawny: "in style and manner I shall approach as near our great dramatist as my feeble powers will permit," and "King Lear is my model, for that is nearly perfect" ("Shelley's *Charles the First*," 222–23; "Recollections of the Last Days of Shelley and Byron" in *The Life of Percy Bysshe Shelley*, ed. Humbert Wolfe [London: J. M. Dent; New York: E. P. Dutton, 1933], 198). Woodings provides an overview of Shakespearean echoes (222–27), including an interesting entry from "one of Shelley's own rare additions" to summaries of his historical sources: "Monopolies & taxes. See Richard 2d—See Hume 206. & consider the present times" (224; Bodleian MS Shelley adds. e. 7. 251). This comment

4: TRANSITORY ACTIONS, MEN BETRAYED 157

reveals Shelley consciously considering his theme's relevance to contemporary politics.

29. Kemble is quoted without source in Vera Watson's *Mary Russell Mitford* (London: Evans Brothers, 1950), 173.

30. *Banned!: A Review of Theatrical Censorship in Britain* (London: MacGibbon & Kee, 1967), 56. Findlater's chronology of this episode is hard to follow; for clarification see Watson, 172, 195–96, 207.

31. Marjorie Astin, *Mary Russell Mitford: Her Circle and Her Books* (London: N. Douglas, 1930), 32–34. For commentary on Mitford's dramatic style, and on *Julian, Foscari,* and *Rienzi,* see Fletcher, *English Romantic Drama,* 155–56.

32. Quoted without date or source in William James Roberts, *Mary Russell Mitford: The Tragedy of a Blue Stocking* (London: A. Melrose, 1913), 254.

33. Thomas Babington Macaulay, "Parliamentary Reform," *Selected Writings*, eds. John Clive and Thomas Pinney (Chicago: University of Chicago Press, 1972), 168, 447, 171, 175–79 (hereafter cited as *Selected Writings*).

34. *The Life of Mary Russell Mitford*, 2d ed., ed. A. G. L'Estrange, 3 vols. (London: R. Bentley, 1870), 3: 143.

35. *The Works of Mary Russell Mitford: Prose and Verse* (Philadelphia: Crissy and Markley, 1846), 652 (hereafter cited in the text).

36. Both Macready's failure in producing the play and the poet's shortcomings as dramatist have been better rehearsed in Browning scholarship and folklore than the play itself. Audiences liked the play, but financial difficulties and the withdrawal of a principal actor evidently resulted in its closure after only five performances. Edmund Gosse wrote a detailed account of these circumstances in the December 1881 issue of *The Century*.

37. *The Brownings' Correspondence*, eds. Philip Kelly and Ronald Hudson (Winfield, Kans.: Wedgestone Press, 1984), 3: 320.

38. *A Browning Handbook* (New York: F. S. Crofts, 1935), 77. For a detailed analysis of Browning's liberalism, including comment on "The Lost Leader" and Shelley's political influence, see Trevor Lloyd's "Browning and Politics," *Robert Browning,* ed. Isobel Armstrong (Athens: Ohio University Press, 1975), 142–67. John Maynard mentions that the edition of Shelley's poetry Browning devoured as a young man included *Charles the First (Browning's Youth* [Cambridge: Harvard University Press, 1977], 200). It is likely that he also knew Mitford's play.

39. *Robert Browning: The Poems*, eds. John Pettigrew and Thomas J. Collins, 2 vols. (New Haven: Yale University Press, 1981), 1: 410.

40. To Rev. Alexander B. Grosart, 24 February 1875; *Letters of Robert Browning, Collected by Thomas J. Wise,* ed. Thurman L. Hood (New Haven: Yale University Press, 1933), 166–67. See a similar response in a letter written in September of the same year (Orr, *Life and Letters of Robert Browning,* 123).

41. Without connecting it with *Strafford,* D. M. de Silva cites the poem as evidence of Browning's radicalism and notes that mention of Milton is a reminder "that the source of Browning's political inspiration went beyond Shelley . . . to the seventeenth-century Puritans" ("Salvation, Politics, and the Truth in History: A Reading of Browning's *Strafford,*" in *A Salzburg Miscellany: English and American Studies, 1964–84,* ed. James Hogg, 2 vols. [Salzburg: Institut fur Anglistik und Amerikanistik, Universitaet Salzburg, 1984], 2: 5). D. C. Sommerville makes a passing reference to "The Lost Leader" echo of Pym's lines in "An Early Victorian Tragedy," *London Mercury* 16 (1927): 175. De Silva's essay provides a valuable close reading of the play, but does not supplant Sommerville's brief but exceptionally lucid commentary. For another reading of the play, see Ashok Sengupta, "*Strafford* Reconsidered," in

Studies in Nineteenth-Century Literature, ed. James Hogg (Salzburg: Instut fur Anglistik und Amerikanistik, Universitaet Salzburg, 1979), 3–19.

42. *The Complete Works of Robert Browning*, ed. Roma King et al., 9 vols. to date (Athens, Ohio: Ohio University Press, (1970–   ), 2: 5–115; vol. 2 contains *Strafford*, ed. Gordon Pitts, and *Sordello*, ed. John Berkey. Anneliese Meidl supplements this edition of the play with analysis of a manuscript not considered by Pitts in "A *Strafford* Manuscript in the Lord Chamberlain's Office Records," *Browning Institute Studies* 12 (1984): 163–88. The play was licensed, she reports, "without any comment or objection by the Examiner of Plays, Charles Kemble" (163). Meidl finds the manuscript to be "less antiroyalist than the first edition," undoubtedly toned down by Macready for the stage (172; see 171, 186).

43. In an introduction to the play the historian Samuel Gardiner wrote, "We may be sure, therefore, that it was not by accident that Mr. Browning, in writing this play, decisively abandoned all attempt to be historically accurate. . . . The real Strafford was far from opposing the war with the Scots at the time when the Short Parliament was summoned. To anyone who knows anything of the habits of Charles, the idea of Pym or his friends entering into colloquies with Strafford, and even bursting unannounced into Charles's presence, is, from the historical point of view, simply ludicrous." Nevertheless, he concludes, "For myself, I can only say that, every time I read the play, I feel more certain that Mr. Browning has seized the real Strafford. . . . Charles too, with his faults perhaps exaggerated, is nevertheless the real Charles" (*Strafford: A Tragedy*, ed. E. H. Hickey [London: Bell, 1892], xiv–xvi).

44. *Robert Browning's Prose Life of Strafford*, introd. C. H. Frith (London: Kegan Paul, 1892), pp. 143, 240. This work appeared in 1837 as volume three in John Forster's *Lives of Eminent British Statesmen*, 7 vols. (London: Longman, Orme, Brown, Green & Longmans, 1836–39). In the play, see 1.1.109–20; in the *Life*, 240. C. H. Frith cites the original passage from Dr. James Welwood's *Memoirs of the Most Material Transactions in England for the Last Hundred Years Preceding the Revolution of 1688* (1700; see Frith, *Robert Browning's Prose Life of Strafford*, lxiii).

45. "The Life of Strafford: Browning's Apprenticeship in Biography," *Studies in Browning and His Circle* 8 (1980): 50–51.

46. Review in *the Examiner*, 7 May 1837. Busby points out that the tradition of friendship between Pym and Strafford and the "Apostasy of Wentworth" are emphasized in Forster's biography of Pym (46). Busby argues convincingly that the tone of apology in the biography of Strafford is inconsistent with Forster's views expressed elsewhere and thus is probably Browning's, but he overstates the case when asserting, "Clearly Browning and Forster held nearly opposite opinions of the Earl of Strafford" (47).

5
The English Pamphlet War of the 1790s and Coleridge's *Osorio*

Marjean D. Purinton

Although it appears that by 1796, Samuel Taylor Coleridge's politics were supplanted by religious, domestic, and philosophical concerns, his political arguments are actually rooted in deeper ideological questions.[1] Contrary to the standard critical judgment, Coleridge had not withdrawn from radical politics by the time that he wrote *Osorio* in 1797, but rather his politics became more deeply submerged in his writing. Prior to 1797, Coleridge's associates and activities were blatantly revolutionary. His prose from 1793-99 reflects radical content and polemical patterns expressed in the contemporary political pamphlets. Moreover, his radical views and revolutionary ideas become embedded as latent content in his poetry and drama.

To unveil Coleridge's displaced radicalism, we must consider the ways in which it is encoded. One of Coleridge's Notebook entries from 1797 gives us a clue about how to read his works. Commenting on the running water of a stream in the Quantocks, Coleridge writes: "There is not a new or strange opinion—Truth returned from banishment—a river run under ground."[2] Like the natural stream forced underground by its surrounding environment, so Coleridge's "truth" or radicalism is forced, concealed below the surface of the literature's manifest content by its ideological context.

The subtext of *Osorio* is guided by oppositional ideology. The tragedy exposes how subjected populations mistake the culturally constructed tyrannical forms for external forms founded in absolute truths. Although fiction-making process is humanly unavoidable and although it may not necessarily produce oppressive forms (such as tyranny), it can be examined, evaluated, and altered. Like other political and philosophical writings of the early nineteenth century—specifically the polemical discourse in England during the aftermath of the French Revolution—Coleridge's works point to a recognition that surface-level changes are fundamentally ineffective in generating freedom from oppressive forms. Like the manifest content of the pamphlets, the radical ideology inscribed in Coleridge's *Osorio* maintains that until changes occur in the way humankind thinks collectively, humankind cannot be liberated. A mental revolution must precede a social revolution; in other words, humankind must first become aware of delusions masked as freedom. One government's succession by another government offers no improvement if tyranny continues to dictate policy and practice.

As instruments that direct societal thinking and behavior, human-constructed fictions can enslave or liberate. *Osorio* dramatizes the ways in which ideology permeates all societal functions and institutions. To alter those institutions and operations, as well as the fiction-making process that perpetuates their hegemony, ideology must be changed. A dialogical form, *Osorio* unmasks oppressive ideology by revealing the obvious and submerged constraints on mental freedom. It is not surprising then that in *Osorio*, Coleridge makes a radical appeal for ideological transformations that result in societal and political restructurations rather that replacements.

Osorio is by no means an isolated instance of Coleridge's radical appeal for ideological change. In his last issue of *The Watchman*, Wednesday, 27 April 1796, Coleridge alleges that both Royalists and Jacobins have "veiled the face of Liberty."[3] He argues that the anarchists are "indefatigable in seducing the minds of the multitude by preaching up doctrines" that are totally impractical because the majority are not mentally prepared for them (288). In a poem often identified as an expression of Coleridge's retreat from political matters, "Ode to the Departing Year" (1796), the persona challenges readers to devote themselves to the cause of human nature, ideological reform, and to rise from the delusions of privacy. Encouraging readers to revive from the illness and imprisonment of complacency, the persona proclaims that Nature is struggling "in portentous birth."[4] Birth is a trope for revolution, and revolution is a time pregnant with human destiny. Read in the context of the English pamphlet war, Coleridge's drama *Osorio* stages a response to the French Revolution by suggesting an alternative that restructures societal and political systems at their foundations. The radical nature and message of the play lie in the ideological criticisms reconstructed from the polemical discourse of revolutionary prose.

Coleridge's revolutionary politics are embedded in *Osorio*'s dramatizations of domestic struggles, sibling rivalry, and religious persecution. Set in Granada and during the reign of Philip II (1156–98), *Osorio* begins at the close of the Spanish civil wars with the Moors.

The action takes place during a period of intense religious persecution analogous to the period of political repression in England during the 1790s.[5] Because the political issues and the polemical rhetoric of the English pamphlet war are displaced in *Osorio*'s setting, the tragedy's embedded meanings suggest interpretative paradigms that include the French Revolution and its aftermath—including the Pitt Ministry during the especially repressed period of 1793–98.

The prose discourse of the 1790s repeatedly calls for an ideological revolution of the sort called for in the latent content of *Osorio*. In *The Rights of Man* (1791), Thomas Paine claims that "Rights of Man is called a levelling system. . . . It is a system of mental levelling."[6] In *An Historical and Moral View of the Origin and the Progress of the French Revolution* (1795), Mary Wollstonecraft argues that the mind must be changed before humankind can change the system. She believes that a revolution in opinion can overturn the empire of tyranny.[7] Richard Price's 1789 sermon to the Revolution Society declares that the revolutionaries' endeavors to enlighten must have ultimately in view a reformation of manners and virtuous practice.[8] Similarly, William Godwin's *Enquiry Concerning Political Justice* (1793) calls for a revolution of opinions: "We must change the nature of the mind."[9] In the "Introductory Essay" of the first edition of *The Watchman*, Tuesday, 1 March 1796, Coleridge writes: "Men always serve the cause of freedom by *thinking*" (13). The same mental tyrannies and revolutions that appear in the English polemical discourse about the French Revolution emerge as reconfigurations of dramatic conflict in *Osorio*. Conversely, the manifest content of the play opens onto ideological concerns expressed in the English pamphlet war.

In the opening scene of the play, a seemingly private, domestic dispute suggests latent political meanings. A commanding father-guardian, Lord Velez, entreats his ward Maria, an orphan of fortune, to love and to wed his younger son Osorio. Steadfastly, Maria refuses; instead, she faithfully awaits the return of Albert, Osorio's brother who is presumed dead. Sharp words to Velez accompany her defiant actions:

> For mercy's sake
> Press me no more. I have no power to love him!
> His proud forbidding eye, and his dark brow
> Chill me, like dew-damps of the unwholesome night.[10]

Maria refuses to marry against her will.

Maria's bold rejection suggests political meanings more complicated than a maiden's pining for a lost love. As an orphaned young woman, she democratically defies an established and aged patriarch. She opposes the hegemonic powers of gender, class, and age. She is much like France, orphaned from its parentage (both king and queen had been guillotined), but resisting pressure to unite with the heir apparent (another potential monarch) and refusing to believe that its true love is dead (democratic reform). This domestic scene parallels the international political scene; in both situations, young upstarts challenge the ancien regime. What Maria enacts on a domestic and personal level has just occurred on a political and collective level in France. Like other audacious revolutionaries, she holds out against obedience to a mandate that enslaves her.

It is significant that the opening scene of the play depicts a challenge to authority in the configuration of a parent/child conflict. In the political pamphlets of the 1790s, the ancien regime is often figured as a tyrannous parent and revolutionaries as disobedient children. In *An Historical and Moral View*, Wollstonecraft demonstrates how the child liberty is moving beyond blind submission and obedience to its parents, despotism and superstition (259). The polemical prose urges a dissolution of rank, including the superiority of parent to child. Godwin argues that readers divest themselves of the shackles of infancy—a reverence for superiors—and that readers judge for themselves unfettered by the prejudices of education or institutions (2: 121-24). In *Vindication of the Rights of Men* (1790), Wollstonecraft alleges that parents too often treat their children like slaves—much as aristocrats force commoners into a system of obedience and punishments.[11] In his *Letter to the Bishop of Llandaff* (1793), William Wordsworth says: "We are wrongly taught from infancy that we were born in a state of inferiority to our oppressors, that they were sent into the world to scourge and we to be scourged. Accordingly we see the bulk of mankind actuated by these fatal prejudices, even more ready to lay themselves under the feet of *the great*, than the great are to trample upon them."[12] Similarly, Price's sermon maintains: "Ignorance is the parent of bigotry, intolerance, persecution and slavery" (15). Paine's *Rights of Man* specifically connects France to the parent/child analogy in suggesting that France no longer needs the titles indicating and inculcating superiority: "France has outgrown the baby cloaths of Count and Duke and breeched itself in manhood" (1: 59).

In addition to recapitulating the parent/child dichotomy figured in the political pamphlets, *Osorio* dramatizes the dissolution of the French fraternity during the Reign of Terror as the rivalry between brothers Osorio and Albert. Just as France had literally led its patriarchal father (Louis XVI) to the guillotine, Osorio figuratively beheads the patriarchal authority of the family in his manipulations of Velez. Not wanting to share his power, Osorio knows that his claim to authority depends on the demise of his brother. Albert reappears to challenge his brother's usurpation. This sibling rivalry serves as a domestic analogue to the demise of the political brotherhood in France. Lynn Hunt asserts that "fraternity" was the least understood of the values in the revolutionary triad of "liberty, equality, and fraternity." Competition, conflict, and violence among the brothers became an undeniable part of the French Revolution.[13] Similarly, the plot of *Osorio* emanates from fraternal conflict.

The sibling rivalry characteristic of surface-level revolution appears in the political pamphlets and the poetry of the 1790s. In his 1798 poem "Fears in Solitude,"' Coleridge laments the dissolution of the French fraternity which he had dramatized in the fratricide of the Velez brothers. The poem's subtitle identifies it as one written during the alarm of an invasion, and the persona identifies humankind turned viciously upon itself:

> And all our dainty terms for fratricide;
> Terms which we trundle smoothly o'er our tongues
> Like mere abstractions, empty sounds to which
> We join no feeling and attach no form![14]

The promises and slogans of the political fraternity have become meaningless words. The political changes in France remain firmly planted in an oppressive ideology never transformed. From this foundation, new tyrants, such as Robespierre, Napoleon, Pitt, or Osorio, emerge. Discontent breeds competition for power. Disillusioned by the fiction of freedom, brothers attack and usurp brothers. The suspicion, distrust, and unfaithfulness among the political revolutionaries appear dramatically in *Osorio* as a private dispute among brothers.

While the manifest content of the play disguises its radical political meanings, characters themselves appear in disguised forms. Albert appears disguised as a Moresco, despite a law forbidding the wearing of Moorish garments. Like Maria, he asserts his rebellion against authority in his blatant disregard for a law that holds one ethnic group subservient to another. Even though he could be punished by death, Albert challenges, as do the Jacobins of the 1790s, the tyranny of the class system.[15] Hoping to discover whether Maria played a part in the conspiracy to have him killed, Albert veils the account of his supposed assassination as though it were a dream. Both his costume and his words conceal his true identity and meaning to

Maria. Readers nonetheless perceive the character hidden by the robes, the story camouflaged as a dream, and the political meanings concealed as familial conflicts.

Ideological change cannot occur as long as revolutionary thought is subverted by hegemonic forms—even disguised as freedom. The French Revolution helped to unveil the powerful influence mental tyrannies exerted on political and social conditions. The physical disguises and the linguistic concealments of Osorio point to the submerged criticisms of the oppressive ideology. The darkness of ignorance is powerfully oppressive, and the drama discloses the importance of knowledge to the revolutionary process. After listening to the Moor's sad tale, Maria offers her sympathy and her help in dragging the "undiscover'd wrongs" (1.343) that oppress him "into light" (1.344).

Repeatedly, throughout the pamphlets of the 1790s, oppression is shown to end with enlightenment. In the *Letter to the Bishop of Llandaff*, Wordsworth writes: "It is the province of education to rectify the erroneous notions which a habit of oppression . . . may have created" (1: 34). The Revolution Society's first concern must be to enlighten the country, says Price. Nations of the world are patient under despotism because they are kept in darkness and want knowledge (14). In *An Historical and Moral View*, Wollstonecraft claims that humankind will recover its liberty only after it has been taught how to think (239). When a nation changes its opinion and habits of thinking, argues Paine in *Rights of Man*, it is no longer to be governed as before (2: 276). In *Enquiry Concerning Political Justice*, Godwin claims that social and institutional improvements will advance in a "just proportion to the illumination of public understanding" (1: 273). Coleridge's first Bristol Lecture, *A Moral and Political Lecture* (1795), asserts that "whatever contributes to increase discussion must accelerate the progress of liberty."[16] Like his prose, Coleridge's play contributes to the political discussion encouraging a radical restructuring of society. Because *Osorio's* multivalent meanings impel readers to think beyond the manifest content of the drama, it initiates the same kind of mental revolution called for in the polemical pamphlets.

* * *

Operating concurrently with the familial conflict of *Osorio*, a plot involving religious and ethnic persecution unfolds. Francesco, the Dominican Inquisitor, plans to destroy all the Moors. A Moresco chief who pretends to be a Christian, Ferdinand and his wife Alhadra are suspects. Five years earlier, Alhadra had been imprisoned at Holy

Brethren by Francesco solely on the basis of her complexion. She describes the conditions:

> They cast me, then a young and nursing mother,
> Into a dungeon of their prison house.
> There was no bed, no fire, no ray of light,
> No touch, no sound of comfort!
> (1.1.207–11)

The dramatic tropes of dungeons and prisons represent the antithesis of enlightened revolution. Coleridge recognizes in his prose that imprisonment can numb the desire for freedom. In "Insensibility of the Public Temper" (1798), Coleridge remarks: "What is familiar to the imagination ceases to be terrible; and what ceases to be terrible we no longer feel a strong inducement to resist."[17] His prose and drama indicate the ways in which enlightened ideological change can be suppressed at both physical and mental levels.

While Alhadra fears for the physical well-being of her husband, she also fears the extinction of freedom's light that the dungeon figures. She knows firsthand how the dungeon can quell the spark of hope for religious or political freedom. Willing to conceal her religion, she entreats Lord Velez, Maria, and Osorio to vouch for them as Christians:

> A month's imprisonment would kill him . . .
> . . . He hath a lion's courage,
> But is not stern enough for fortitude.
> Unfit for boisterous times, with gentle heart
> He worships Nature in the hill and valley.
> (1.241; 243–45)

Ferdinand's peril on the personal and religious level parallels France's condition on the public and political level. Like France, Ferdinand is not yet prepared for the "boisterous times" of change, the momentary chaos and hardships accompanying political restructuration. Wollstonecraft, Paine, Wordsworth, and Godwin all point out that the inefficacy of the French Revolution was due in part to the unpreparedness of France to evolve from despotism to republicanism. These nineteenth-century political applications are, however, concealed in terms of a Catholic ideology that marks Moors as unenlightened "other."

Juxtaposing religious and political oppression, the drama's statement about religious freedom is played out in the persecution of Alhadra and Ferdinand. Just as Osorio dramatizes the fiction-making process of political oppression, it exposes the oppressive forms of culturally produced myths termed "religion." The manifest conflict enacts a critique of any oppression under the guise of religious sanctions rather than an indictment of any one religion. Referring to the disguised Albert in his Moorish robes, Alhadra comments: "These renegade Moors—how soon they learn / The crimes and follies of their Christian tyrants!" (1.286–87). Tyranny is tyranny—whether disguised in Moorish robes or Christian dogma.

In both France and England, national religions had become political weapons. In *Rights of Man,* Paine alleges: "Persecution is not an original feature in any religion . . . but it is always the strongly-marked feature of all religions established by law" (1: 68). In *The Age of Reason* (1794), Paine maintains that all national institutions of churches are merely human inventions "set up to terrify and enslave mankind, and monopolize power and profit."[18] Price's sermon predicts: "That gloomy and cruel superstition will be abolished which has hitherto gone under the name of religion and to the support of which civil government has been perverted" (15). Godwin terms the system of religious conformity a system of blind submission that makes men hypocrites (2: 233–34). According to Wordsworth's *Llandaff Letter,* the ministers of the church of England are merely advocates of civil and religious slavery (1. 31). Coleridge's contributions to *The Watchman* record his outrage at the religious persecutions of the Catholics in Ireland. In the Wednesday, 9 March 1796, issue, Coleridge writes:

> It was a persecution conceived in the bitterness of bigotry, carried on with the most ferocious barbarity, by a banditti, who being of the religion of the State, had committed with the greater audacity and confidence the most horrid murders, and had proceeded from robbery and massacre to extermination. (2: 75–76)

The play and the pamphlets indict any religious system that dupes believers into submissive positions or that assumes superiority over other systems of belief.[19]

The familial conflicts of the play and the plot involving religious persecution converge in the dramatic trope of disguise. Suspicious of the so-called Christian who wears Moorish robes, Osorio plots to disguise Ferdinand and to unmask this mysterious stranger among them. Osorio is mystified by the disguised Albert's characterization of himself as "he that can bring the dead to life again" (2.2.217). Seeking to gain enlightenment about this enigmatic claim, Osorio retorts: "You are no dullard, / But one that strips the outward rind of things" (2.2.218–19). Like Coleridge's notebook entry from 1797, Osorio's response discloses a way of reading the play. The interpretative frameworks of the drama multiply when a reader "strips the outward rind of things" and considers the roots, the ideology, of the manifest conflicts. By stripping the outward rind of things, readers are less likely to become imprisoned by their own conceptions, to be limited by the interpretative lines in which they confine themselves. Just as Albert is undressed in the play, readers can unveil the English pamphlet war dramatically recast (even disguised) in *Osorio*'s conflicts.

A similar metaphor of unmasking appears in Coleridge's *A Moral and Political Lecture*. At the end of the polemic, Coleridge urges his audience to "peel away the layers of error and prejudice which time and ignorance have engendered" (613). Coleridge's letter to his brother George on 10 March 1798 indicates that he has himself endeavored to "peel away the layers of error and prejudice" to consider the roots, or the collective mentality, dictating political activity. He writes: "I have for some time past withdrawn myself almost totally from the consideration of *immediate* causes, which are infinitely complex & uncertain, to muse on fundamental & general causes."[20] Those "fundamental and general causes" had been played out in *Osorio* where he reveals the fiction-making process capable of producing oppressive forms. Coleridge's radicalism is constituted in his concern with foundation of the "isms" and "ologies" that appear to shape social and political activities.

Paine's, Wollstonecraft's, and Coleridge's prose all clearly indicate that their attacks are similarly aimed not at persons but at processes and principles. In *An Historical and Moral View*, Wollstonecraft asserts that "certain opinions, planted by superstition and despotism . . . have taken such deep root in our habits of thinking" (6). In *The Rights of Man*, Paine claims: "*Principles* and not *persons* were the meditated objects of destruction of the French Revolution" (1: 23). In *Vindication of the Rights of Men*, Wollstonecraft says: "I attack the foundation" (124). In *A Moral and Political Lecture*, Coleridge assures his audience that the "object is to destroy pernicious systems, not their misguided adherents" (612), and he suggests that in deep and strong soil they fix their roots (605). Even Edmund Burke's pamphlet *Reflections on the Revolution in France* (1790) admits that when "your foundation is choked up and polluted, the stream will not run long or clear."[21] He cites human passions as the real vices, "which cannot be rooted out by destroying the leaders in a society" (162). These political pamphlets assert and *Osorio* dramatizes that for social restructuring to occur, changes must be made in the oppressive ideology, not just the leaders momentarily empowered.

* * *

As a dramatic character, Albert performs what Coleridge's play and his own prose direct. To get to the "roots" of his attempted assassination, however, he, too, must conceal his true identity. Disguised in his sorcerer's robes, Albert appears to Maria and swears to "uncover all concealed things" (3.1.8). Osorio believes that this wizard will convince Maria of Albert's death by producing a portrait of herself—one she gave to Albert, and which Osorio later confiscated from Ferdinand. Substituting a picture of his attempted assassination for Maria's portrait, Albert reveals his brother's wickedness. Osorio soon learns that he has been tricked, but Lord Velez, who is unaware of the substitution, believes that Maria is convinced of Albert's death. Velez chides Osorio for allowing affections to "give reality / To these your contrivings (3.1.240–41) Sarcastically, Osorio responds: "You see through all things with / *your* penetration" (3.1.243). Albert sees through all things except his self-deception, his uncanny ideological resemblance to his brother.[22]

At a metacritical level, readers may see the limitations that mere appearances and manifest content offer. As readers uncover the disguises, machinations, and intrigue, they also discover where ideology becomes the subject of the play. Poems that Coleridge wrote in the years just prior to *Osorio* convey parallel metacritical themes. Political content disguised in poetical form, for example, similarly appears in Coleridge's *The Destiny of Nations: A Vision* (1796). Here, as in the drama, corporeal forms disguise shadows, words conceal meanings, and reality shades symbolism:

> For all that meets the bodily sense I deem
> Symbolical, one mighty alphabet
> For infant minds; and we in the low world
> Placed with our backs to bright Reality,
> That we may learn with young unwounded ken
> The substance from its shadow.[23]

The subtext of the poetry indicates a commitment to the public arena of politics plus an interpretative clue about how to read its disguised messages.[24] "Religious Musings" (1795) also announces its own interpretative framework: "For the great / Invisible (by symbols only seen)."[25] The faces of the oppressed inscribe the mental (and therefore invisible) tyrannies of the systems that oppress them. The poems as well as the play insist that humankind has become enslaved to the fictions and systems it has created.

In the latent content of the play and in his own prose, Coleridge warns readers about delusionary forms of freedom. In questioning the forms hidden by the drama's disguised characters, readers learn to question the tyrannies concealed by the political system's fictions. These broader, ideological issues and the drama's familial theme are conflated in a soliloquy. Concealed as a sorcerer, Albert pretends to conjure up the soul of Albert. In his spell, the sorcerer implores the soul:

> Ye, as ye pass, toss high the desert sands,
> That roar and whiten, like a burst of waters,
> A sweet appearance, but a dread illusion,
> To the parch'd caravan that roams by night.
> And ye build up on the becalmed waves
> That whirling pillar, which from earth to heaven
> Stands vast, and moves in blackness.
>
> (3.1.25–31)

At the dramatic level, we perceive that Albert's supposedly dead soul is in need of reviving, and at the ideological level, we recognize that the revolutionary fervor of the 1790s is in need of resuscitating. This incantation could easily be voiced to the spirit of freedom and liberty that had scattered the sands of antique customs and that had offered "a sweet appearance" only to transform into "a dread illusion." Expatriots still roamed by night seeking the light of liberation promised by the *illuminati* and other revolutionary societies. Recognizing the need to breathe new life into the impetus for radical change, Coleridge laments in "Euthanasia of the Constitution" (1798): "The people have lost the spirit and relish of liberty."[26] The essay indicates Coleridge's concern about England's retaining even a shadow of liberty if it forfeits the substance. Like Osorio, many potential revolutionaries are impelled by the desire of acquiring wealth and power. This selfish principle has been fatal to the cause of freedom.

No matter how attractively packaged, any system that limits thought enslaves those deluded into believing that they are free. Coleridge knew firsthand the oppressions of the Pitt ministry, and his reading well documented the delusions of freedom promised by Robespierre and later by Napoleon. In "France: An Ode" (1798), Coleridge's persona observes:

> The Sensual and the Dark rebel in vain,
> Slaves by their own compulsion! In mad game

> They burst their manacles and wear the name
> Of freedom, graven on a heavier chain![27]

Coleridge's prose, poetry, and *Osorio* demonstrate the enslaving and static results of accepting appearances. Failure to strip the outward rind of things leaves humankind subjugated, but unlike the poem, *Osorio* dramatizes a new vision. The sorcerer's (Albert's) spell beseeches the spirit to build a "whirling pillar" to function much like a lighthouse illuminating the way in darkness even for waters no longer tempestuous.[28] The political implications are now obvious, but the "whirling" nature of this pillar suggests that the structure is not even so literal as the French National Assembly, the English Parliament, the Anti-Slavery Bill, or a Napoleon Bonaparte; the ubiquitous nature of this supportive structure implies an ideological framework. Any changes at the surface-level of political institutions become mere illusions. A new form of tyranny replaces the old.

This concern for the illusionary nature of surface-level changes likewise occurs in the political pamphlets. In *The Rights of Man*, Paine warns: "What we formerly called Revolutions were little more than a change of persons, or an alteration of local circumstances" (1: 133). Wollstonecraft points out in *An Historical and Moral View* that the French Revolution failed to shake up the foundation of the old system of government (508). Conversely, it was precisely this fundamental renovation that Burke feared. He says: "The French have slain the *mind* in their country" (55). He hopes that although names have been changed, many things may remain in the same shape (162-63). In his *Remonstrance to the French Legislators*, Wednesday, 27 April 1796, Coleridge laments that tyranny in France merely wears a new name, because no ideological renovations occurred: "But the effects of Despotism could not be instantly removed with the cause: and the Vices, and the Ignorance, and the Terrors of the multitude conspired to subject them to the tyranny of a bloody and fanatic faction."[29] Coleridge is aware of how the Republic now dons the cloak of Tyranny, new vestments for old abuses, and he encourages reform in the spirit or ideology of revolution which does not simply substitute one oppressive government for another: "Legislators of France! in the name of Posterity we adjure you to consider, that misused success is soon followed by adversity, and that the adversity of France may lead, in its train of consequences, [to] the slavery of all Europe!" (273).

The final actions of the play emphasize the latent content of the ideological revolution called for in the pamphlets. Osorio urges Ferdinand to a dark cavern. His sleep already haunted by dreams, Ferdinand protests that he fears not man but the cavern: "But this inhuman cavern / It were too bad a prisonhouse for goblins" (4.1.50–51). The dramatic trope of the cavern suggests mentality—a turning inward to the dark recesses of thought not yet enlightened by change. Ideological revolution will liberate thought held captive. Cast in a Gothic trope, seemingly privatized imagination is actually ideological and political.[30]

Within the cavern, the linear action of the play develops through dramatic tropes of play acting and fiction making. Adopting the mask of a third-person narrator, Osorio relates to Ferdinand the story of his life, a fiction he has come to believe as an absolute and fixed truth. His history—his fantasy—ends with the destruction of what he believes to be his traitor, and he thrusts Ferdinand down the cavern's chasm. Drawing his sword, Osorio fiercely concludes:

> That which his wisdom prompted.
> He made the traitor meet him in this cavern,
> And here he kill'd the traitor.
> (4.1.131–33)

Both Ferdinand and Osorio are unmasked for the fiction makers and political principles they represent. Just as characters' fictions have been revealed, so the oppressive ideology that engenders tyrants (Velez, Osorio, Louis XVI, Robespierre, Pitt) and repressive acts (religious persecution, gender discrimination, sibling rivalry, international war) are also uncovered. Paradoxically, it is during the scene in the cave (interior locality) that "the outward rind of things" is stripped away for readers. The oppressive ideology is unmasked in its multivalent forms.

Like other Romantic dramas (*The Borderers, The Cenci, John Woodvil*), *Osorio* suggests that an ideology predicated on the cycle of tyranny/revenge generates no societal changes. Coleridge similarly recognizes the futile nature of superficial changes in *A Moral and Political Lecture* when he warns: "Let us beware that we be not transported into revenge while we are levelling the loathsome pile with the ground, lest when we erect the temple of freedom we but vary the style of architecture, not change the materials" (612). The English pamphlet of the 1790s, which included contributions by Coleridge, argues voraciously what the drama stages: only an ideological revolution will change the nature, rather than the mere name, of tyranny.

While Albert's actions suggest a way to break the tyranny/revenge cycle, Velez's and Francesco's strategies reify the legitimation of their own power positions. Velez orders the recalcitrant Maria to a convent: "Repent and marry him—/ Or to the convent" (4.2.274–76). Life at the convent not only signals a death of Maria's womanhood, but it, too, is a place of isolation—a type of dark cavern signifying unenlightened mentality. Hearing Velez's pronouncement, Francesco vehemently approves. As a representative of Church authority, he knows the threat posed by daughters' disobeying fathers and the laity's disobeying priests. On a metacritical level, readers may now see that, by extension, this demonstration of power suggests the consequences of disobedience to the king by anti-ministerial clubs, such as the sansculottes. Both "fatherly" tyrants in the play quell any form that could shatter the social structure which empowers and privileges them.

Maria is not the only force to subdue, however. Francesco claims to have secured fresh evidence that Ferdinand and Alhadra are infidels, and he asserts: "We are not safe until they are rooted out" (4.3.310). Boldly, Maria questions his hypocrisy:

> Thou man, who call'st thyself the minister
> Of Him whose law was love unutterable!
> Why is thy soul so parch'd with cruelty,
> That still thou thirstest for thy brother's blood?
> (4.3.311–14)

Maria points out the discrepancy between Francesco's vows and his actions. His perversion of Christian principles is not, however, the only link in the unfolding chain of tyranny and revenge. Learning that Osorio has killed her husband, Alhadra vows revenge. Her hypocrisy appropriates the Hebraic "eye for an eye" code to exact justice. The mercy and forgiveness taught by both Jesus Christ and Mahomet have been perverted by systems that encode these qualities as enslaving laws. This unmasking of priests and religious dogma similarly appears in Wollstonecraft's *Vindication of the Rights of Men.* The political tract poses a question similar to Maria's indictment of Francesco's actions as church father: "Was not the separation of religion from morality the work of priests" (94)? The radical criticisms embedded in these scenes points toward those systems of human creation which have enslaved humankind. Disguised as Christianity, monarchy, commerce, republicanism, family, and class, these systems need to be "rooted out" in a revolution at the ideological level.

* * *

In the climactic conflict between Albert and Osorio, we see the dramatic enactment of the political polemics in English pamphlets.

Like the meeting between Osorio and Ferdinand, the final action between Albert and Osorio occurs in a dungeon. This location reminds readers of the metaphorical link between the dungeon and the unenlightened mind—the mental revolution encouraged by both the polemics and the play. In a soliloquy that Coleridge later extracted from the play and inserted along with "The Foster-mother's Tale" in the 1798 *Lyrical Ballads,* Albert muses about the political and social condition of humankind:

> And this place my forefathers made for men!
> This is the process of our love and wisdom
> To each poor brother who offends against us—
> Most innocent, perhaps—and what if guilty?
> Is this the only cure?
>
> (5.2.107–11)

Albert speculates whether the process through which humankind has sought amelioration and reform has yielded any substantial benefits. Is a vicious cycle of oppression and rebellion the only cure for the disease of enslavement? Albert's mental activity occurs in a closed space—a reminder to readers of the imprisoning power of thought. Albert ponders the illness of enslavement in his soliloquy:

> Each pore and natural outlet shrivel'd up
> By ignorance and parching poverty,
> His energies roll back upon his heart,
> And stagnate and corrupt till changed to poison,
> They break out on him like a loathsome plague-spot!
> Then we call in our pamper'd mountebanks—
> And this is their best cure!
>
> (5.2.112–18)

Albert's words seem at once personal (a reflection of his own struggle) and universal (the plight of humankind's existence); they also signal contemporary political comments that are historically and geographically displaced. His words can be applied to the diseased condition of France in the aftermath of the French Revolution or to the turbulence and repression marked by the Pitt administration in England. Even the best-intended reformers' efforts had failed to eliminate poverty and ignorance. Substantially unchanged, the systems continue to corrupt and to defile.

This fiction-making process aptly describes the French Revolution's degeneration into the Reign of Terror and then eventually to Robespierre's own death at the guillotine. In *The Age of Reason,*

Paine declares: "What a fool do fabulous systems make of Man!" (449). Just as one government's usurpation of another does not necessarily offer political freedom, so one system's replacement by another does not necessarily yield beneficial ideological change. Paine, Coleridge, and other thinkers of the period well knew that the purge of poisoned revolutionaries merely enabled commercial tyrannies to exist. The French monarchy was destroyed, for example, but now the Directory reigned; the substitution offered no cure for oppression.

The conclusions that Albert reaches at the end of his meditation echo the ideological disputes of the polemical pamphlets of the 1790's. Rising slowly from a bed of reeds, Albert invokes the healing and illuminating spirit of Nature, for humankind lies in a mental prison of uncomforted

> And friendless solitude, groaning and tears,
> And savage faces at the clanking hour
> Seen thro' the steaming vapours of his dungeon
> By the lamp's dismal twilight!
>
> (5.2.119–22)

Although Albert's words reflect his preoccupation with his own personal world, they also point toward contemporary social responses to political activities. The auspicious expectations of the dawn of the French Revolution had dwindled to dismal twilight, but still light shines, for wisdom is to be gained from this lesson. The "light," "wisdom," or "truth" gained from the historical experience (encoded by the pamphlets) and staged by the dramatic action (encoded by *Osorio*) is that the process of superficial change, of exchanging a crown for a Directory, a pope for an episcopacy, landlords for merchants, perpetuates a master/slave dichotomy and the cycle of oppression/rebellion.

The polemical pamphlets likewise insist that the process generating significant changes in societal conditions must occur at an ideological level. Optimistically, Wollstonecraft writes in *An Historical and Moral View*: "Out of this chaotic mass a fairer government is rising than has ever shed the sweets of social life on the world" (73). Reluctantly, Burke admits: "Many parts of Europe are in open disorder . . . and in many others there is a hollow murmuring under the ground. A confused movement is felt that threatens a general earthquake in the political world" (179). Enthusiastically, Paine announces in *Rights of Man*: "From the Revolutions of America and France, and the symptoms appearing in other countries, it is evident that the opinion of the world is changed with respect to systems of Government. A general Revolution in the principle and construction of Government is necessary" (1: 132–33). Insightfully, Coleridge proclaims in *A Moral and Political Lecture*: "A revolution in other parts of Europe is not far distant. Oppression is grievous—the oppressed feel and complain. Let us profit by the example of others; devastation has marked the course of most revolutions" (612). In petitioning for ideological revolution, Coleridge notes that if the horrors of other recent revolutions have made nations wise—"if a great people shall from hence become adequately illuminated for a Revolution bloodless" (605), then political and social restructuring is possible.

Osorio gives readers glimpses of possibilities for ideological revolution. At the end of the play, Albert tries to arrest the cycle of oppression by refusing to enact revenge against Osorio. He also tries to thwart Osorio's attempts at suicide. Dashing a goblet of poisoned wine to the ground, Albert implores Osorio to seek remorse and to be saved, to admonish that impulse, socially inculcated, that turns one brother against another. It is time, he insists, to abandon those customs and habits of mind that enslave humankind. As he reveals his identity to Maria, Albert seeks forgiveness and reconciliation from his brother and his betrothed.

Maria, too, endeavors to break those culturally contrived patterns by participating in this mental revolution. Convinced that Albert is an infidel who must escape Francesco's interrogation, Maria plots to help the sorcerer escape. Entering the dungeon, she says:

> I have put aside
> The customs and the terrors of a woman,
> To work out thy escape.
>
> (5.2.228–30)

Because she refuses to adhere to the hegemonic ideology that holds one gender subservient to another, Maria continues to defy the systems of oppression. She refuses to play the part of a "woman" defined by a delimiting system or culturally constructed category.[31] Furthermore, she is willing to risk her own life to help the Moor, a member of an oppressed and marginalized group, to escape. She is able to grow beyond race and gender privileges operating within the oppressive ideology.

Osorio is, however, unable to alter the custom of revenge and retribution that prevents his participation in this mental revolution. He can only see himself as a villain, his own tormentor. He offers himself to Albert so that his brother may become the unquestionable hero. Unable to loosen the shackles of his mental tyrannies, Osorio curses remorse and attempts to fall on his sword. He fails to grow beyond the limitations of dualities of the prevailing ideology. If Albert is the hero, he reasons, then he must be the villain.

Entrapped by bifurcated thinking that engenders vengeance, Alhadra demands Osorio's life for Ferdinand's. Maria pleads for mercy, but Alhadra, like Osorio, is not yet ready to participate in a mental revolution that exacts forgiveness rather than revenge.[32] Alhadra agrees to spare everyone except Osorio, and momentarily she ponders whether the more satisfying revenge might be for him to live as an outcast, a self-accusing and self-tormenting spirit. The Moors deny mercy and descend on him. As Osorio is slain, Alhadra utters these final words:

> I thank thee, Heaven! thou hast ordain'd it wisely,
> That still extremes bring their own cure. That point
> In misery which makes the oppressed man
> Regardless of his own life, makes him too
> Lord of the oppressor's! Knew I an hundred men
> Despairing, but not palsied by despair,
> This arm should shake the kingdoms of this world;
> The deep foundations of iniquity
> Should sink away, earth groaning from beneath them;
> The strong holds of the cruel men should fall,
> Their temples and their mountainous towers should fall;
> Till disclarion seem'd a beautiful thing,
> And all that were and had the spirit of life
> Sang a new song to him who had gone forth
> Conquering and still to conquer!
>
> (5.2.307–21)

At an epistemological level, these lines recapitulate the Romantic notion that humankind is incapable of understanding as long as its spirit (*Geist*, mind) is not free. At a political level, these words reify the precarious human interactions that separate the oppressed and the oppressor when the collective mentality engenders bifurcated thinking. At a societal level, this speech indicates the inefficacy of humankind's mighty institutions, its temples and towers of tyranny. The destruction of these edifices (for example, the Bastille) and their leaders (for example, Danton, Robespierre, Saint-Just) merely enables other structures to be built (such as La Guillotine) and to be controlled by another group of cruel authorities (such as Bonaparte). Alhadra longs for changes in the social order, but she cannot yet exercise societal transformations, because she has not come to realize that reform must occur at the "deep foundations" of social interaction. The physical revolution that her revengeful act incites merely perpetuates the cycle that the English pamphlet war of the 1790s seeks to redefine by advocating mental or ideological revolution. *Osorio* enacts what the polemics reprove; its radicalism lies in its portrayal of the consequences of political reform not based on ideological revision.

Notes

1. Among critics claiming that Coleridge retreated from political engagement are Richard Holmes, *Coleridge: Early Visions* New York: Viking, 1989), 156–58; George Watson, "The Revolutionary Youth of Wordsworth and Coleridge," *Critical Quarterly* 18 no. 3 (1976): 54; Nigel Leask, *The Politics of Imagination in Coleridge's Critical Thought* (New York: St. Martin's Press, 1988), 1–45; John Beer, "The 'Revolutionary Youth' of Wordsworth and Coleridge: Another View," *Critical Quarterly* 19 no. 2 (1977): 79–87; Carl Woodring, *Politics in the Poetry of Coleridge* (Madison: University of Wisconsin Press, 1961), 204–5. Marilyn Butler argues that Coleridge left politics as early as 1793, *Romantics, Rebels, and Reactionaries: English Literature and its Background 1760–1830* (Oxford: Oxford University Press, 1981), 70–78.

Some scholars are convinced of Coleridge's retreat from political involvement, but they maintain that this position occurs closer to 1798. Nicholas Roe argues that Coleridge's revolutionary fervor survived until the French invasion of Switzerland in February 1798 (*Wordsworth and Coleridge: The Radical Years* [Oxford: Oxford University Press, 1988], 237). In the "Introduction" to Coleridge's *Essays on His Times* (Princeton University Press, 1978), David V. Erdman says that by March/April 1798, Coleridge want into political retirement or "secession" (l: x). Similarly, Daniel P. Watkins asserts that Coleridge's commitment to the rebel cause remained "more or less firm until 1798" and the French invasion of Switzerland. See "'In That New World': The Deep Historical Structure of Coleridge's *Osorio*," *Philological Quarterly* 69 no. 4 (Fall 1990): 495.

In a number of recent studies, however, we are seeing more hesitancy about proclaiming Coleridge's self-removal from the political arena. John Morrow cautions that Coleridge was willing to criticize French policies, but he did not reject the aspirations underlying the French Revolution. See *Coleridge's Political Thought: Property, Morality and the Limits of Traditional Discourse* (New York: St. Martin's, 1990), 36. In "*Osorio*'s Dark Employments: Tricking Out Coleridgean Tragedy," *Studies in Romanticism* 33 no. 1 (1994): 119–60, Parker Reeve asserts that as "spectral airing" (120), *Osorio*'s ghosts were part of the shadowy afterlife of revolutionary sympathies Pitt's ministry had tried to suppress. In *Coleridge's Submerged Politics: "The Ancient Mariner" and "Robinson Crusoe"* (Columbia: University of Missouri Press, 1994), Patrick J. Keane says: "I am not fully persuaded that Coleridge's tyrant-hating appetite for 'vengeance' in the form of political activism on behalf of national regeneration was either appeased or totally sublimated during the Stowey retirement." (252). In her engaging study of Coleridgean drama, *In the Theatre of Romanticism: Coleridge, Nationalism, Women* (Cambridge: Cambridge University Press, 1994) Julie A. Carlson asserts: "Coleridge's plays examine the problematics of action in a revolutionary age more comprehensively than any of his other writings" (99–100). Although Daniel P. Watkins, *A Materialist Critique of English Romantic Drama* (Gainesville: University Press of Florida, 1993), situates the drama within the postrevolutionary, antiaristocratic context, he maintains that it is politically conservative; see 21–38.

2. Samuel Taylor Coleridge, *Notebooks—The Notebooks of Samuel Taylor Coleridge*, ed. Kathleen Coburn, 3 vols. (Princeton: Princeton University Press, 1957–73) 1: 176.

3. Samuel Taylor Coleridge, *The Watchman*, ed. Lewis Patton (Princeton: Princeton University Press, 1970), 288. Further citations are identified in the text.

4. Samuel Taylor Coleridge, "Ode to the Departing Year," *The Complete Poetical Works of Samuel Taylor Coleridge*, ed. E. H. Coleridge, 2 vols. (1912; reprint, Oxford: Oxford University Press, 1968), 1: 161, line 31.

5. Terry Eagleton argues that a fiction's "history" is imaginary, because it negotiates a particular ideological *experience* of real history. See *Criticism and Ideology: A Study of Marxist Literary Theory* (London: NLB, 1976), p. 77. As Daniel P. Watkins has shown, the world of medieval Spain exists as the product of a representational process that signifies not "medieval Spain" as such, but as the basis for a displaced commentary on the British government of the 1790s. See "'In That New World,'" 497–98.

In contrast, Michael Fischer contends that Coleridge seeks a displacement of history to see "idealization." See "Morality and History in Coleridge's Political Theory," *Studies in Romanticism* 21 (1982): 457–60. In "The Politics of the Imagination," R. F. Storch claims that Coleridge's philosophical idealism gradually reduced historical events to a mere shadow of a spiritual drama, *Studies in Romanticism* 21 (1982): 451. Barbara R. Friedman proposes that although Coleridge renders events as dramatized scenes, he believes history must be understood as prophecy and interpreted as allegory. See *Fabricating History: English Writers of the French Revolution* (Princeton: Princeton University Press, 1988), 18–23. In "The French Revolution in the English Theatre," Jeffrey N. Cox argues that in his fleeing the troubling historical realities of his day, Coleridge displaced revolutionary acts into a Gothic framework (*History and Myth: Essays on Romantic Literature,* ed. Stephen C. Behrendt [Detroit: Wayne State University Press, 1990], 33–52).

I agree with Lynn Hunt, however, who says that the revolutionaries' passion for the allegorical, the theatrical, and the stylized was not an aberration but an essential element in their effort to free humanity. See *Politics, Culture, and Class in the French Revolution* (Berkeley: University of California Press, 1984), 55. I also agree with John David Moore who claims that *Osorio* reflects the continental Gothic and the English Jacobinical traditions. As Gothic, the play reveals Pitt as the British Robespierre; as Jacobinical, the play suggests that tyranny masquerading as liberty must be violently removed. The public themes of the play are disguised as private ones. See "Coleridge and the 'Modern Jacobinical Drama': *Osorio, Remorse* and the Development of Coleridge's Critique of the Stage, 1779–1816," *Bulletin of Research in the Humanities* 85 (1982): 443–54. For a discussion of the political and philosophical context of Coleridge's writings during 1797–98, see Keane, *Coleridge's Submerged Politics,* 212–48.

6. Thomas Paine, *The Rights of Man* (1791; reprint, New York: Dutton, 1951), 2: 167. Further citations are identified in the text.

7. Mary Wollstonecraft, *An Historical and Moral View of the Origin and Progress of the French Revolution and the Effect It Has Produced in Europe* (1795; reprint, Delmar, N.Y.: Scholars' Facsimiles & Reprints, 1975), 12. Further citations are identified in the text.

8. Richard Price, *A Discourse Delivered on the Love of Our Country, Delivered on Nov. 4, 1789, at the Meetinghouse in the Old Jewry, to the Society for Commemo-

rating the Revolution in Great Britain (1789; reprint, Boston: Edward E. Powers, 1790), 17. Further citations are identified in the text.
   9. William Godwin, *Enquiry Concerning Political Justice and Its Influence on Morals and Happiness*, ed. S. L. Priestley, 3 vols. (Toronto: University of Toronto Press, 1946), 2: 462. Further citations are identified in the text.
   10. Samuel Taylor Coleridge, *Osorio: A Tragedy, The Complete Poetical Works of Samuel Taylor Coleridge*, ed. E. H. Coleridge, 2 vols. (1912; reprint, Oxford: Oxford University Press, 1962), 2: 522, 1.1.78–81. Further citations are identified in the text.
   11. Mary Wollstonecraft, *A Vindication of the Rights of Men* (1790; reprint, Delmar, N.Y.: Scholars' Facsimiles & Reprints, 1975), 45. Further citations are identified in the text.
   12. William Wordsworth, *A Letter to the Bishop of Llandaff on the Extraordinary Avowal of his Political Principles Contained in the Appendix to [his] Late Sermon by a Republican, The Prose Works of William Wordsworth*, eds. W. J. B. Owen and Jane Worthington Smyser, 3 vols. (Oxford: Oxford University Press, 1974), 1: 36. Further citations are identified in the text.
   13. Lynn Hunt, *The Family Romance of the French Revolution* (Berkeley: University of California Press, 1992), 12, 88. Interestingly, in "1798: The Sex of Revolution," David Punter notes that England wanted to believe that it had achieved a stable maturity, that her revolutionary disturbances of adolescence were already over (the English Civil War). Although Punter claims that this English myth repeats itself in the texture of literary history, I argue that *Osorio* dramatically questions this very fiction (*Criticism* 24 [1982]: 210–17.
   14. Samuel Taylor Coleridge, "Fears in Solitude," *The Complete Poetical Works of Samuel Taylor Coleridge*, ed. E. H. Coleridge, 2 vols. (1912; reprint, Oxford: Oxford University Press, 1968), 1: 135, lines 113–16.
   15. Daniel P. Watkins cogently argues that familial struggles for power energize the deep historical structure of the play. He maintains that *Osorio* demonstrates the making of the middle class and its bourgeois set of values. See "'In That New World,'" 495–515; and *A Materialist Critique of English Romantic Drama*, pp. 21–38. Paul Magnuson argues that *Osorio* presents the victory of the oppressed as a class over the intolerable tyranny of the aristocrats. See *Coleridge and Wordsworth: A Lyrical Dialogue* (Princeton, N.J.: Princeton University Press, 1988), 60–61.
   16. Samuel Taylor Coleridge, *A Moral and Political Lecture, Lectures 1795: On Politics and Religion*, eds. Lewis Patton and Peter Mann (Princeton, N.J.: Princeton University Press, 1977), 613. Further citations are identified in the text.
   17. Samuel Taylor Coleridge, "Insensibility of the Public Temper," in *Essays on His Times*, ed. David V. Erdman, 3 vols. (Princeton: Princeton University Press, 1978), 1: 22.
   18. Thomas Paine, *The Age of Reason, The Thomas Paine Reader*, eds. Michael Foot and Isaac Kramnick (1794; reprint, Hammondsworth: Penguin, 1987), 449.
   19. In "Political and Biographical Background of Coleridge's *Osorio*," Arnold B. Fox shows how Coleridge parallels the Inquisition to the despotic English government and parallels the Inquisitor Francesco to Pitt, *Journal of English and Germanic Philology* 61 (1962): 258–67. In "Coleridge and the English Revolution," John Morrow argues that Coleridge promoted an extension of the seventeenth-century English Revolution cut short by the Commonwealth. He claims that Coleridge advocated a weakening of the Anglican monopoly (*Political Science* 40 [1988]: 128–41. Keane similarly links the tyranny of the Spanish Inquisition with the tyranny of Pitt, the "British Robespierre" (*Coleridge's Submerged Politics*, 247).
   20. Samuel Taylor Coleridge, *Collected Letters of Samuel Taylor Coleridge*, ed.

E. L. Griggs, 6 vols. (Oxford: Oxford University Press, 1956–71), 1: 397. Further citations are identified in the text.

21. Edmund Burke, *Reflections on the Revolution in France and on the Proceedings in Certain Societies in London Relative to that Event,* ed. Thomas H. D. Mahoney (New York: Liberal Arts, 1955), 90. Further citations are identified in the text.

22. Parker analyzes how tropes of deception and disguise govern *Osorio.* He considers the veiled narrations, veiled allegory, veiled bodies, and veiled images that contribute to the ambiguity crucial to Coleridge's dramatic enterprise; see "*Osorio's* Dark Employments: Tricking Out Coleridgean Tragedy," 119–60. Carlson argues that the plots of *Osorio/Remorse* are obsessed with questions of mistaking identity (not simply mistaken identities). She emphasizes the role-playing trope in *Osorio,* which, she maintains, is a part of subjectivity for the drama's characters; see *In the Theatre of Romanticism,* 110–17.

23. Samuel Taylor Coleridge, *The Destiny of Nations: A Vision, The Complete Poetical Works of Samuel Taylor Coleridge,* ed. E. H. Coleridge, 2 vols. (1912; reprint, Oxford, Oxford University Press, 1968), 1: 132, lines 18–23. Further citations are identified in the text.

24. According to A. C. Goodson, Coleridge's subliminal imagery cannot be devoid of political concerns. See *Verbal Imagination: Coleridge and the Language of Modern Criticism* (New York: Oxford University Press, 1988), 155–56.

25. Samuel Taylor Coleridge "Religious Musings,," in *The Complete Poetical Works of Samuel Taylor Coleridge,* ed. E. H. Coleridge, 2 vols. (1912; reprint, Oxford: Oxford University Press, 1968), 1: 109, lines 9–10.

26. Samuel Taylor Coleridge, "Euthanasia of the Constitution," in *Essays on His Times,* ed. David V. Erdman, 3 vols. (Princeton, N.J.: Princeton University Press, 1978), 1: 27.

27. Samuel Taylor Coleridge, "France: An Ode," in *The Complete Poetical Works of Samuel Taylor Coleridge,* ed. E. H. Coleridge, 2 vols. (1912; reprint, Oxford: Oxford University Press, 1968), 1: 247, lines 85–88.

28. Keane interprets Albert's "whirling pillar" in terms of revolution/revelation imagery. He argues that Coleridge borrowed the biblical imagery from Hosea for his political positions in the Bristol lectures and *The Watchman*; see *Coleridge's Submerged Politics,* 263.

29. Samuel Taylor Coleridge, *Remonstrance to the French Legislators, The Watchman,* ed. Lewis Patton (Princeton, N.J.: Princeton University Press, 1970), 269. Further citations are identified in the text.

30. According to Raimonda Modiano, Coleridge's metaphysics gave him the protective support he needed to exert his political freedom. See "Metaphysical Debate in Coleridge's Political Theory," *Studies in Romanticism* 21 (1982): 465–74. Although Morton D. Paley argues that the poems Coleridge wrote during the 1790s represent contemporary history in apocalyptic terms, he also argues that Coleridge's poetry oscillates between public and domestic concerns. See "Apocalypse and Millennium in the Poetry of Coleridge," *Wordsworth Circle* 23 no. 1 (1992): 24–34. In *Coleridge's Submerged Politics,* Keane identifies Coleridge as "an obviously involved author" (306), an author who identifies with Alhadra—the character ready for action (263), with Albert—an advocate of repentance rather than physical punishment (305); and with Ferdinand—the publicly "unfit" character afraid of prisons (305–6). My analysis suggests less personal identification between Coleridge and the characters, including what they represent, and more ideological affinities between the drama and the political discursive arena from which it emerges.

31. My reading of Maria's role compares with that of Carlson who argues that

Maria does not fully conform to the era's feminine ideal. Carlson notes that Maria's renunciation of the convent as just rewards for disobeying Velez and her willingness to save the sorcerer (Albert in disguise) come straight out of Wollstonecraft. See *In the Theatre of Romanticism,* 116–17.

32. My reading of Alhadra's "heroism" differs from that offered by Keane; see *Coleridge's Submerged Politics,* 263. Carlson contends that Alhadra's color and religion disqualify her, "a potential man" (104), from exemplifying the play's dominant values; see *In the Theatre of Romanticism,* 116. I argue, on the other hand, that Alhadra's actions, rather than her race, religion, or gender, preempt her representation of the postrevolutionary "new woman."

6

Scott the Dramatist

Daniel P. Watkins

Walter Scott's interest in drama has been almost entirely ignored by scholars and general readers alike, both because his accomplishments in fiction and poetry tend to overshadow his other literary activities and, more broadly, because his dramatic work belongs to a genre that has seldom been regarded as worthy of serious critical attention. Nevertheless, his creative and critical work in the area of dramatic literature is important, because it provides a useful avenue into Romantic literary and social history and, by so doing, helps to create the necessary conditions for reconsidering the aesthetic and ideological dimensions of Romantic literature. Scott not only translated several dramas from German into English,[1] and wrote a lengthy (over one-hundred pages) historical sketch on the history of Western drama, but he also wrote four original dramas of his own. Although all of these works must eventually be given full scholarly and critical consideration, the original dramatic compositions offer a manageable and enlightening starting point for the study of Scott the dramatist.

Halidon Hill, Macduff's Cross, Auchindrane, and *The Doom of Devorgoil* display many of the characteristic traits found in Scott's poetry and fiction, ranging from a nostalgic recollection of a now-faded Scottish past to an often-sentimental vision of Scottish culture and an intense interest in the power relations defining personal and public life in moments of large-scale historical transformation. If the meaning of the dramas can be contained in a single, workable explanation, it is perhaps that they acknowledge the power and direction of historical change over the three hundred years immediately preceding Scott's own day, as well as the emergence of certain bourgeois structures of value and belief during that period, but attempt to negotiate history in such a way as to preserve what Scott considered to be universal bedrock assumptions about human experience and meaning. Put slightly differently, desiring stability and yet unable to deny the reality of social and historical turmoil, Scott seeks ways in his dramas to contain the flow of history and to shape and define the significance of what cannot be contained. The dramas frankly acknowledge the passing, for example, of feudalism and its aristocratic cultural expression, but at the same time insist that certain values undergirding feudalism and aristocracy can and must be brought forward into the new world order to assure its stability, integrity, and meaningfulness. In their effort to negotiate history in this manner, the dramas are culturally and ideologically conservative, but at the same time, they display respect for, and knowledge of, the deep energies and strange contours of social and historical reality.

Because I have written about *Halidon Hill* elsewhere,[2] I want to concentrate here on Scott's other dramas, with the intention of briefly sketching their handling of several historically charged issues and thereby suggesting some of the ways Scott appropriates and imaginatively seeks to control the difficult pressures of history by placing them in the service of his own conservative vision. The discussion that I offer is by no means complete, but it is meant to be merely a first step toward a serious critical assessment of these neglected dramas.

* * *

Macduff's Cross (composed 1821; published 1823) is a very short dramatic piece recounting a legend that Scott had collected earlier in *The Minstrelsy of the Scottish Border.* Scott summarizes that legend in a brief preface to the drama, noting that "the Cross was a place of refuge to any person related to Macduff, within the ninth degree, who, having committed homicide in sudden quarrel, should reach this place, prove his descent from the Thane of Fife, and pay a certain penalty" (964).[3] The Cross was seen, that is, as a sort of refuge from turmoil for individuals related to the preserver of the Scottish crown. As the introduction states further, however, "The shaft of the Cross was destroyed at the Reformation . . . The Cross bore an inscription, which is transmitted to us in an unintelligible form by Sir Robert Sibbald" (964). According to the introduction, only the pedestal upon which the Cross was mounted has been preserved, constituting (like the unintelligible inscription) a mere trace of the Cross, its history, and its power.

One simple historical explanation of the legend of Macduff's Cross is that its destruction marks the loss of a refuge from turmoil that an earlier age had enjoyed, presumably, therefore forcing individuals of Scott's day to face hard struggles without hope of escape. In the "Prelude" to the drama, addressed to Joanna Baillie, Scott uses a reference to personal aging to emphasize this view of cultural and historical change: "Our time creeps on, / Fancy grows colder as the silvery hair, / Tells the advancing winter of our life" (866). But this simple explanation becomes complicated by the fact that the same Scott who states matter-of-factly in the introduction that the Cross no longer exists imaginatively reconstructs, in his play, the Cross and its tremendous healing powers. This process of imaginative reconstruction, moreover, itself produces, in the form of nostalgia, a sort of refuge from the historical world whose undeniable triumph is implicitly acknowledged in the introduction. The story of Macduff's Cross, that is, reinstitutes the meanings associated with the alleged *history* of the Cross.

One broad issue that is therefore central to interpretation of the drama involves the tension between the historical record represented in the introduction and the nostalgic recollection of the past presented in the drama itself. What, for instance, is the relation between the fact of the destruction of the Cross and the poetic reconstruction of its powers? Is the pull of nostalgia a refusal to accept the authority of the historical fact described in the introduction and reinforced in the "Prelude," even as that fact is acknowledged? Or, in its imaginative portrayal of events surrounding the Cross, might the drama be said to offer a sign of hope that even extreme turmoil is negotiable? Although at the level of theory these questions may have only partial answers, at the level of the drama itself they provide a useful starting point for the critical effort to specify Scott's dramatic appropriation and portrayal of history.

The story of Macduff's Cross that the drama presents is brief and simple. Two monks (Waldhave and Ninian) ascend to a rocky pass where the Cross is situated. Their conversation eventually includes discussion of a conflict that had occurred years before between two Scottish barons, when one of the barons, Maurice Berkeley, apparently kills the other (Louis Lindesay) in a fight over the latter's young wife, who is also killed in the fight. Shortly after this conversation, a man being closely pursued by another seeks refuge at Macduff's Cross; it is soon revealed that the fleeing man is Maurice Berkeley, and that he is being pursued by Richard Lindesay, who seeks to avenge the death of his brother. In the lengthy exchange that follows the arrival of the two enemies, Berkeley discloses that he never committed adultery with Lindesay's wife, as everyone, including Louis Lindesay, had assumed; even in death, Berkeley says, she possesses "The purity of . . . [a] martyr'd saint." With Berkeley's pronouncement of the woman's innocence, one of the monks (Waldhave) reveals his true identity as Louis Lindesay, who had somehow survived his earlier fight with Maurice Berkeley. Berkeley and Lindesay, both of whom are "sick of war," make peace, and Berkeley secures the peace by bestowing his daughter to Richard Lindesay in marriage "To inhibit farther bloodshed"; then, with Louis Lindesay, he withdraws from public life to pass his remaining years as a monk.

The events of the drama suggest, of course, that even the severest personal and political difficulties (as exemplified in the conflict between Lindesay and Berkeley, which is both personal and political insofar as it is a conflict not simply between individuals but between two ruling families) can be resolved by religion and marriage. In the time when Macduff's Cross carried authority, the drama seems to suggest, religion and marriage were the necessary permanent foundation for social stability and hence human happiness. Their portrayal as the medium and expression of social harmony constitutes one important dimension of the drama's nostalgia, because implicit in that portrayal are both the effort to preserve a perceived fundamental social function of religion and marriage and an implicit acknowledgment that that function has been lost or forgotten, declining—along with its preeminent symbol, Macduff's Cross—into social and cultural obscurity. From this perspective, the nostalgic desire articulated in the drama is not simply for the preservation of marriage and religion; it is, rather, a Burkean desire for the placement of these institutions at the center of social life, under the assumption that their authority will assure stability, human integrity, and a smooth transition from one historical age to the next. That such a vision is expressed against the historical backdrop of the demise of Macduff's Cross may be seen as one sign that nostalgia sometimes carries within it not only desire but also dread.

Another way of specifying the operations of nostalgia and history is to consider the relation between the descriptions of religion and marriage at the conclusion of the drama to descriptions that appear much earlier. For example, while Berkeley's final speech approvingly sees marriage as one way of achieving personal fulfillment and securing peace in society, Waldhave's comments much earlier offer a very different view. When Ninian begins the tale of the Berkeley-Lindesay quarrel by noting that "Louis Lindesay, had a wife," Waldhave (Lindesay) interrupts with the comment that "Enough is said, indeed,— since a weak woman, / Ay, and a tempting fiend, lost Paradise, / When man was innocent" (1). And, although at the end of the drama Lindesay and Berkeley withdraw together as brothers to spend the remainder of their lives in prayer, earlier Waldhave states quite emphatically that his religious commitment does not well suit him:

> ... But for myself,
> Retired in passion to the narrow cell,
> Couching my tired limbs in its recesses,
> So ill-adapted am I to its limits,
> That every attitude is agony.
>
> (1)

The scenes cited here demonstrate that the concluding vision of the drama constitutes an imaginative resolution rather than permanent truth. That is, both religion and marriage are at first problematic for Lindesay, only gradually coming to be seen as embodiments and expressions of virtuous human sentiment. The importance of this point lies in its suggestion that the direction of meaning in the text of the drama reduplicates the more general operations of nostalgia. The final vision of Berkeley and Lindesay is an ideal reconstruction of social relations and institutions, which, in their manifestation earlier in the drama, are conflicted and, at times, even disabling. Just as the drama itself negotiates and settles the social and historical uncertainties associated with the destruction of Macduff's Cross, so the story told in the drama negotiates and settles conflicted internal details that are undeniable, but that are nevertheless unsuitable to a nostalgic vision of the world as a place held together and given meaning by Christian religion and aristocratic notions of marriage as a stabilizing social institution.

There is, of course, a utopian dimension to nostalgia, and in *Macduff's Cross* utopian desire is clearly present in the portrayal of the human potential to overcome conflict and to construct a personal and social life wherein meaning, value, and fulfillment are possible.[4] But in Scott's drama desire is ideologically burdened in ways that locate it securely within the same conservative political framework responsible for the very difficulties that would be overcome.[5] The drama is unable to imagine social relations other than they presently exist, that is, governed by an aristocratic worldview, patriarchal familial relations, and patriarchal religion. Under such circumstances, utopian desire is necessarily transformed into a vision which repeatedly returns to the real sources of alienation under the (mistaken) assumption that those sources can be cleansed of their alienating features without compromising their social function. The inevitable result is that alienating social relations and structures of authority are preserved even as, at the level of desire, alienation appears to have been overcome.

Perhaps the most obvious instance of the reduplication of alienating authority can be found in the drama's portrayal of gender.[6]

Waldhave's remark (cited above) early in the play about the loss of Paradise being the fault of "a weak woman" may be easily read as a comment reflecting personal bitterness over domestic unhappiness. But within the context of other representations of gender in the drama, the comment must be seen as symptomatic of a larger structural social situation. Gender, after all, is at the center of the dramatic action: the quarrel between Lindesay and Berkeley revolves around the question of who controls the affections of a woman; the severest insult that Richard Lindesay can imagine to cast at Berkeley is to say that Lindesay's wife (and Berkeley's beloved) was an "adulteress" (ii); and the woman at the source of the conflict is (unintentionally) killed in the fight between Berkeley and Lindesay, prompting both men to withdraw from public life.

A commonplace feminist explanation of events such as these would include recognition of the fact that, although the woman is presented as a source of turmoil, she herself is conspicuously absent, identified as a "martyr'd saint" or "adulteress" only by men who have something to gain from defining her according to their own needs and on their own terms. The conflict between Lindesay and Berkeley, on this view, is about the appropriation and use of feminine identity for the purpose of constructing masculine identity and securing masculine authority. The death of Lindesay's wife during the quarrel between the two men stands as hard evidence of the sacrifice of women by men motivated by self-interest and struggling for personal and public advantage.

Another dimension of gender in the drama involves the different relation that each man had with the now-deceased woman. As Berkeley remarks during his quarrel with Richard Lindesay, "I loved this lady fondly—truly loved—/ Loved her, and was beloved, ere yet her father / Conferr'd her on another" (ii). Although Berkeley is motivated by love—and is loved in return—Lindesay displays a stricter aristocratic sensibility; he is "Honour'd and fear'd . . . but little loved" (i) by his friends, and his marriage to the woman Berkeley loves is the result of an arrangement with the woman's father, not romantic commitment. Each man is drawn in such a way as to register different social assumptions about marriage and love, with Lindesay accepting the absolute authority of the father and estate to determine all matters with respect to marriage and Berkeley displaying a more bourgeois notion about individual choice in matters of marriage. As different as these relations are, however, they are again, from a feminist point of view, identical insofar as they refuse any real acknowledgment of feminine choice, or even the human status of women. In fact, although Berkeley vehemently defends the integrity of love and personal affection, at the same time he fully displays the same absolute masculine authority as Louis Lindesay or the deceased woman's father. In the final passage of the drama, in his effort to assure peace between the two warring families, he tells Richard Lindesay:

> It is the will
> Of Heaven, made manifest in thy preservation,
> To inhibit farther bloodshed: for De Berkeley,
> The votary Maurice lays the title down.
> Go to his halls, Lord Richard, where a maiden,
> Kin to his blood, and daughter in affection,
> Heirs his broad lands;—If thou canst love her,
> Lindesay,
> Woo her, and be successful.
>
> (2)

The point here, of course, is that even as the drama portrays the passing of aristocracy—Berkeley not only announces the values of an emergent, and antiaristocratic, individualism; he goes so far as to give up his title—it insists on the permanence of certain values and structures of authority (in this case, patriarchy) that had helped to ground an aristocratic worldview.[7] In a very real sense, the murdered woman at the center of the quarrel between Lindesay and Berkeley is a graphic example of what Berkeley does to his own daughter at the end of the play, when (contrary to his own actions regarding the woman he loved) he promises her to Richard Lindesay as a gesture of goodwill. At least with respect to gender relations, the difference between aristocratic and bourgeois structures of authority is minimal, as the fates of the two women in the drama emphatically demonstrate.

One final observation may help to clarify the social definition of gender in the drama. Behind the portrayal of Lindesay's deceased wife and Berkeley's daughter, the latter of whom is promised in marriage, lies the symbolic presence of Macduff's Cross, which stands as a visible reminder of the noble and durable values that the drama articulates and defends. In describing to his fellow Monk the story of the Cross, Ninian speaks to Weldhave of the time

> when fell Macbeth beneath the arm
> Of the predestined knight, unborn of woman,
> Three boons the victor ask'd, and thrice did Malcolm,
> Stooping the sceptre by the Thane restored,
> Assent to his request.
>
> (1)

Like Shakespeare, Scott calls attention to the fact that Macduff was "unborn of woman," thus calling into play the possible assumption that the preserver of the Scottish throne owes his greatness and blessedness to his uniquely masculine identity. In some respects, it is this idealized masculinity that Lindesay and Berkeley both uphold (by withdrawing, hand-in-hand, to a sort of all-male Paradise at the end of the drama) and pass along to the future, from the older men to Richard Lindesay and from an aristocratic to a bourgeois world. The triumph and authority of masculinity are imagined to be the guarantors of peace. Although the strong historical understanding informing the drama captures the passing of a world, its equally strong ideological commitments insist on the durability of values that, history shows, create strife and produce alienation and loneliness.

* * *

Auchindrane; or The Ayrshire Tragedy (composed late 1829; published early 1830) is Scott's most serious and impressive dramatic piece, one that strives to offer a historical vision of why the Scottish barony lost its hold on power. Prefaced to the drama is a lengthy and detailed historical sketch describing the demise of one family line due solely to the corruption of its own members. The drama itself offers an imaginative poetic version of the family's demise, articulating many details and nuances of individual and social power that are absent from (or only partly accounted for in) the preface.

The preface shows a clear sense of specific historical conditions, speaking plainly of "the violence of our ancestors" (965) and of "the complicated crimes" (965) in which they often engaged; and it attempts to distinguish those conditions from those defining and controlling the modern world. One major difference between the world of the early seventeenth century (in which the drama is set) and the world of the early nineteenth century, Scott says, is that modern criminals are motivated by "Mammon" (966), by thirst for monetary gain, whereas crimes in the past were often the result of "pride, ambition, and love of vengeance" (966). Moreover, the modern world enjoys the authority of universal law, which criminals may elude but cannot deny; criminals in the past, particularly when they were barons, were often very strong, and freely and openly defied a relatively weak legal structure, thus terrorizing the country almost at will.[8]

Although one general intent of these descriptions in the preface is doubtless to applaud the superior legal system of the modern world, at the same time they contain a sentimental view of crime in old Scotland by implying that modern criminals lack the stature, or grand character, of criminals in the past. As the preface puts it, "The criminals . . . of former times, drew their hellish inspiration from a loftier source than is known to modern villains. The fever of unsated ambition, the frenzy of ungratified revenge . . . stigmatized by our jurists and our legislators, held life but as passing breath; and such enormities as now sound like the acts of a madman, were then the familiar deeds of every offended noble" (966). The "loftier source" of crime in old Scotland may bespeak greater terror, but it also bespeaks life on a scale unknown to the modern world; and it is precisely this larger-than-life feudal and aristocratic past that the preface seems to admire and that the drama approvingly depicts.

The detailed attention in the preface to the grandeur associated with past crimes and criminals does not bespeak Scott's admiration for aristocratic life outside the law, just as his comment that modern crime as driven by Mammon does not reflect his belief that modern criminals are too limited in their motives and goals. Rather, the preface seems to admire the force and sheer boldness identified with the aristocratic criminals of the past. The absence of these qualities among modern criminals, the preface implies, marks a general diminishment of one part of personal and cultural life. Even as modern law is better situated to contain crime, that is, it does so at the expense of the grandeur and expansiveness of which human life is capable. Whereas in the preface Scott acknowledges the passing of a world, and admits that historical change has brought certain advances in holding criminal activity in check, at the same time his view of the past is nostalgic, expressing a deep longing for a world unconstrained by the life-deflating hard code of modern law. On this view, the portrayal of crime, in the preface and in the drama, extends beyond crime itself into a general vision of culture and society, both of how they have changed over time and what values should be defended and preserved as essential to the fullness of human life.

The story told in the drama is considerably less complex than the history sketched in the preface.[9] It begins with the return of Quentin Blane (the fictional representation of Dalrymple, who is discussed in the preface) to Scotland after having spent six years at war in the Netherlands. Because Blane possesses information that would implicate his master, John Mure of Auchindrane, in the assassination of the earl of Cassilis, Mure has sent him off to the wars in hopes that he will be killed. Having survived, however, he returns to Scotland, not only to face the continuing wrath of Mure but also to find that the woman whom he loves (Marion) has married an old rival (Neil MacLellan). Mure and his son, Philip, plot Blane's murder, which is carried out by Philip with the assistance of MacLellan; Philip then murders MacLellan, the only witness to the crime against Blane. Blane's body, which had been thrown into the sea, washes up on shore and, at the approach of MacLellan's daughter, begins to bleed—a sign that Blane had been murdered by a relative of the innocent girl. John and Philip Mure are arrested by the earl of Dunbar, confess their crimes, and accept their fates, both their imminent executions and the demise of the house of Auchindrane.

By rewriting the historical account of Auchindrane as drama, and in the process changing slightly some of the characters and even some of the details, Scott opens a creative space for expanding his interest in the "loftier sources" of criminal activity, mentioned in the preface, to include consideration of the ideological dimensions of an aristocratic worldview. The drama seems to take for granted the grandeur of life in feudal Scotland—a grandeur that (the drama seems to suggest) surpasses the fact of isolated historical details—and it uses that grandeur as a fundamental assumption in articulating a nostalgic, and inherently conservative, vision of culture and society. This is not to say that historical fact is unimportant to Scott. To the contrary, the historical facts offered in the preface are essential—and unavoidable—as context. But, as the drama clearly shows, their meaning is not transparent; it is, rather, a process of negotiation, a process of filtering facts through different sets of culturally mediated desire, belief, and need.

A further preliminary (and very general) observation about the relation between the preface and the drama may throw additional light on the historical dimension of Scott's dramatic imagination. Like Byron (and like Godwin in *Caleb Williams*), Scott recognizes that core cultural values present their greatest challenge and demand closest consideration, at the precise moment when they are violated, for here they stand exposed and their durability is seriously tested. Probably for this reason he follows Byron in writing about crime as a way of writing about history, culture, and society.[10] In other words, the interest of the drama does not reside entirely in its portrayal of John Mure's criminal activities and their punishment but rather in the demise of the house of Auchindrane and the conditions that promoted that demise. Mure's character and crimes are symptoms of, and avenues into, much larger, and historically more interesting, issues.

One of the most difficult issues treated in the play involves social stability, which would seem entirely unavailable to a historically informed imagination seeking to represent forthrightly John Mure's crime and the ensuing demise of his entire family line. Certainly the plot of the drama does not avoid any of the transgressions cataloged in the preface, and even intensifies their horror by drawing into the action some of the most precious features of private or domestic life: marriage and children. Nor does it gloss over the impact of crime on innocent people, for not only are the criminals caught and punished; innocent individuals caught against their will in the web of criminal activity suffer greatly, as witnessed in the murder of Quentin Blane, the destruction of Marion MacLellan's marriage, and the shock of the young Isabel upon discovering Blane's corpse.[11] No one escapes the deeds of John Mure, for they filter through society touching and helping to shape every aspect of personal and public life.

Despite the emphasis on pervasive disruption, however, the desire for social stability remains the drama's most powerful issue. In fact, the drama seems to insist that stability can and should be carried forward as an attainable goal and durable value even in the face of social decline. The conclusion of the drama makes this point emphatically, when the Earl of Dunbar enters with John and Philip Mure under arrest. It is not simply the arrest and promise of punishment that raise the possibility of peace; it is, rather, the confession of both criminals to their crime, and their acceptance of both their individual and family fates. As Philip says to his father in the final passage of the drama:

> Father, 'tis fitter that we both should die,
> Leaving no heir behind. The piety
> Of a bless'd saint, the morals of an anchorite,
> Could not atone thy dark hypocrisy,
> Or the wild profligacy I have practised.
> Ruin'd our house, and shatter'd be our towers,
> And with them end the curse our sins have merited!
>
> (3.3)

This is a public statement, which implicitly acknowledges the integrity of the prevailing structure of social authority and assumes that social unrest is attributable only to ungrateful and foul individuals such as themselves. In effect, the particular direction of the confession collapses all the drama's actions into a large, all-encompassing social order, defined not so much by the military superiority of Dunbar as by the recognition, even by criminals, of the necessary claim that society has on all individuals.[12]

It may be worth remarking, briefly, that the sentiments voiced in the drama's conclusion seem to contradict (or at least to depart from) several important historical points put forward in the preface. For example, the preface notes that the elder Mure "was at length brought to avow the fact [of his crime], but in other respects died as impenitent as he had lived" (970); it also states plainly that the modern legal system is superior to the older in preventing individuals from open defiance of the law. In the final scene of the drama, John Mure is not in the least defiant but rather speaks lovingly as a father of his desire to have his own execution "pay the ransom" (3.3) for his son's imminent execution. And the question of the legal system is set aside entirely in favor of confessions meant to endorse public authority and order over individual interest—it is not so much law as it is a rigorous and clearly-defined structure of social values that assures peace and stability.

These departures from the preface are important, because they help to focus the ideological bent of the drama. Historical fact is acknowledged, but it is then rapidly (and impressively) negotiated in such a way as to leave standing a quite conservative notion of the relation of the state to the individual—a notion that in fact disables historical questions having to do with the nature and function of legal systems from one historical moment to the next, or with the meaning of continued defiance of state authority even after certain crimes have been admitted. By rewriting the preface as dramatic action, specific questions about the nature and conditions of social stability—in the past *or* the present—are successfully obscured by a nebulous but powerful desire to have stability.

Several particular issues reflect the drama's anxiety over the question of durable values within a context of rapidly changing personal and public circumstances. Like *Macduff's Cross, Auchindrane* gives considerable attention to gender relations. Unlike the earlier drama, however, its interest in heterosexual love is directed to nonaristocratic individuals, using a lower social class as the basis for articulating a vision of marriage, reproduction, women, and the relation of the institution of marriage to other social institutions.

One underlying assumption of the drama seems to be that the marriage of Marion to Neil MacLellan is ill-suited, doomed from the beginning, and that true love had existed between Marion and Quentin Blanc. This assumption is seen not only in the nostalgic longing that marks the meeting of Marion and Blanc, after six years' separation, but also in the portrayal of Marion as an emotionally and physically abused wife. The abusive nature of the relationship between Marion and her husband, Neil MacLellan, is stated directly in the young Isabel's comment to her mother that she understands quite clearly how jealousy operates in marriage: "Ay, but I know already! Jealousy / Is, when my father chides, and you sit weeping" (1.2).

Such details do more than promote nostalgic interest in an ideal love between Marion and Blane that never was allowed to flourish;

they also acknowledge a rift in the most personal corner of life, which is homologous to the larger family and political turmoil seen in John Mure's relation to the earl of Cassilis, the earl of Dunbar, and James VI of Scotland. The connection between marriage and its social context is further suggested in the depiction of Marion's husband, who is described by one of Dunbar's officers as a man who hangs "on our fiercer barons, / The ready agents of their lawless will" (3.1). The violence and moral emptiness of MacLellan that are implicit in this description are manifested equally in the ranger's marriage, constituting a single thread of personal and social life, one that binds marriage ineluctably to a larger network of social and political relations.

The relation of marriage to society, as described here, is particularly masculine, defined largely by MacLellan's duplication of public aggressiveness and violence in the private sphere of marriage. But the values, beliefs, and actions that define John Mure's world and that are duplicated in the character of MacLellan have specific consequences for women, who are relegated entirely to a passive existence in the private sphere. (Unmistakable evidence of this fact is seen in John Mure's comment that the proper place for Marion is the home and that her concerns should be entirely domestic.[13]) One consequence is that Marion, denied her own voice and person within the prevailing structures of belief and authority, attempts to generate from out of the narrow sphere that she inhabits a positive vision of life, free of masculine domination and violence.

For instance, she teaches her daughter, Isabel, the rites of a pagan religion, which the two females practice rather than the dominant religion, Christianity, of their society, and despite an emphatic warning from their master to give over their pagan activities. John Mure tells Marion:

> Linger such dregs of heathendom among you?
> And hath Knox preach'd, and Wishart died, in vain?
> Take notice, I forbid these sinful practices,
> And will not have my followers mingle in them.

(3.1)

The situation regarding religion helps to elucidate both the power dynamics of patriarchy in feudal Scotland and the indomitable spirit of women who suffer gravely, and virtually invisibly, at its hands. In its portrayal of these dual components of social life, the drama brings a strong judgment to bear on one sort of corruption that existed in the past, namely, a wild and energetic criminal masculinity so hypocritical that it even uses the vocabulary of Christianity to maintain and extend its authority. And at the same time it offers a brief glimpse, in the characters of Marion and Isabel, of innocence and hope of meaningful spiritual expression, despite the oppressiveness of masculine authority.

But the drama neither dismisses patriarchy nor embraces paganism; rather, it uses the latter as one ideological means of canceling the oppressive elements within the former. When the drama ends, Marion and Isabel survive, while MacLellan and John and Philip Mure do not; but they survive under the protection of the Earl of Dunbar, who reinstates both patriarchy and Christianity, though apparently cleansed of the atrocities evident in the actions of John Mure and Neil MacLellan. The Earl of Dunbar is identical to John Mure, except that he is from a slightly higher social class and is a more palatable example of the values and codes of authority governing feudal Scotland. He steps forward to terminate the private tyranny exercised by John Mure over his followers and to restore a more acceptable exercise of the very values that Mure held but had abused. Meanwhile, Marion's final scene depicts her submissively obeying John Mure's command to return home, and Isabel's final scene depicts her fainting at the sight of Quentin Blane's murdered corpse. As the play concludes, the women are silenced and rendered invisible, and masculine authority reasserts itself, presumably representing values that are perdurable, capable of surviving even the most severe assaults.

An equally important issue involves the question of education, or literacy, in relation to prevailing aristocratic structures of authority. As a poor orphan boy, Quentin Blane won the favor of John Mure, who "took a kindly charge / For my advance in letters" (1.2), enabling Blane to become in the military what one of his fellow soldiers disparagingly calls "the colonel's scribbling drudge" (1.1). Ironically, his status as "Quentin the quillman" proves to be his salvation in the military, for although John Mure gives specific instructions that Blane (as Hildebrand puts it) is to be "thrust . . . on some desperate service, / Which should most likely end thee" (1.1), the education with which the young orphan has been provided causes him to be assigned "More peaceful tasks than the rough front of war, / For which my education little suited me" (1.1). Upon his return from Scotland after the wars, Blane sees his education as the continuing means of his preservation, as he plans to "teach writing and grammar" (1.1.) in some isolated corner of the kingdom, far removed from the circumstances that heretofore have battered him.

The many comments about Quentin Blane's literacy, which is both cultivated and then destroyed by John Mure of Auchindrane, add an important dimension to the drama, helping to charge its vision with political significance. By distinguishing Blane from everyone else in the drama—that is, by presenting him as a scholar temperamentally unsuited to the violent conduct exercised by all of the other male characters—and then placing him at the center of a sweeping conflict involving even the king of Scotland,[14] Scott effectively situates writing among the powerful currents and turmoil of social life, showing its inescapable relation to cultural value, political authority, and social conflict. But that relation is ideologically burdened, for although the drama insists that education and scholarship do not occupy a sphere apart from society, at the same time it idealizes them. The learned Blane is temperamentally unsuited for the life pursued by other men in the drama, and if he is ultimately destroyed by the violence around him, he nevertheless embodies and projects values, interests, and integrity that are immune to the destructive forces of his world. The issue of Blane's learning, on this view, is one of value rather than power; the drama idealizes Blane's integrity, while acknowledging that literacy alone is incapable of assuring social stability.

One of the curious and important ironies associated with the portrayal of Quentin Blane is the fact that the authority that enables him to cultivate interests and talents ill-suited to a world governed by violence is the very authority that murders him. This contradictory situation again reflects the difficult historical and ideological territory that the drama attempts to negotiate. The historical fact is that the violent and often lawless world of feudal Scotland provided a context for the development of scholarship and learning, and one sign of the historical integrity of the drama is that it acknowledges this fact. At the same time, however, even as Blane is securely situated within a network of social exchange, he is removed from it, presented as innocent, learned, and ideologically free of the controlling codes and values of his world. In portraying Blane in this manner, the drama effectively works within the frames of historical fact, while at the same time articulating a utopian desire for an educated imagination unencumbered by social and political turmoil. The difficulty of credibly asserting such a vision as this is quite clearly presented in *The Doom of Devorgoil,* where the question of the relations between learning and social authority dissolves into satire.

The effort of the drama to negotiate the difficult territory of history, culture, and society, without actually denying their authority, can be seen as well in two instances of nostalgic longing. In the first, Quentin Blane describes his (naive) desire, after the wars, to live quietly outside the mainstream of Scottish life:

> I had a hope,
> A poor vain hope, that I might live obscurely
> In some far corner of my native Scotland,
> Which, of all others, splinter'd into districts,
> Differing in manners, families, even language,
> Seem'd a safe refuge for the humble wretch
> Whose highest hope was to remain unheard of.
>
> (1.1)

In the second, old Hildebrand, an Englishman, offers Blane refuge from the Scottish tyranny that threatens his life:

> Mark me, Quentin.
> I took my license from the noble regiment,
> Partly that I was worn with age and warfare,
> Partly that an estate of yeomanry,
> Of no great purchase, but enough to live on,
> Has call'd me owner since a kinsman's death.
> It lies in merry Yorkshire, where the wealth
> Of fold and furrow, proper to Old England,
> Stretches by streams which walk no sluggish pace,
> But dance as light as yours. Now, good friend Quentin,
> This copyhold can keep two quiet inmates,
> And I am childless. Wilt thou be my son?
>
> (1.1)

These expressions of desire—one for a peaceful refuge in Scotland, the other for a peaceful refuge in England—may be placed alongside Marion's practice of pagan religion as judgments against certain atrocities that the drama portrays as occupying the center of Scottish feudal society. At the same time, however, their emphasis on retreat (which implies the impossibility of transforming social life and assumes that value, hope, and integrity therefore must be sought in a nonsocial sphere) is discredited by the larger structure of events in the drama. With Blane's murder, the utopian dream of life outside society is destroyed, effectively reinstating questions of human meaning within the spheres of history, culture, and society—effectively reinstating, that is, the central structures of authority and belief that the drama has put under scrutiny.

Auchindrane is ideologically complex in its efforts to articulate a workable set of human values within a historical framework. Scott chooses the social life of crime as his primary subject, using this as a means of looking unflinchingly at the rough and violent dimensions of Scottish feudal society. But, unlike Byron, he produces a drama that seems incapable of imagining a fundamental structural transformation of that society as a necessary means of ending oppression, tyranny, and violence. Although it rejects the notion of a sphere of meaning and possibility apart from society, the drama also leaves feudal structures of authority entirely intact, presumably under the assumption that the historical record can be interpreted in such a way as to distinguish apparently isolated criminal activities in feudal society from a durable core of noble aspiration and beliefs. The drama is driven by the logic of nostalgia, which cleanses the past of its real power dynamic, asserting in its place a redemptive vision of unconflicted value. In this respect, the drama duplicates, at the level of ideology, the same nostalgic longing expressed by Quentin Blane and Hildebrand that, at the level of plot, it rejects. The demise of the Scottish barony, according to this vision, resulted from its abandonment of certain durable values—represented in various ways by Marion, Quentin Blane, and the Earl of Dunbar—that are essential to social stability, cultural integrity, and historical continuity.

* * *

The Doom of Devorgoil (written 1817; published 1830) is Scott's only attempt at comedy in drama. The genre enables him to explore the same subject matter as *Auchindrane*, that is the demise of a Scottish barony—in quite different terms.[15] In *Devorgoil* as in *Auchindrane* a barony is threatened with extinction, though in this instance it is ultimately preserved from destruction. A series of comic and seriocomic episodes reveal the causes of social decline, which are corrected just in time to prevent the destruction of the Devorgoil castle by flood. The preservation of the castle is accompanied by the sudden acquisition of extreme wealth, which reinvigorates the Devorgoil barony and provides the context for the satisfaction of personal desire as well, as the younger members of the Devorgoil family prepare to enter marriages of their choice. The play concludes with a song celebrating personal happiness, public stability, and enduring honor.

The happy conclusion of the play is reached through a complex and enlightening portrayal of events and personal exchanges, which, despite the happy ending, suggest intense, even debilitating, anxiety over the direction of personal and social life. *Devorgoil* moves nervously between history and hysteria, presenting a search for pleasure and hope capable of sustaining human life faced with insurmountable hardships and under the threat of continuing, rapid decline. That search brings the drama face to face, once more, with all the major issues that occupy Scott's imagination in his other dramas—including even the issue of literacy and education—and humorously turns them on their head, thereby effectively revivifying their cultural significance by injecting them with the pleasures of the imagination.

One of the primary ingredients in the comic portrayal of hardship, anxiety, and social decline is the supernatural, the portrayal of which not only allows Scott to consider, through a new vocabulary, the cultural and historical significance of religion, social stability, and class relations, but also (as I want to argue, below) to present more sharply than in his other dramas the problematic issues of literacy and gender. Further, the strong presence of supernatural elements in *Devorgoil* provides an important means by which the drama can negotiate the difficult path between history and hysteria and produce a social vision, finally, of hope and stability without subjecting its characters to the excruciating violence that inevitably accompanies historical fact. Put differently, in *Devorgoil*, Scott finds a means of preserving and articulating historically constituted values without having to subject those values entirely to the authority of the historical record, as he does in all three of his other poetic dramas.[16]

Devorgoil tells the story of a baron and his family living in extreme poverty and facing the imminent death of the family line and hence their estate. The baron, Oswald, has presumably brought much of the disgrace onto the family by marrying Eleanor, a woman of obscure parentage. As Eleanor herself describes the situation to their daughter, Flora:

> Your father's fortunes were but bent, not broken,
> Until he listen'd to his rash affection.
> Means were afforded to redeem his house,
> Ample and large—the hand of a rich heiress
> Awaited, almost courted, his acceptance;
> . . . .
> And he forsook the proud and wealthy heiress,
> To wed with me and ruin.
>
> (1.2)

In an effort to provide her daughter with at least some material security in the face of the family's imminent demise, Eleanor presses her to marry a dull-witted student named Gullcrammer, whom Flora does not love—she sees him, in fact, as "the fop, / The fool, the low-born, low-bred, pedant coxcomb" (1.1)—preferring instead the affections of a ranger named Leonard, to whom she has secretly promised herself. Eleanor's young niece, Katleen, who is a poor but proud cottage girl, now lives with the family and serves as a sort of hysterical commentator on the personal and social situation of the Devorgoil estate; as she puts it, she is "hysteric on the subject" (1.1) of the excruciating poverty that the aristocratic family suffers. Katleen is in love with a friend of Leonard, a ranger named Lancelot Blackthorn.

The plot follows these individuals through an evening at the Devorgoil estate and revolves mainly around Katleen's playful effort to frighten Gullcrammer, who stays the night due to bad weather. Her strategy for instilling fear in the dull-witted scholar requires that she and Lancelot Blackthorn assume the role of ghosts (named Owlspiegle and Cockledemoy), who haunt Gullcrammer's chambers. Gullcrammer proves to be an excellent dupe; believing wholeheartedly that he is being visited by spirits, for example, he allows Blackthorn to cut his hair in a ridiculous manner. After Katleen and Blackthorn complete their practical joke and leave Gullcrammer's chambers, they encounter a real ghost in the form of a Palmer, who warns them to leave the castle because "There is a fate on't" (3.3). When Katleen refuses to heed the warning, the Palmer leaves a key in her possession, with instruction to "wait the even with courage" (3.3).

Shortly thereafter, a second spirit appears to Lord Oswald and the others, who are assembled in a chamber in a distant part of the castle. This spirit is in the form of Lord Erick of Devorgoil, whose tale is related earlier in the drama by Oswald:

> My grandsire, Erick, doubled human strength,
> And almost human size—and human knowledge,
> And human vice, and human virtue also,
> As storm or sunshine chanced to occupy
> His mental hemisphere. After a fatal deed,
> He hung his armour on the wall, forbidding
> It e'er should be ta'en down. There is a prophecy,
> That of itself 'twill fall, upon the night
> When, in the fiftieth year from his decease,
> Devorgoil's feast is full. This is the era.
>
> (2.2)

The spirit of Erick shows Oswald and his companions a treasure chamber full of wealth and promises it all to Oswald on condition that he abandon his lower-class wife: "This do, / And be as great as ere [sic] was Devorgoil / When Devorgoil was richest!" (3.4). When Oswald refuses, the lake around the castle begins to rise, threatening to flood the castle. Just before the castle is destroyed, Leonard takes the key in Katleen's possession and opens the gate to the treasury, whereupon the flood immediately subsides. Leonard turns out not to be a forester at all, but rather the Heir of Aglionby, and his noble lineage, linked to the estate of Devorgoil by marriage to Flora, preserves the Devorgoil family line in faith, constancy, and virtue (3.4).

The events of the drama move headlong toward the same conclusion presented in *Auchindrane*—for example, the disintegration and termination of a barony—until supernatural elements are introduced, which lift the plot out of the violent certainty of history and enable a vision of a preserved aristocracy and aristocratic value. But the use of supernatural means to construct a vision of aristocratic survival is not itself particularly remarkable; the real genius of the drama lies in the way the supernatural is used to secure certain bourgeois structures of belief within a larger aristocratic worldview. Oswald, after all, does not abandon Eleanor to preserve his estate, but remains tied to her through affection and love; nor is Flora forced at last to marry Gullcrammer but instead wins the man of her heart (Leonard). The primacy of personal sentiments evident in these relations suggests certain features of *Macduff's Cross,* but here, more forcefully than in the shorter drama, those sentiments are lifted into the aristocratic world, actually serving as a strong support for the estate, as personal relations are not grounded upon expediency but upon the stronger bond of love.

Although the manipulation of events by means of supernatural machinery veers far afield from historical fact, it serves an important ideological function of creating a bridge between past and present. The supernatural machinery is a means by which the downward spiral of feudal and aristocratic authority is arrested, and an aristocratic worldview is reinvigorated with the energy of deeply held assumptions about the integrity of personal life more characteristic of the early nineteenth century than the age of Scottish feudalism. Moreover, the supernatural machinery enables the drama to suggest that the political violence of the past, embodied in the spirit of Erick, can be defeated utterly by personal affection; or, put in more broadly ideological terms, it allows the drama to imagine (or dream) that a seamless flow of history, untarnished by violent upheaval, is possible.

Several smaller issues take particular meaning within this larger set of ideological concerns. One of the more interesting of these, at least when placed against the grim vision of *Auchindrane,* involves education. Put simply, Gullcrammer is no Quentin Blane, and the fact that he is not suggests a certain ambiguity on Scott's part over the role and nature of learning under the hard hand of historical change. *Auchindrane* offers a compelling portrait of the tense and difficult relation of learning to social and political circumstance, emphatically refusing to allow even learned individuals a position on the backside of history. *Devorgoil* seems to mock book-learning unrestrainedly, as virtually every character in the play has a go at the underbred Gullcrammer, and the scholar Gullcrammer himself seems to take every opportunity, without aid, of displaying his unmatched dimness.

The problematic details relating to Gullcrammer's character, and its relation to Quentin Blane, among other things, clearly present an idea that is left rather vague in *Auchindrane*, namely that formal education has little bearing on the deep structures of authority and belief that define culture and society. Like Byron's Manfred, the drama seems to assume that "The Tree of Knowledge is not that of Life" (1.1.12);[17] it seems to assume, that is, that the important and controlling codes of culture reside not in (false or true) intellect but rather in values, love, and constancy—in the very virtues that triumph in the drama. On this view, the comic portrayal of Gullcrammer steadfastly writes formal education out of the formula for social stability.

A second (and perhaps more complex) social issue concerns gender relations. Like Scott's other dramas, *Devorgoil* presents a fairly straightforward picture of patriarchy, though here Scott depicts more carefully some of its subtle modifications at the hands of a bourgeois sensibility. But what is striking is not just the portrayal of a slightly more modern version of patriarchy, but rather the construction of an elaborate—and very funny—set of sexual metaphors for describing historical tension and transformation.

A strong reading of the plot suggests that the entire dramatic situation is a veiled description of sexual intercourse. Numerous small details suggest—sometimes only very obliquely—sexual play. For instance, while disguised as Cockledemoy and Owlspiegle, and during the trick on Gullcrammer, Katleen and Lancelot Blackthorn sing songs that are full of double entendres. In the early stages of their trick, Owlspiegle (Lancelot) sings to Cockledemoy (Katleen) that "Now the pole-star's red and burning," to which Cockledemoy responds in song, "Lift latch—open clasp, / Shoot bolt—and burst hasp!" (3.2). Shortly thereafter, Owlspiegle, in song, plays upon his own name to invite Cockledemoy into sexual play; he asks Cockledemoy: "Wilt thou ride on the midnight owl?" (3.2). Still later, in a less suggestive song, Cockledemoy describes her ride on a dragonfly and invites Owlspiegle to join her: "She [the dragonfly] has four wings and strength endow, / And her long body has room for two," to which Gullcrammer (listening to the song) responds, "Cockledemoy now is a naughty brat" (3.2). Finally, near the end of their trick, Cockledemoy sings that she has fallen into the lake, and the description of her return to safety carries unmistakable sexual overtones: "Now merrily, merrily, row I to shore, / My bark is a bean-shell, a straw for an oar." Owlspiegle's response to Cockledemoy's safe return hovers ambiguously between relief and sexual release: "My life, my joy, / My Cockledemoy!" (3.2).

Sexual overtones carry over into the major plot as well. After a long speech in which Oswald describes the respect he has lost as a result of his poverty, Eleanor scolds him, calling his complaints "but empty declamation" (1.2). Rather than respond directly to his wife's criticism, he unsheathes his sword and, as the stage direction notes, "addresses the rest of the speech to it":

> Yes, trusty friend, my father knew thy worth,
> And often proved it—often told me of it.
> Though thou and I be now held lightly of,
> And want the gilded hatchments of the time,
> I think we both may prove true metal still.
> 'Tis thou shalt tell this story, right this wrong:
> Rest thou till time is fitting.
>
> (1.2)

To this speech, Eleanor responds, "my dearest husband," while Flora exclaims "My dear father," (1.2); both women abandon the sort of strong statements that they had earlier made to Oswald, becoming more submissive and expressing feminine support for their beleaguered master.[18] The Freudian implications of this bizarre scene are obvious and astonishing, offering an emphatic (and humorous) parallel between masculine sexuality and familial, social, and military power; indeed, Oswald's speech may be regarded as the centerpiece of the drama's portrayal of sexuality and gender accompanying historical transformation.

Phallic or otherwise sexual imagery is most fully realized in the many descriptions of the castle drawbridge, which effectively represents the sexual anxiety of Oswald as his personal and public authority declines. The bridge is sometimes up, sometimes down, but seldom functioning properly, or being used at the right time. For instance, upon his return to the castle, Oswald's first question to his wife is, "why is the drawbridge lower'd?" (1.2), to which Eleanor responds, "The counterpoise has fail'd, and Flora's strength, / Katleen's, and mine united, could not raise it" (1.2). And after his address to his sword, Oswald immediately leaves the company of his wife, Flora, and Katleen, saying "Peace, both!—we speak no more of this I go / To heave the draw-bridge up" (1.2). A bit later, he lowers the bridge to admit Gullcrammer to the castle, but is unable to raise it again, saying, "The counterpoise has clean given way; the bridge / Must e'en remain unraised, and leave us open, / For this night's course at least, to passing visitants" (2.2). Finally, toward the end of the drama, as the flood threatens the castle, the drawbridge becomes submerged, but as the flood recedes, Leonard exclaims that "the drawbridge is left dry!" (3.4), which, read in sexual terms, marks both exhaustion and triumph for the Devorgoil estate.

Deploying a strategy different from that of his other dramas, Scott here uses sexuality to mark historical tension—seen in the simultaneous presence of desire and vulnerability—as well as continuity during historical transformation. Moreover, sexual metaphors both enliven the drama and provide a basis for articulating certain bourgeois values without compromising the larger aristocratic sensibility that the play preserves in its conclusion. That is, the personal affection and sexual play seen in the various love relations—Oswald and Eleanor, Flora and Leonard, and Katleen and Lancelot Blackthorn—violate (even at the level of plot) aristocratic assumptions about the social definition of marriage;[19] and yet aristocracy is not made to pay for this transgression. The castle of Devorgoil is made rich again, and Flora wins the man of her heart. The aristocratic context of social life is brought forward through history, now being served rather than threatened by the individual interests pursued by the characters.

To consider sexuality in the drama from a slightly different (and perhaps too clever) angle: if the plot-level events are read as a displacement of sexual energy and activity, then Oswald's anxieties, Katleen and Lancelot's sexual play, and Flora's sexual longing—all of which are eventually happily resolved—may be regarded as depictions of the hope and pain accompanying the birth of the bourgeoisie, including bourgeois patriarchy. From this perspective, aristocracy provides the necessary (maternal) condition for the appearance of a new social class, and, ideologically, it offers the guidance and (patriarchal) authority necessary to the growth of that new class. Such a reading not only places the drama squarely within a conservative ideological framework consistent with the vision of Scott's fiction; it enables Scott to offer a sentimental view of historical transformation free of the extreme violence and criminality that burdens the social vision of *Auchindrane*, thereby presenting further (ideological) justification for remaining committed to aristocratic definitions of social life, even while acknowledging (and perhaps even welcoming) certain modern modifications of social life. Thus, Flora's song about constancy in love may serve as an enlightening statement about the drama's vision of historical and social transformation:

> When the tempest's at the loudest,
> On its gale the eagle rides;

> When the ocean rolls the proudest,
> Through the foam the sea-bird glides—
> All the rage of wind and sea
> Is subdued by constancy.
> Gnawing want and sickness pining,
> All the ills that men endure;
> Each their various pangs combining,
> Constancy can find a cure—
> Pain, and Fear, and Poverty,
> Are subdued by constancy.
> Bar me from each wonted pleasure,
> Make me abject, mean, and poor;
> Heap on insults without measure,
> Chain me to a dungeon floor—
> I'll be happy, rich, and free,
> If endow'd with constancy.
>
> (1.2)

* * *

The issues sketched here should be investigated more fully from a historical and ideological perspective, along with other important issues in Scott's dramas that I have not considered: particularly class struggle. My purpose has not been to offer an exhaustive analysis but rather simply to suggest that Scott's dramas bear more careful consideration than they have heretofore received. For the dramas not only offer insight into another dimension of Scott's imagination; they provide additional important material for understanding Romantic drama and especially the Romantic vision of history. As that vision is more fully explored, I believe, the place of drama within Romantic literary history will become secure, helping to provide some of the necessary conditions for a complete reassessment of Romantic aesthetics and ideology.

Notes

1. Scott translated Maier's *Fust von Stromberg*, Iffland's *The Wards*, Schiller's *Conspiracy of Fiesco*, Goethe's *Goetz von Berlichingen*, and Steinsberg's adaptation of von Babo's *Otto von Wittelsbach*. For a useful discussion of these translations, see Duncan M. Mennie, "Sir Walter Scott's Unpublished Translations of German Plays," *Modern Language Review* 33 (1938): 234–39.

2. Daniel P. Watkins, *A Materialist Critique of English Romantic Drama* (Gainesville, Fla.: University Press of Florida, 1993), 123–33.

3. All quotations from Scott's dramas and their prefaces are taken from J. Logie Robertson, ed., *Scott: Poetical Works* (1904; reprint, London: Oxford University Press, 1964). Page number references to the prefaces appear parenthetically in the

text. Passages from the dramas are cited parenthetically in the text by act and scene numbers, with the exception of the one-act *Macduff's Cross*, which is cited by scene number only.

4. For a more positive political view of Romantic nostalgia, see Robert Sayre and Michael Lowy's important essay, "Figures of Romantic Anticapitalism," in *Spirits of Fire: English Romantic Writers and Contemporary Historical Methods*, eds. G. A. Rosso and Daniel P. Watkins (Rutherford, N.J.: Fairleigh Dickinson University Press, 1990), 23–68.

5. For a theoretical discussion of the ideological dimensions of utopian thought, see the final chapter of Fredric Jameson's *The Political Unconscious: Narrative as a Socially Symbolic Act* (Ithaca: Cornell University Press, 1981), 281–300.

6. For an excellent study of gender relations in Scott's fiction, see Ina Ferris, *The Achievement of Literary Authority: Gender, History, and the Waverly Novels* (Ithaca and London: Cornell University Press, 1991).

7. For a useful discussion of Scott's views on feudalism, see Graham McMaster, *Scott and Society* (Cambridge: Cambridge University Press, 1981), esp. 59–69. McMaster's persuasive argument follows a line of thought slightly different from the one I offer here, insofar as it considers Scott's views in relation to the thought of the Scottish Enlightenment.

8. In his novels, Scott is similarly preoccupied with the differences between the legal codes of the past and present. In an excellent discussion of this subject, Daniel Cotton remarks, "In all of Sir Walter Scott's novels the difference between the modern world and the world of the past is defined by the difference between the rule of law and the rule of violence. At every period of history described in these works the progressive elements of civilization are distinguished from the anachronistic on the basis of their commitment to the increasing sublimation of violent conflict within formal regulations, especially the written regulations of law." See *The Civilized Imagination: A Study of Ann Radcliffe, Jane Austen, and Sir Walter Scott* (Cambridge: Cambridge University Press, 1985), 171. See also Bruce Beiderwell, *Power and Punishment in Scott's Novels* (Athens and London: University of Georgia Press, 1992), for a discussion of Scott's portrayal of law in his fiction.

9. Edward Wagenknecht notes that the story of *Auchindrane* "was derived from Robert Pitcairn's record in his *Ancient Criminal Trials* of a 1611 case in the west of Scotland that, in Scott's opinion, afforded 'a perfect picture of the violence of our ancestors.'" See *Sir Walter Scott* (New York: Continuum, 1991), 58.

10. For a discussion of the portrayal of crime in Byron's dramas, see Daniel P. Watkins, "Byron and the Poetics of Revolution," *Keats-Shelley Journal*, 35 (1985): 95–130.

11. For Isabell's reaction to seeing the dead Quentin Blane, see the stage direction near the end of the play: "She goes to aid the SERGEANT with the body, and presently gives a cry, and faints."

12. The confession of crime is, of course, a standard figure in tragedy, but Scott's handling of it is nuanced in such a way as to emphasize the drama's retrogressive vision.

13. When he finds Marion wandering on the beach after sunset, John Mute comments:

> . . . .
> But women
> Should shun the night air. A young wife also,
> Still more a handsome one, should keep her pillow
> Till the sun gives-example for her wakening.

> . . . .
> Please your own husband, and that you may please him,
> Get thee to bed, and shut up doors, good dame.
> Were I MacLellan, I should scarce be satisfied
> To find thee wandering here in mist and moonlight,
> When silence should be in thy habitation,
> And sleep upon thy pillow.
>
> (3.1)

14. In the exchange between John Mure and his cousin, Gifford, about why Mure continues to be prosecuted for his villainous actions, the role of King James is made emphatically clear. The following exchange arises from the news, brought by Gifford, that a new witness (Quentin Blane) is about to be produced to prove Mure's guilt:

> *Auchindrane:*   When they produce such witness, cousin Gifford,
> We'll be prepared to meet it. In the mean while,
> The King doth ill to throw his royal sceptre
> In the accuser's scale, ere he can know
> How justice shall incline it.
>
> *Giford:*   Our sage prince
> Resents, it may be, less the death of Cassilis,
> Than he is angry that the feud should burn,
> After his royal voice had said, "Be quench'd:"
> Thus urging prosecution less for slaughter,
> Than that, being done against the King's command,
> Treason is mix'd with homicide. (2.1)

15. Even though the original version of *Devorgoil* (entitled *The Fortunes of Devorgoil*) was written prior to *Auchindrane*, I place it last here as a comic counterpoint to Scott's other dramas.

16. In *Macduff's Cross*, Scott, of course, had relied heavily on superstition, and in *Auchindrane*, he had made mild use of the supernatural in the final scenes; but in neither drama did the supernatural play a central role, as historical detail provided the primary context for the values being articulated.

17. Jerome J. McGann, ed., *Lord Byron: The Complete Poetical Works*, vol. 5 (Oxford: The Clarendon Press, 1986).

18. The stage direction helps to clarify this point: "The Women look at each other with anxiety during this speech, which they partly overhear. They both approach OSWALD."

19. I am thinking here, of course, of the fact that Oswald violates the aristocratic code of marrying only into aristocracy and that Flora rejects her mother's choice of a husband for her, following her own heart in pursuing Leonard.

7
Percy Bysshe Shelley's *The Cenci* and the Rhetoric of Tyranny

SUZANNE FERRISS

> *The hand of Vengeance found the Bed*
> *To which the Purple Tyrant fled*
> *The iron hand crushed the Tyrants head*
> *And became a Tyrant in his stead*
> —William Blake, "The Grey Monk"

IN "PROLEGOMENON FOR A THEORY OF ROMANTIC DRAMA," TERENCE HOAGWOOD establishes key defining elements of the genre: "the displacement of revolutionary sociopolitical content" geographically and chronologically, and "metadramatic reflection on the problem of representation itself."[1] Percy Bysshe Shelley's *The Cenci* is, by this definition, exemplary. Shelley's tragedy—based on the Italian Renaissance legend of Count Francesco Cenci—in fact refers to contemporary politics, sending a warning to a Regency society on the brink of succumbing to the revolutionary excesses experienced decades earlier by the French.[2] Shelley's allusions to the French Revolution and to the potential for rebellion in Regency England, however, are tied to references to language.[3] By presenting the corruption of revolutionary rhetoric, as well as action, in the characters of Count Cenci and his daughter, Beatrice, the play simultaneously assesses the poet's power to effect change, whether political or intellectual. Shelley pictures the tyrant as a poet, specifically a dramatic poet, and thus extends his postrevolutionary critique to the image of the poet as "unacknowledged legislator," offered contemporaneously in his political tract, *A Philosophical View of Reform* (1819), and subsequently in his own poetic manifesto, *A Defence of Poetry* (1821). As such, *The Cenci* may more properly be called a *post*revolutionary work, not simply by the date of its composition but because it endorses the ideal of liberation while exhibiting a profound skepticism that it may be achieved through revolution—political or poetic.

Written in 1819 during the hiatus between composing the third and fourth acts of *Prometheus Unbound, The Cenci* shares the former work's preoccupation with the question of liberation, both political and intellectual.[4] In *Prometheus Unbound,* Jupiter's despotic dominion is allied with the government of postrevolutionary France, "a disenchanted nation" where "Blood, like new wine, bubbles within / Till Despair smothers / The struggling World, which slaves and tyrants win" (1.567–77).[5] He acts the tyrant less through physical violence than by enslaving human minds. The challenge to his rule then comes from "Heaven-defying minds" (2.3.39), and his fall not only sparks political but intellectual and artistic liberation. In the "great Republic" (4.533) that results, language becomes "a perpetual Orphic song, / Which rules with Daedal harmony a throng / Of thoughts and forms, which else senseless and shapeless were" (4.415–17).

Not only does *The Cenci* serve as a coda to the idealized image of revolutionary potential presented in *Prometheus Unbound;* it questions the potential for language, especially poetic language, to recuperate revolutionary energy and ideals. In the detailed examination of *The Cenci* that follows, I will demonstrate that Beatrice Cenci's murder of her father, a willed response to the sexual and psychic oppression he has imposed through incestuous assaults, is an unwitting perversion of the revolutionary impulse in politics and, ultimately, in language. Her vengeful assault ironically mirrors that which it seeks to counter, her father's despotism. Her parricide is a postrevolutionary act, tracing the historical narrative of the French Revolution's inevitable decline into violent excesses. In shrouding both Cenci's act of incest and Beatrice's act of parricide in silence, the drama further turns the repressive violence of the Reign of Terror onto language itself, which figures as the underscored presence behind a series of documents evoked in the text and used to pattern its action: Beatrice's petition to the Pope, the ill-timed warrant for Cenci's arrest, and Orsino's incriminating letter to Beatrice. The machinations surrounding the passage of these documents and Beatrice's ambiguous defense at her trial recall the manipulative discourse of the Terror, a form of linguistic tyranny practiced under the guise of revolution. Recognition that language aided, abetted, justified, and finally covered up violent excesses casts doubt on the playwright's own attempts to realize revolution in and through poetic language. The manipulations of language and document in the drama thus call into question the very possibility of poetically restoring revolutionary ideals. The play is in fact a "tragedy of language," making the poet a "cooperative participant in the reconsolidation of oppression."[6]

"Beware! For my revenge / Is as the sealed commission of a king"

Early in the play, Shelley imbues his dramatic portrait of the Renaissance count with contemporary political significance. From the standpoint of the "spirit of the age," the aristocratic libertine is transformed into a self-serving promoter of personal liberty. His opening negotiations with the Pope's representative, Cardinal Camillo, cast the Count as a rebel for repeatedly acting with "perilous impunity" (1.1.6), defying moral authority. Openly contemptuous of the Pope for his willingness to sell dispensation, Cenci even appears to be an anarchic, revolutionary figure, as Curran has noted.[7] The Count acknowledges none of the "checks of other men": "I have no remorse and little fear" (1.1.84–85). Dismissive of external dictates, he follows only his own desire: "I please my senses as I list" (1.1.69). Yet his is a corrupted fulfillment of the Revolutionary credo of personal liberty, one made horrific by the emendation: "And [I] vindicate that right with force or guile" (1.1.69–70). His vow to employ violence in the service of rights echoes the actions of those who violently defied all law to uphold a fraudulent notion of personal liberty.

Shelley further complicates Cenci's image as a debased revolutionary figure in depicting the Count's force as only partly physical. As Cenci himself explains:

> I rarely kill the body which preserves,
> Like a strong prison, the soul within my power,
> Wherein I feed it with the breath of fear
> For hourly pain.
>
> (1.1.114–17)

Cenci seeks to impose psychic torture, rather than merely physical terror, on those who presume to obstruct his pursuit of pleasure. As such, he appears a perverted revolutionary, in both political and moral senses, recalling Edmund Burke's critique of revolutionary license as the "degenerate choice of a vitiated mind."[8]

Fittingly, then, in Shelley's drama the Count's revolutionary perversions assume degraded sexual form as the incestuous assault on his own daughter, a palpable image of psychic and physical domination. As a particularly shocking subversion of moral authority, the Count's rape of his daughter couples revolutionary action and renewed oppression, as Shelley calls on popular associations of the Revolution with sexual immorality, including rape and incest.[9] He traces in Beatrice's rape at her father's hands the oppression imposed on the "body politic" by Louis XVI. In *The Social Contract,* Rousseau had redistributed various attributes of the king's body among the fused individuals or "members" who constituted the general will or the "people." In this altered configuration, the king existed authentically only as the people's enemy. As Carol Blum has noted, "the people fused to form one innocent body, the fatherland, menaced by its archetypal Nemesis incarnate in Louis XVI."[10] So Saint-Just proclaimed, "He forced his way into the bowels of the Fatherland with blows of his sword in order to hide himself inside"; "the body of the fatherland, passive and patient in its innocence, had been violated by the aggression of the hated stranger."[11]

In his image of Beatrice as object of this invasive violation, Shelley alters Saint-Just's formulation, figuring the body politic as female.[12] The Count's rape of Beatrice, combined with his verbal and physical abuse of his wife, Lucretia, thus invokes another staple of Revolutionary mythology: the rape of Lucretia. Cenci's violence allies itself with the sexual transgression credited with toppling the Tarquin kings and ushering in the Roman Republic. The Roman myth, immensely popular during the Revolutionary period in France, similarly yokes political and domestic tyranny. Tarquin's rape of Lucretia mirrors his father's oppressive policies.[13] In his dramatic portrait of rape in *The Cenci,* Shelley ironically invokes Revolutionary imagery of the body politic and its violation to highlight the political movement failure. He represents Cenci, the perverted revolutionary, as imposing terroristic violence that echoes and rivals monarchist oppression. His incestuous assault springs simultaneously then from the "vitiated mind" of revolutionary excess criticized by Burke and what his opponent, Thomas Paine, termed the "degraded mind that existed before the Revolution, and which the Revolution is calculated to reform."[14] in Mary Wollstonecraft's paradoxical formulation, Cenci's is "the despotism of licentious freedom."[15]

Significantly, the Count's violence, the product of his doubly dissolute thought, takes shape not in physical form but in language. Though never overtly mentioned, the radically oppressive act of Cenci's incestuous assault does reveal itself in his discourse. The Count's voiced *threat* to violate Beatrice is enough to unhinge her: to Lucretia's question, "What did your father do or say to you?" (2.1.59), Beatrice replies, "It was one word, Mother, one little word" (2.1.63). The oppressive effects of Cenci's verbal threat recall his earlier claim that, like the king, he wields the *lettre de cachet:* after learning of the accidental deaths of his two sons, he warns the remaining members of his family, "Beware! For my revenge / Is as the sealed commission of a king / That kills, and none dare name the murderer" (1.3.96–98). In this reference to the sealed letter, which served as a warrant for arbitrary arrest and imprisonment prior to the Revolution, Shelley further overlays Cenci's rebellion with the political tyranny of eighteenth-century monarchist France. In his portrait of Cenci, the British playwright conflates the rebel and the monarch, presenting the revolutionary figure as tyrannical agent, yoking violence to the arbitrary and manipulative uses of language. Cenci and others of his kind employ a "rhetoric of tyranny" (*Queen Mab, Works,* 1:5.121). The Count guards his despotic power by using language as his shield.

Employing words as weapons of oppression, Cenci also serves as a depraved image of the poet. As Curran has argued, "the Count is an artist, conscious of his every effect."[16] Paradoxically, however, his creation is his tyranny: Cenci speaks of his revenge as an "invention" (1.1.99), as a product of his "fancy." He boasts to Camillo: "Any design my captious fancy makes / The picture of its wish, and it forms none / But such as men like you would start to know" (1.1.87–89). Shelley pictures the Count as a *literary* creator: Camillo accuses Cenci of having written "shame and misery" on the faces of his family (1.1.41–42). More tellingly still, the events depicted in Shelley's drama appear as Cenci's invention. He is a "corrupt dramatic poet," according to Ronald Lemoncelli, plotting his family's ruin:

> One, two;
> Aye . . . Rocco and Christofano my curse
> Strangled: and Giacomo, I think, will find
> Life a worse Hell than that beyond the grave:
> Beatrice shall, if there be skill in hate
> Die in despair, blaspheming: to Bernardo,
> He is so innocent, I will bequeath
> The memory of these deeds, and make his youth
> The sepulchre of hope, where evil thoughts
> Shall grow like weeds on a neglected tomb.
>
> (4.1.45–54)

The remainder of the drama brings Cenci's invention to life: Giacomo suffers real torture on the rack and psychological torture in confessing his part in Beatrice's plan to murder their father; Beatrice's claim that she was fulfilling God's will in murdering her father appears impiously false at her trial and leads to her execution; and Bernardo not only witnesses Beatrice's execution but will forever bear the legacy of his infamous family in his name, "an inheritance to strip / Its wearer bare as infamy" (4.1.61–62). Even Beatrice's parricide fulfills Cenci's vision: "she shall die unshrived and unforgiven, / A rebel to her father and her God" (4.1.89–90). In this way, Shelley's portrait of Cenci as a decidedly literary creator, and more specifically, as a dramatic poet, has profound implications for his contention elsewhere that poets are "the unacknowledged legislators of the world" (*A Philosophical View of Reform, Works*, 7:20; *A Defence of Poetry*, 508).

In fact, Shelley's portrait of the Count as a corrupted literary artist and failed revolutionary undermines his own comments about the poet's revolutionary role in his political essays. Cenci's boast that his fancy produces radically unfamiliar visions, images other men "would start to know" (1.1.89), appears gruesomely ironic when compared with Shelley's comment on poetry's ethical potential in his *Defence*. There he argues that "the great instrument of moral good is the imagination" (488).[17] Poetry, as "the expression of the imagination" (480), especially "strengthens that faculty which is the organ of the moral nature of man" (488):

> It awakens and enlarges the mind itself by rendering it the receptacle of a thousand unapprehended combinations of thought. Poetry lifts the veil from the hidden beauty of the world, and makes familiar objects be as if they were not familiar; it reproduces all that it represents, and the impersonations clothed in its Elysian light stand thenceforward in the minds of those who have once contemplated them, as memorials of that gentle and exalted content which extends itself over all thoughts and actions with which it coexists. (487)

But Cenci can imagine what the decorous poet finds "unspeakable": his unnatural creation of incest and parricide undermines this idealized image of poetry as Elysian visions. The dissolute products of his vitiated and degraded mind pervert both political and literary revolution.

"A child's prone mind"

Initially, Beatrice retaliates against the Count's dual corruption of the revolutionary impulse. Silenced by Cenci's rhetoric of tyranny, she first attempts to voice her oppression through her former suitor, Orsino. In her earliest appearance, she entrusts Orsino with a petition to the Pope requesting intervention from Rome. Shelley pictures Beatrice's spurned lover as an untrustworthy "deliverer," for Orsino arbitrarily decides *not* to present Beatrice's "eloquent petition" (1.2.68) to the Pope, fearing the Pope will marry Beatrice to another to get her away from her father. Like Cenci, Orsino deliberately bypasses the Pope's authority, manipulating the course of Beatrice's letter to realize his own desires. He exploits the potential of correspondence, like revolutionary energy, to evade control, though only to enforce his own power over Beatrice. Aptly, then, Orsino's machinations over the petition are confounded with Cenci's oppression: Beatrice mistakes the approaching steps of Orsino's servant, who bears the unopened petition, for Cenci's. She feels her father's threat just as she learns she has failed to extricate herself from his grasp. Orsino's diversion of the petition and Cenci's incestuous assault are both attempts to safeguard despotic designs by silencing Beatrice.

Consequently, Beatrice's public plea for aid against her father's oppression appears as an attempt to appropriate speech and to silence her father; hers is an ideal revolutionary subversion of his (and Orsino's) linguistic tyranny. Beatrice pleads,

> I do entreat you, go not, noble guests;
> What although tyranny, and impious hate
> Stand sheltered by a father's hoary hair?
> What, if 'tis he who clothed us in these limbs
> Who tortures them, and triumphs? What, if we,
> The desolate and the dead, were his own flesh,
> His children and his wife, whom he is bound
> To love and shelter? Shall we therefore find
> No refuge in this merciless wide world?
>
> (1.3.99–107)

Her repeated questions counter the decisive certainties of Cenci's threat. The anaphora of Beatrice's questions, "What" and "What, if" further underscores the movement of her remarks from statement of fact to supposition. Her exposé of Cenci's domestic violence takes the form of speculation rather than direct accusation: "What, if we . . . were his own flesh, / His children and his wife?" In this nearly absurd contradiction of fact, Beatrice at once reveals Cenci's horrific designs and veils her charge under the cloak of fiction.

She makes a similarly subversive assault against her father's oppression in asking the guests to envision empathetically the events that have provoked her outburst: "Oh, think what deep wrongs must have blotted out / First love, then reverence in a child's prone mind / Till it thus vanquish shame and fear! O think!" (1.3.108–10). The crescendo produced by the repeated imperative, "O, think!" gives way as Beatrice begins a more constrained listing of her efforts to find release from Cenci's tyranny:

> I have borne much, and kissed the sacred hand
> Which crushed us to the earth, and thought its stroke
> Was perhaps some paternal chastisement!
> Have excused much, doubted; and when no doubt
> Remained, have sought by patience, love and tears
> To soften him, and when this could not be
> I have knelt down through the long sleepless nights
> And lifted up to God, the father of all,
> Passionate prayers: and when these were not heard
> I have still borne . . .
>
> (1.3.111–20)

The rhythmic catalog of Beatrice's endeavors, marked by "have" ("have borne," "have excused," "have sought," "have knelt"), not only establishes her stoicism but, by opposition, reveals the extent of Cenci's libertine oppression. In her emendation—"until I meet you here, / Princes and kinsmen, at this hideous feast" (1.3.120–21)—she cleverly places all responsibility for her release from both forms of endurance onto others.

But Beatrice's pleas go unheeded, because the men she exhorts for help are simply more representatives of paternal tyranny. From the perspective of linguistic and legislative order, her speech appears the product of a "wild girl" (1.3.132), an "insane girl" (1.3.160), just as the uncontained and uncontainable Revolution had appeared to conservatives as "a madman, who has escaped from the protecting restraint and wholesome darkness of his cell."[18] As the Revolution had appeared to its critics as a perversion of thought, so Beatrice's discourse appears a distortion of thought's expression. As a subversive assault on the sociosymbolic law of the father, Beatrice's plea remains unacknowledged and uncomprehended.[19]

In the final moments of her speech, however, Beatrice retreats from her subversive stance and directly attacks her father. She issues a series of commands to Cenci: "Retire thou, impious man! Aye hide thyself" (1.3.146), "Frown not on me" (1.3.151), "Cover thy face from every living eye" (1.3.154), "Seek out some dark and silent corner" (1.3.157), "Bow thy white head before offended God" (1.3.157). This string of imperatives, borrowed at once from the language of religious exorcism and political propaganda, bears traces of force and so subverts her earlier revolutionary stance—in both political and poetic terms. Beatrice rejects the revolutionary possibility of language to confront the rhetoric of tyranny and in so doing fails as an artist, as well as a revolutionary. She appropriates the speech of linguistic tyranny and joins Cenci in doubly corrupting the revolutionary impulse.

Employing the rhetoric of tyranny herself, Beatrice silences Cenci. Accosting her after the banquet, the Count admits that "inarticulate words / Fell from [his] lips" (2.1.112–13), that his daughter had struck him "dumb" (2.1.119). Cenci resorts to actual violence in response to her challenge to his own rebellious designs. He again relegates Beatrice to silence, making her the object of his discourse and not the subject of her own.

He succeeds, at least temporarily, in subjecting and silencing Beatrice. Ellipses mark each of her attempts to describe Cenci's assault: "I imagined . . . no, it cannot be!" (3.1.50); "never fancy imaged such a deed / As" (3.1.55–56). She can neither imagine nor name the deed that has transformed her:

> What are the words which you would have me speak?
> I, who can feign no image in my mind
> Of that which has transformed me. I, whose thought
> Is like a ghost shrouded and folded up
> In its own formless horror. Of all words,
> That minister to mortal intercourse,
> Which wouldst thou hear? For there is none to tell
> My misery: if another ever knew
> Aught like to it, she died as I will die,
> And left it, as I must, without a name.
> (3.1.107–116)

Not only does Beatrice lack a name for Cenci's act; she feels stripped of her own: "Oh, what am I? / What name, what place, what memory shall be mine?" (3.1.74–75). She associates formlessness of thought and silence with death, suggesting that "without a name" she will be placeless and remain exiled from humanity, metaphorically and literally. She recognizes that she can achieve relief only by naming the crime she has suffered and her assailant:

> If I could find a word that might make known
> The crime of my destroyer; and that done
> My tongue should like a knife tear out the secret
> Which cankers my heart's core. . . .
> (3.1.154–57)

She would secure "assured redress" (3.1.166) by attaching a word to Cenci's deed. Instead, Beatrice cannily employs silence to seek revenge against her father, turning the knife not toward her own heart but his.

Beatrice vows that "something must be done" (3.1.86). Her unnamed deed threatens at once the law of language and the law of the courts; she will reverse even "nature's law" (3.1.334). She argues,

> In this mortal world
> There is no vindication and no law
> Which can adjudge and execute the doom
> Of that through which I suffer.
>
> (3.1.134–37)

But in bypassing the law, as Cenci's self-appointed judge and executioner, Beatrice acts much like her father. She similarly evades all external authority in pursuing her rebellious designs. Like the agents of the Terror, she justifies suspending the law in the name of revolutionary action. She appeals to a higher law, one outside the reach of men: "The crimes which mortal tongue dare never name / God therefore scruples to avenge" (4.4.128–29). As Cenci had earlier attributed the fortuitous deaths of his sons to God's agency, Beatrice argues that Cenci's death is God's will. She claims that Marzio, the assassin she hires, commits "a high and holy deed" (4.2.35), acting as "a weapon in the hand of God / To a just use" (4.3.54–55).

Beatrice's parricidal designs, then, represent a retreat from the revolutionary stance upheld in her banquet speech. Not only does she betray the revolutionary potential of language; she disavows it entirely. As the revolutionary impulse is transferred from language to physical action, it is corrupted. Her parricide marks a descent into physical violence, an embodiment of the implied violence contained in her verbal threats against Cenci. Barbara Groseclose asserts that "if parent-child incest is symbolic of tyrannical oppression, then the parricide must represent the possibility of eliminating tyranny through violence,"[20] but Beatrice's act in fact debases the revolutionary impulse, for it, too, is a tyrannical instance of oppressive force. Marjean Purinton has convincingly argued that Beatrice remains trapped within the same binary pattern of thinking that grounds all oppressive relationships.[21] Moreover, her murder of her father clearly invokes popular representations of revolutionary action as "a kind of oedipal killing of the old, paternal régime."[22] Such references to the political parricide committed by the French were by no means positive, however, and instead meant to censure the French for their excessive use of violence, as Burke does when he upbraids "those children of their country who are prompt rashly to hack that aged parent in pieces."[23] Beatrice's attempts to veil her parricide in discourse invoking patriarchal authority, here God's, only compounds its violence. Like her father and Orsino, she, at least temporarily, uses language as a defensive and repressive structure to defend rebellious action.

"O blood, which art my father's blood, / Circling through these contaminated veins"

The warrant for Cenci's arrest is central to Shelley's drama and to interpretations of Beatrice's act of violence against her father. Stuart Sperry identifies the arrival of the warrant for Cenci's arrest and execution only moments after the Count's murder as the most obvious and dramatic piece of irony in the play, and its crux.[24] The arrest warrant assumes added importance when read in comparison to Beatrice's petition, for, unlike the petition, the arrest warrant is not diverted. It makes an untimely appearance, but it does arrive at its appointed destination. Beatrice's parricide, however, obviates its effects. She usurps its power to pass sentence against her father. Although Curran initially argues that Savella's arrival with the warrant is the sole instance in the play that suggests Beatrice had no need to take justice into her own hands, he later rejects this reading: Cenci is "ordered killed by the irrational command of a capricious tyrant who had refused aid to the distraught family"; Beatrice could not rationally expect help from the Pope, and the sudden arrival of Savella with the warrant "does not at all obviate the imperative by which Beatrice murders the Count."[25] And although Curran rightly alludes to Orsino's diversion of the petition and its disastrous effects on subsequent events, he overlooks the implications of Beatrice's equally arbitrary use of power. For as Ronald Tetreault argues, "By taking revenge and killing her father, she usurps the paternal power of the state and of God, playing out a hubris which is a tragic reflection of her father's megalomania."[26] Viewed in the wake of the warrant's arrival, Beatrice's parricide appears as an arbitrary usurpation of the warrant's power to submit Cenci to judgment, as an uncanny echo of her father's own boast that his revenge "is as the sealed commission of a king / That kills" (1.3.97–98). Tragically and ironically, it is *Beatrice*, and not Cenci, who now appears to wield the *lettre de cachet*.[27]

The Count's incestuous assault becomes a metaphor for Beatrice's corruption and for the perversion of the revolutionary impulse. In his earlier political essays, Shelley, like Mary Wollstonecraft, repeatedly describes tyranny and oppression in terms of infection and disease.[28] In the incomplete "Essay on Christianity," he argues that "the whole frame of human things is infected by the insidious poison. Hence it is that man is blind in his understanding, corrupt in his moral sense, and diseased in his physical functions" (*Works*, 6: 249–50). In *A Philosophical View of Reform*, he laments the "contaminating tyrannies" spreading through Europe (*Works*, 7: 11) like a "social disease" (*Works*, 7: 51). But Shelley's comments also partake of the imagery of disease and overmedication applied by the Revolution's critics: Burke writes that the Revolution is an "opiate of amnesty," a "distemper of remedy," and an "unnecessary physic," or else a "plague" that necessitates "quarantine."[29]

In *The Cenci*, Shelley similarly envisions incest as a contagion, a palpable transference of the Count's oppressive power. It is at once a "clinging, black, contaminating mist" (3.1.17), "poisoning / The subtle, pure, and inmost spirit of life" (3.1.22–23) and the blood passing within her body, as Beatrice imagines her father's presence within her: "O blood, which art my father's blood, / Circling through these contaminated veins" (3.1.95–96). The product of their mingling fluids becomes the child of Cenci's curse:

> That if she ever have a child; . . .
> . . . May it be
> A hideous likeness of herself, that as
> From a distorting mirror, she may see
> Her image mixed with what she most abhors,
> Smiling upon her from her nursing breast.
>
> (4.1.141–49)

The child produced is Beatrice herself, contaminated and distorted by Cenci's oppression. As her father had earlier predicted, "what she most abhors / Shall have a fascination to entrap / Her loathing will" (4.1.85–87). She falls prey to the temptation to challenge Cenci's tyranny with a still more radical violence and so becomes a product of "what she most abhors," her father's despotism.

Shelley's use of "child" here gives his portrait of Cenci's offspring added political relevance. In "An Address to the People on the Death of Princess Charlotte," he had argued that the "child" produced by "misrule" is anarchy, the "enemy of freedom," and "the last flash before despotism" (*Works*, 6: 79). As William Keach explains, "For Shelley, anarchy is . . . a deadening, perverted disorder that takes the form of authoritarian rule."[30] The legacy of revolutionary disorder, then, is renewed oppression. Shelley's formulation echoes at once William Godwin's maxim that "revolution is engendered by an indignation against tyranny, yet is itself evermore pregnant with tyranny" and Burke's vision (as Steven Blakemore describes) of "revolutionary forces unleashing an excremental sexuality, deluging Europe with a revolutionary offspring that is illegitimate and unnatural."[31] In political terms, Beatrice's vengeful assault, the offspring of Cenci's violence, ironically appears as a mirror-image of that which it seeks to counter, her father's despotism. Her action is reflected in the distorted mirror of revolution and liberty held up by Cenci.

In *A Philosophical View of Reform*, Shelley pictures poets and philosophers as "mirrors of gigantic shadows which futurity casts upon the present" (*Works*, 7: 20). And in his *Defence*, he argues, "poetry is a mirror which makes beautiful that which is distorted," unlike prose, which as "the story of particular facts is as a mirror which obscures and distorts that which should be beautiful" (p. 485). In *The Cenci*, however, the mirror distorts: Cenci envisions the child of his incestuous coupling with Beatrice as "a hideous likeness of herself," as an image seen from "a distorting mirror" (4.1.146–47). Beatrice's tragedy is that she unwittingly becomes the image of her father. She assumes his art and his artfulness, similarly perverting the revolutionary possibility of poetic language.

"This bloody knife / With my own name engraven on the heft"

Aptly, then, Beatrice's speeches at her trial betray the extent of her corruption by Cenci. The "contaminating mist" of their incestuous coupling becomes an "undistinguishable mist / Of thoughts" (3.1.170–71) and words. Beatrice immediately announces the change: "—My brain is hurt; / My eyes are full of blood; . . . / I see but indistinctly" (3.1.1–3). She describes profound psychic effects; most significantly, her vision has been altered. In Shelley's drama, the change registered itself in Beatrice's perception of events. As Laurence S. Lockridge notes, "following the rape she begins to speak in a way that reveals her own moral contamination. She has absorbed her oppressor's poison."[32] Camillo's declaration that "She is as pure as speechless infancy!" (5.2.69) becomes an ironic commentary on Beatrice's efforts to defend herself, for she slyly twists words to deny her father and, in turn, reject the charge of parricide. She argues, "I have no father" (3.1.40) and, therefore, "'Tis most false / That I am guilty of foul parricide" (4.4.145–46). If she has no father, then she cannot have murdered him. Her manipulation of language to cast guilt on the man who was following her orders, even if this manipulation is unconscious, contradicts her bid for clemency:

> My Lords, if by my nature I had been
> So stern, as to have planned the crime alleged,
> Which your suspicions dictate to this slave,
> And the rack makes him utter, do you think
> I should have left this two edged instrument
> Of my misdeed; this man, this bloody knife
> With my own name engraven on the heft,
> Lying unsheathed amid' a world of foes,
> For my own death? That with such horrible need
> For deepest silence, I should have neglected
> So trivial a precaution, as the making
> His tomb the keeper of a secret written
> On a thief's memory?
>
> (5.2.93–105)

Beatrice's outright denial of Marzio as her agent in Cenci's death badly contradicts events depicted in Shelley's drama and reveals the full extent of her corruption.

The terms of her denial, moreover, undermine her defense. For Beatrice's description of Marzio as a "two edged instrument" of her misdeed recalls her earlier claim that the world is a "two-edge lie, / Which seems, but is not" (4.4.115–16). The phrase she used earlier to describe patriarchal oppression now characterizes her own claims of innocence. Her image of Marzio as a "bloody knife" ironically echoes her earlier depiction of him as "a weapon in the hand of God / To a just use" (4.4.54–55). In place of God's hand, though, we find her signature: the bloody knife carries her "own name engraven on the heft." Wielding ambiguous formulations as her own weapon, Beatrice simultaneously admits to and denies "arming" Marzio. She addresses him in the discourse of the Terror, which Mme. de Staël had described as "speeches sharp as daggers, that held death in every word":[33]

> . . . art thou the accuser? . . .
> If thou hast done murders, made thy life's path
> Over the trampled laws of God and man,
> Rush not before thy Judge, and say: "My maker,
> I have done this and more; for there was one
> Who was most pure and innocent on earth;
> And because she endured what never any
> Guilty or innocent endured before:
> Because her wrongs could not be told, not thought;

> Because thy hand at length did rescue her;
> I with my words killed her and all her kin."
>
> (5.2.131–43)

While accusing Marzio herself, Beatrice skillfully makes Marzio *her* unjust accuser. She voices Marzio's confession only to cast guilt on him for putting "words" to "her wrongs," the doubly silenced incestuous and patricidal assaults.

She speaks for him, just as the incriminating letter sent to her by Orsino (bequeathing Marzio and his accomplice Olympio to her service in Giacomo's name) had earlier spoken her guilt for her (3.2.71–73). Shelley transforms the note that was, in the historical account, Beatrice's note to Orsino, changing it to *his* letter to *her:* "She ordered them [Olympio and Marzio] to repair to Monsignore Guerra with a note, in which they were desired to murder Francesco, in consideration of a reward of a thousand crowns" ("Relation of the Death of the Family Cenci," *Works,* 2:161). Although in the "Relation" manuscript a bloodstained sheet betrayed Beatrice and Lucretia, in Shelley's drama Orsino, or more specifically his letter, reveals their culpability. Beatrice appears still victimized by the rhetoric of tyranny, as Orsino's lines speak *for* her:

> "To the Lady Beatrice.
> That the atonement of what my nature
> Sickens to conjecture may soon arrive,
> I send thee, at thy brother's desire, those
> Who will speak and do more than I dare
> Write. . . .
>   Thy devoted servant, Orsino."
>
> (4.4.90 – 095)

Ironically, his conspiratorial silence identifies Beatrice as the plot's author.

The letter's introduction itself provides Beatrice with another opportunity to exploit the ambiguous nature of accusation and become an oppressor herself through speech. To the judge's question, "Know you this paper, Lady?" (5.3.171), Beatrice replies:

> Entrap me not with questions. Who stands here
> As my accuser? Ha! wilt thou be he,
> Who art my judge? Accuser, witness, judge,
> What, all in one? Here is Orsino's name;
> What is Orsino? Let his eye meet mine.
> What means this scrawl? Alas! ye know not what,

> And therefore on the chance that it may be
> Some evil, will ye kill us?
>
> (5.3.171–79)

Beatrice demands that the incriminating signature be verified by Orsino's presence, for she recognizes that "this scrawl" bears dubious significance at best. She craftily exploits the potential ambiguity of language to effect the desired execution of their enemy while abdicating all responsibility. To the question, "Art thou guilty of thy father's death?" Beatrice counters that the judge has himself invented the crime, that he has "called" it her father's death (5.3.83), and sidesteps the charge:

> Which is or is not what men call a crime,
> Which either I have done, or have not done;
> Say what ye will. I shall deny no more.
> If ye desire it thus, thus let it be,
> And so an end of all. Now do your will;
> No other pains shall force another word.
>
> (5.3.84–89)

Beatrice again turns the accusation against another and again her deliberately ambiguous response resists formulation. As the judge recognizes, "She is convicted, but has not confessed" (5.3.90). Retreating into silence once again, she challenges others to read events as they will and invites them to interpret her acts. Thus, Beatrice comes full circle, accusing her accusers of linguistic tyranny while exploiting its devices herself: "Beatrice ironically submits to Cenci's despotism by using his terrorizing tactics and by employing language to deceive herself and others. She, in effect, becomes a moral and poetical tyrant."[34]

Again her discursive manipulations contradict the image of poetic revolution and legislation offered in *A Philosophical View of Reform* and *A Defence of Poetry*. As Shelley argues in his *Defence*, "Poetry cannot be made subservient. Poetry is a sword of lightning, ever unsheathed, which consumes the scabbard that would contain it" (491). By contrast, Beatrice's image of Marzio as a "bloody knife / With my own name engraven on the heft, / Lying unsheathed amid's a world of foes" (5.2.98–100) allies her parricide and poetic creation as postrevolutionary acts, images of revolutionary ideals perverted and corrupted.

I do not mean to suggest that Shelley completely denigrates the potential of poetry to effect change but that he complicates the issue in his graphic presentation of the poet's difficulties through the characters of Cenci and Beatrice. Just as Beatrice becomes an unwitting reflection of her father, and revolutionary action a distorted image of tyrannical oppression, so the aesthetic revolution risks mirroring linguistic tyranny. Shelley's portraits of literary creation in *The Cenci* underscore the dangerous possibility that actions, filtered through the prism of a discredited, postrevolutionary language, may become distorted. More generally still, Shelley's invention of a series of misdirected documents—Beatrice's petition, Orsino's letter, the Pope's arrest warrant—highlights the potential of words, including those of the poet, to mislead. If (as Dawson has remarked) "the spirit of poetry must incarnate itself in the letter,"[35] then the poet's expression is itself subject to distortion.

What *The Cenci* demonstrates through the palpable image of incestuous rape is the contamination of revolution by that which it seeks to overturn. The example of Robespierre and the Terror had demonstrated that political revolution perpetuated oppression. With the added example of Napoleon before him, that "minister" of "Treason, Slavery, Rapine, Fear, and Lust" ("Feelings of a Republican on the Fall of Bonaparte," *Works*, 1: 206), Shelley's denunciation is more radical still. In his political essays, Shelley describes the inevitable turn of revolution toward a renewed despotism, and he employs images strikingly similar to those of *The Cenci*. As he reveals in *A Philosophical View of Reform*, the example of the French Revolution demonstrates the futility of revenge: the oppressed's "desire to wreak revenge, to this extent, in itself a mistake, a crime, a calamity, arose from the same source as their other miseries and errors, and affords an additional proof of the necessity of that long-delayed change which it accompanied and disgraced" (*Works* 7:13). In "On the Punishment of Death," he further argues that "it is sufficiently clear that revenge, retaliation, atonement, expiation, are rule and motives" that do not deserve "a place in any enlightened system of political life" (*Works*, 6: 185). Employing the same terms in his Preface to *The Cenci*, Shelley warns, "revenge, retaliation, atonement, are pernicious mistakes. If Beatrice had thought in this manner she would have been wiser and better" (240).

He adds an important qualification to his apparent condemnation of Beatrice, however. Had she repressed her retributive urge "she would never have been a tragic character: the few whom such an exhibition would have interested could never have been sufficiently interested for a dramatic purpose" (240). Shelley has "a dramatic purpose" in designing his tragedy so his denunciation of Beatrice is incomplete; as we have seen, the drama at once enlists and undermines the audience's sympathy for her cause. His ambivalent portrait of Beatrice echoes, then, the ambivalence about revolution expressed in letters, such as this one, to Elizabeth Hitchener: "Popular insurrection and revolutions I look upon with discountenance; if *such things must be* I will take the side of the People, but my reasonings shall endeavor to ward it from the hearts of the Rulers of the Earth, deeply as I detest them" (*Letters*, 1: 221). He thus directs his reasoning and his tragedy toward fostering an alternative revolution in opinion or a revolution in thought.[36] Shelley offers no positive portrait of revolutionary action—political or aesthetic—within his drama and instead employs drama to demonstrate the need for moral change.

Through the example of Beatrice, Shelley questions the possibility of *any* revolutionary action following the disillusioning example of France. He passes both poetic creation and political revolution through the postrevolutionary prism of his drama. In Beatrice's arbitrary use of violence and, above all, in the discourse she employs to justify and veil this act, *The Cenci* casts doubt on the possibility that the revolutionary ideals betrayed in France by the Terror and Napoleon's rise to power may be recuperated in Regency England either politically or poetically. Her language is decidedly not the "perpetual Orphic song" of the "great Republic" in *Prometheus Unbound*.[37] Instead, the revolutionary potential of both political action and poetic production bear the brunt of Shelley's skepticism in this radical questioning of the legislator's potential to effect positive change, whether functioning as the people's recognized political representative or their "unacknowledged" advocate, the poet.

Notes

1. Terence Allan Hoagwood, "Prolegomenon for a Theory of Romantic Drama," *Wordsworth Circle* 23 (Spring 1992): 49–64.

2. Stephen C. Behrendt argues, "*The Cenci* is a play about revolution, and the insidious combination of circumstances that engender it" ("Beatrice Cenci and the Tragic Myth of History," *History and Myth: Essays on English Romantic Literature*, ed. Stephen C. Behendt [Detroit: Wayne State University Press, 1990], 214).

Rolf P. Lessinich argues that "Shelley's attitude to revolution and tyrannicide was most clearly expressed in *The Cenci*" ("Godwin and Shelley: Rhetoric versus Revolution," *Studia Neophilologica* 47 [1975]: 51), and P. M. S. Dawson that "again and again in his comments on the French Revolution [Shelley] argued that the attempt to overthrow the old order by violent revolution merely perpetuated the spirit of that order, and *The Cenci* was written to prove just that point" (*Unacknowledged Legislator: Shelley and Politics* [Oxford: Clarendon, 1980], 6). Hoagwood identifies the poet's own citation of lines from *The Cenci* in a letter discussing the Manchester massacre as evidence that "his poetic work and his political interests and activities condition and reflect one another" (*Skepticism and Ideology: Shelley's Political*

Prose and its Philosophical Context from Bacon to Marx [Iowa City: University of Iowa Press, 1988], 164). For Shelley's thoughts on revolution, also see Hoagwood's more recent *Politics, Philosophy, and the Production of Romantic Texts* (DeKalb: Illinois. Northern Illinois Press, 1996), 57–58.

For a thorough investigation of the Italian origins of the text, see Alan M. Weinberg, *Shelley's Italian Experience* (New York: St. Martin's Press, 1991), 71–100.

3. On the linguistic preoccupation of the drama and representations of language in the play, see Michael Worton, "Speech and Silence in *The Cenci*" in *Essays on Shelley*, ed. Miriam Allott (Totowa, N.J.: Barnes and Nobles, 1982), pp. 105–24; Anne McWhir, "The Light and the Knife: Ab/Using Language in *The Cenci*," *Keats-Shelley Journal* 38 (1989): 145–61; Michael O'Neill, *The Human Mind's Imaginings: Conflict and Achievement in Shelley's Poetry* (Oxford: Clarendon Press, 1989); and Stuart Peterfreund, "Seduced by Metonymy: Figuration and Authority in *The Cenci*," *The New Shelley: Later Twentieth-Century Views*, ed. G. Kim Blank (New York: St. Martin's Press, 1991), 184–203.

4. Stuart Curran, *Shelley's Annus Mirabilis: The Maturing of an Epic Vision* (San Marino, Calif: Huntington Library, 1975), 121.

5. Unless otherwise indicated, all references to Shelley's poetry and prose are to *Shelley's Poetry and Prose*, eds. Donald H. Reiman and Sharon B. Powers (New York: W. W. Norton and Company, 1977). References to works not included in this edition are to *The Complete works of Percy Bysshe Shelley*, eds. Roger Ingpen and Walter E. Peck (1926–30; reprinted, New York: Gordian Press, 1965), abbreviated as *Works* followed by individual volume and page number where appropriate. For Shelley's letters and notebooks I refer to *The Letters of Percy Bysshe Shelley*, ed. Frederick L. Jones, 2 vols. (Oxford: Clarendon, 1964); and *Notebooks of Percy Bysshe Shelley* vol. 2 (New York: Phaeton Press, 1968), hereafter *Letters* and *Notebooks*, respectively.

6. William A. Ulmer, *Shelleyan Eros: The Rhetoric of Romantic Love* (Princeton: Princeton University Press, 1990), 127.

7. Stuart Curran, *Shelley's* The Cenci: *Scorpions Ringed with Fire* (Princeton: Princeton University Press, 1970), 75.

8. Edmund Burke, *Reflections on the Revolution in France* (New York: Bobbs-Merrill, 1955),p. 77.

9. See Peter Brooks, "The Revolutionary Body," in *Fictions of the French Revolution*, ed. Bernadette Fort (Evanston, Ill: Northwestern University Press, 1991), 39. Brooks notes that during Marie-Antoinette's trial her crimes against the Republic were allied with charges of sexual immorality, including incestuous relations with her son, the Dauphin. Brooks further points out that in Jacobin rhetoric Old Régime rulers were denounced for their sexual immorality as well as their tyranny (42).

10. Carol Blum, *Rousseau and the Republic of Virtue: The Language of Politics in the French Revolution* (Ithaca: Cornell University Press, 1986), 179. For a brief survey of traditional definitions of the "body politic," see John O'Neill, *Five Bodies: The Human Shape of Modern Society* (Ithaca: Cornell University Press, 1985), 68–72. On the French Revolution's redefinition of the "body politic," see Dorinda Outram, *The Body and the French Revolution: Sex, Class, and Political Culture* (New Haven: Yale University Press, 1989).

11. Quoted in Blum, *Rousseau and the Republic of Virtue*, 180.

12. Shelley thus invokes Revolutionary symbolism; imagery for the Republic was typically represented as female. See Maurice Agulhon, *Marianne into Battle* (Cambridge: Harvard University Press, 1981); and Lynn Hunt, *Politics, Class and Culture in the French Revolution* (Berkeley and Los Angeles: University of California Press,

1984). Shelley was also undoubtedly influenced by early English fears of the Revolution, for, as David Punter has argued, among British authors "some of the fears that well up through the responses to 1789 are of sexual violation" and "some of the popular poetry of the period refers to Britain as female, and suggests that the unloosed virility of the Jacobins is about to pose a threat to social and sexual integrity" ("1789: The Sex of Revolutions," *Criticism* 24 [Summer 1982]: 213).

13. See Ian Donaldson, *The Rapes of Lucretia: A Myth and Its Transformations* (Oxford: Clarendon, 1982), 105–9.

14. Thomas Paine, *Rights of Man* (New York: Penguin, 1984), 59.

15. Mary Wollstonecraft, *An Historical and Moral View of the Origin and Progress of the French Revolution and the Effect It Has Produced in Europe,* in *A Wollstonecraft Anthology,* ed. Janet Todd (New York: Columbia University Press, 1989), 132.

16. Curran, *Shelley's* The Cenci, 73. Elise M. Gold notes Cenci's "aesthetic tyranny" but overlooks the decidedly *dramatic* character of Cenci's aesthetics ("*King Lear* and Aesthetic Tyranny in Shelley's *The Cenci, Swellfoot the Tyrant,* and *The Witch of Atlas,*" *English Language Notes* 24 [September 1986]: 59). McWhir does argue that Cenci acts as "the playwright of a drama in which he is also an actor" ("The Light and the Knife," 153) and Ronald L. Lemoncelli that Cenci is a corrupt dramatic poet and that he resembles the description of this specific type of poet in the *Defence* ("Cenci as Corrupt Dramatic Poet," *English Language Notes* 16 [December 1978]: 103–17). Both, however, downplay the implications of this insight for Shelley's own creation in *The Cenci.*

17. Although *A Defence of Poetry* was written nineteenth months after *The Cenci* (February–March 1821), the two works may still reasonably be compared for, as Lemoncelli has argued, "in the *Defence* Shelley used many of the same ideas, and sometimes the same key words, as Cenci uses in creating and performing his drama. Since the *Defence* is an empirical and cumulative statement of Shelley's aesthetics, it often repeats ideas, words, and phrases from Shelley's earlier works" ("Cenci as Corrupt Dramatic Poet," 106).

18. Burke, *Reflections,* 8.

19. Even before Lacan's "law of the Father" captured the critical imagination, commentators have focused on *The Cenci* as an indictment of patriarchy. See Eugene R. Hammond, "Beatrice's Three Fathers: Successive Betrayal in Shelley's *The Cenci,*" *Essays in Literature* 8 (1981): 25–32, and Jerrold E. Hogle, *Shelley's Process: Radical Transference and the Development of His Major Works* (New York: Oxford University Press, 1988), 147–62.

20. Barbara Groseclose, "The Incest Motif in Shelley's The Cenci," *Comparative Drama* 19 (1985): 230.

21. Marjean Purinton, *Romantic Ideology Unmasked: The Mentally Constructed Tyrannies in Dramas of William Wordsworth, Lord Byron, Percy Shelley, and Joanna Baillie* (Newark: University of Delaware Press, 1994), 96.

22. Steven Blakemore, *Burke and the Fall of Language: The French Revolution as a Linguistic Event* (Hanover, N.H.: University Press of New England, 1988), 43. Burke argues that, according to the French revolutionaries, "Regicide, and parricide, and sacrilege are but fictions of superstition, corrupting jurisprudence by destroying its simplicity. The murder of a king, or a queen, or a bishop, or a father are only common homicide; and if the people are by any chance or in any way gainers by it, a sort of homicide much the most pardonable, and into which we ought not to make too severe a scrutiny. On the scheme of this barbarous philosophy, which is the offspring of cold hearts and muddy understandings, and which is as void of solid wisdom as it is destitute of all taste and elegance, laws are to be supported

only by their own terrors and by the concern that each individual may find in them from his own private speculations or can spare to them from his own private interests" (*Reflections*, 87–88).

23. Burke, *Reflections*, 109.

24. Stuart Sperry, "The Ethical Politics of Shelley's *The Cenci*," *Studies in Romanticism* 25 (1986): 416.

25. Curran, *Shelley's* The Cenci, 142–43.

26. Ronald Tetreault, *The Poetry of Life: Shelley and Literary Form* (Toronto: University of Toronto Press, 1987), 132. Compare Tetreault's remarks with Sperry's contention that we cannot "escape the irony that in the end she becomes her father's child in a way she was not at the outset of the play. . . . The fact that at the last she is unwilling or unable to see the way she has been in fact perverted only makes the essence of her tragedy the more compelling" ("Ethical Politics," 422).

27. Stephen Behrendt, *Shelley and His Audiences* (Lincoln: University of Nebraska Press, 1989), 155.

28. See Mary Wollstonecraft, *An Historical and Moral View*, pp. 139–44. In her *Journals*, Mary Shelley makes frequent references to Shelley's reading of Wollstonecraft; he was especially influenced by *An Historical and Moral View*, particularly its analysis of revolutionary violence. See Moira Ferguson and Janet Todd, *Mary Wollstonecraft* (Boston: Twayne, 1984), 87.

29. Burke, *Reflections*, 72, 81, 101.

30. William Keach, "Radical Shelley?" *Raritan* 5 (1985): 120–29.

31. William Godwin, *Enquiry Concerning Political Justice* (London: Penguin, 1976), 269; Blakemore, *Burke and the Fall of Language*, 59.

32. Laurence S. Lockridge, "Justice in *The Cenci*," *Wordsworth Circle* 19 (spring 1988): 95–98. Tetreault views Beatrice's manipulations of language more generally as a problem endemic to patriarchy. "What the tragic discourse of Beatrice's world excludes is any alternative to the prevailing ideology of patriarchal power" (*The Poetry of Life*, 132–33). "Having no access to an alternative discourse, Beatrice locks herself into tragedy by embracing the ideology of vengeance embedded in the prison-house of her father's language" (141). Hogle similarly characterizes Cenci's language as patriarchal and argues that Beatrice retreats from a feminine alternative to his discourse and instead mistakenly employs patriarchal rhetoric herself. Tetreault's and Hogle's emphases on sexual politics, however, may obscure the larger implications of Beatrice's language for revolutionary practice.

33. Germaine de Staël, *Considerations on the Main Events of the French Revolution*, in *An Extraordinary Woman: Selected Writings of Germaine de Staël*, ed. Vivian Folkenflik (New York: Columbia University Press, 1987), 367.

34. Gold, "*King Lear* and Aesthetic Tyranny," 63.

35. Dawson, *Unacknowledged Legislator*, 257.

36. Sperry suggests that "in arranging Beatrice before her judges, in forcing us to adjudicate between her lies and their hypocrisy, Shelley places us in an intolerable situation. It is a strategy deliberately contrived to compel us to recognize the bankruptcy of conventional kinds of ethical discrimination, to force upon us the necessity of ascending to a higher level of moral awareness" ("Ethical Politics," 425).

37. Jeffrey N. Cox, *In the Shadows of Romance: Romantic Tragic Drama in Germany, England, and France* (Athens: Ohio University Press, 1987), 160.

Index

Absalom and Achitophel, 86
Aeschylus, 64
Albion, and Evening Advertiser, The, 118, 121, 122, 125
Allen, Woody, 23; *The Purple Rose of Cairo,* 23
Analytical Review, 33, 35, 36
"Anarchists, The," 122
Annual Review, The, 66
Anti-Jacobin, or Weekly Examiner, 86, 122
Anti-Jacobin Review, 74, 86, 88, 89, 90, 103, 104, 119, 122
Antoinette, Marie, 35, 92, 93, 94, 136
Aristophanes, 48; *The Birds,* 48
Association for Preserving Liberty, 86
Ast, Friedrich, 41
Atheista Fulminato, 40
Austen, Jane, 13, 35; *Mansfield Park,* 26, 35; *Sense and Sensibility,* 35

Baillie, Joanna, 16, 26, 28, 30, 31, 32, 40, 47, 63, 64, 72, 183; *Constantine Paleologus,* 16, 28, 31, 32; *DeMonfort,* 30, 40, 47, 48, 50
Balzac, Honoré de, 117
Bartholomew, John, 85, 93; *Fall of the French Monarchy; or, Louis XVI,* 17, 85, 93
Bate, Walter Jackson, 65
Baum, Joan Mandell, 22, 132, 133
Beaumont, Francis, 65, 67, 75
Beauties of the Anti-Jacobean, or Weekly Examiner, 122
Beddoes, Thomas Lovell, 56, 58, 62, 63, 64, 65, 76, 77; *Death's Jest-Book,* 41; *The Letters of Thomas Lovell Beddoes,* 56
Behn, Aphra, 38; *The Rover,* 38
Behrendt, Stephen, 23
Bell, John, 67; *British Theatre,* 67
Bellini, Vincenzo, 117; *I Puritani,* 117

Bindman, David, 93
Birch, Samuel, 16, 36, 38, 44; *The Adopted Child,* 16, 32, 36, 37, 38, 40, 44, 50
Black Dwarf, The, 29, 30
Blackwood's Edinburgh Magazine, 56, 60, 62, 64, 65, 69, 73
Blake, William, 85
Blakemore, Steven, 220
Blum, Carole, 211
Boaden, James, 25, 43
Bonaparte, Napoleon, 86, 100, 101, 118, 144, 163, 169, 170, 176, 224
Bonnor, Charles, 87; *Picture of Paris in the Year 1790,* 87
Borges, Jorge Luis, 26
Boyd, Henry, 85, 86; *Helots,* 86; *Royal Message,* 85
Brewer, John, 86
British Critic, 62
British Drama, The, 68
British Museum, 68
Brooks, Peter, 98
Brougham, Henry, 145
Browning, Elizabeth Barrett, 142
Browning, Robert, 17, 116, 117, 135, 145, 146, 149, 150, 151, 152; *Life of Strafford* (co-authored with John Forster), 149; "The Lost Leader," 146, 151; *Paracelsus,* 146; *Strafford: An Historical Tragedy,* 17, 145–53
Buchner, Georg, 101; *Danton's Death,* 101
Bugaboo, The. A Dramatic Poem. by R.S., 29
Bulwer-Lytton, Edward George Earle Lytton, 107, 117
Burke, Edmund, 34, 37, 72, 88, 91, 92, 93, 94, 98, 99, 121, 167, 170, 174, 211, 219, 220; *Letter to a Member of the National Assembly,* 92; *Reflections on the Revolution in France,* 37, 91, 93, 121, 167

Burwick, Frederick, 44, 48, 49
Busby, Bruce, 149
Butler, Marilyn, 84
Byron, George Gordon, Lord, 13, 26, 34, 35, 40, 58, 63, 64, 72, 76, 77, 89, 101, 102, 131, 145, 146, 191, 197; *Cain*, 63, 101; *Heaven and Earth*, 63; *Letters and Journals*, 58; *Manfred*, 13, 15, 31, 34, 44, 63, 64; *Marino Faliero*, 63, 64, 65, 69; *Sardanapalus*, 76 *Ulric and Ilvina*, 63; *Werner*, 28, 40, 41, 63
Byron, Lady (Annabella Milbanke), 34

Cameron, Kenneth Neil, 130; *Shelley and His Circle*, 129, 130
Canning, George, 89, 119
Carlson, Julie, 14, 23, 40, 57
Cave, Richard Allen, 22
Charles I, 34, 107, 117, 132, 133, 134, 135, 138, 140, 141, 142, 143, 144
Charles II, 40, 69, 101, 119, 123, 125, 126, 127, 128, 130
Chenevix, Richard, 70, 72
Chenier, Marie Joseph, 103; *Charles IX*, 103
Cibber, Colley, 60
Cobbett, William, 91
Coleridge, Samuel Taylor, 13, 19, 26, 28, 31, 34, 36, 38, 39, 40, 41, 60, 61, 64, 72, 74, 76, 85, 87, 89, 102, 116, 117, 118, 119, 122, 131, 137, 141, 159–77; *Biographia Literaria*, 39, 75, 76, 87; *The Destiny of Nations: A Vision*, 168; "Euthanasia of the Constitution," 169; *The Fall of Robbespierre*, 28, 61, 116, 118; "Fears in Solitude," 163; "Foster-mother's Tale, The," 173; "France: An Ode," 169; "Insensibility of the Public Temper," 165; *Moral and Political Lecture*, 38, 164, 167, 171, 175; "Ode to the Departing Year, 160"; *Osorio*, 18, 28, 31, 32, 41, 159–77; "Religious Musings," 168; *Remonstrance to the French Legislators*, 170; *Remorse*, 28, 41, 61, 64; *The Watchman*, 160, 161, 166; *Zapolya*, 40, 41, 61
Colman, George, the Younger, 14, 26, 27, 28, 43, 44, 46, 68, 107, 108, 140, 141
Condorcet, Marquis de, 34, 46; *Historical View of the Progress of the Human Mind*, 46
Corday, Charlotte, 95, 105

Cornwall, Barry, 64, 65, 71, 72; *Mirandola*, 65
"Coronation, The," 27
Courtney, Winifred, 119, 121, 122; *Young Charles Lamb*, 121,122
Covent Garden, 32, 58, 63, 73, 87, 105, 141, 145
Cox, Jeffrey N., 14, 17, 20, 22, 57, 74; *In the Shadows of Romance*, 74
Critical Review, 71
Cromwell, Oliver, 30, 117, 118, 138, 139, 141, 142, 143, 144, 145
Cross, Gilbert, 97, 98
Cross, J. C., 88; *Julia of Louvain; or, Monkish Cruelty*, 88, 97
Crown and Anchor Society, 86
Cruikshank, George, 86; "The Contrast," 86
Cuomo, Mario, 23
Curran, Stuart, 212, 218

Danton, Georges Jacques, 176
Darwin, Erasmus, 87
Davenant, Sir William, 130, 131, 132, 133, 134, 151; *Gondibert*, 131
Davies, Robertson, 109
Dawson, P. M. S., 224
Declaration of Rights (French), 37
Defoe, Daniel, 125; *Roxana*, 125
Dekker, Thomas, 67
Democratic Rage, 17
Dent, John, 74, 87, 90, 91, 97; *The Bastille*, 74, 87, 90, 91, 97
DeQuincey, Thomas, 13
DeVane, William, 145, 146
Dialogues of the Gods, 30
Dilthey, Wilhelm, 16, 42, 43
Dodsley, Robert, *Selection of Old Plays*, 67
Donohue, Joseph W., Jr., 57
Doubleday, T., 69; *Babington*, 69
Dramatic Review, 68, 70
Drury Lane, 26, 27, 36, 58, 63, 64, 73, 86, 87, 108, 119, 125, 141

Eliot, T. S., 25, 46; "Shakespeare and the Stoicism of Seneca," 46
Elizabeth I, 66, 69, 70, 77, 116
Ellis, George, 89, 119
English Revolution, 17, 19, 30, 43, 116
Erdman, David, 63
Examiner of Plays, 26, 27, 28, 140

Eyre, Edmund John, 85, 94, 105, 106, 107; *Maid of Normandy; or, The Death of the Queen of France*, 85, 94, 95, 97, 105, 106, 107

Fenwick, John, 122, 125
Ferriss, Suzanne, 19, 20
Findlater, Richard, 140
Fletcher, John, 65, 67, 75
Fletcher, Richard, 152
Ford, John, 65, 67, 70
Fox, Charles James, 30, 33, 103, 130; *History of the Early part of the Reign of James the Second*, 130
French Revolution, 17, 18, 19, 26, 61, 72, 84, 85, 86, 88, 91, 98, 101, 102, 103, 107, 116, 129, 136, 141, 152, 159, 161, 163, 164, 165, 167, 173, 174, 208, 219, 224
Frere, John Hookham, 89, 119
Friends of Liberty, 86

Gallic Freedom; or Vive la Liberté, 27
Gaull, Marilyn, 22, 58
Genest, John, 86
George III, 27, 28, 34, 93, 130
George IV, 141
Gifford, William, 68, 89, 91; *Baviad*, 91
Gillray, James, 33, 92, 98, 119, 121, 122; "A Family of Sans-Culotts refreshing after the fatigues of the day," 98; *French Telegraph making Signals in the Dark*, 33; "New Morality," 119, 122
Godwin, William, 17, 28, 34, 35, 40, 117, 118, 119, 121, 122, 125, 126, 127, 129, 130, 131, 132, 133, 134, 144, 145, 150, 151, 152, 161, 162, 164, 165, 166, 191, 219; *Caleb Williams*, 191; *Enquiry Concerning Political Justice*, 126, 161, 164; *Faulkner*, 17, 28, 40, 41, 125, 126, 127, 131, 132; *History of the Commonwealth*, 131; "Interview of Charles the First and Sir William Davenant in the Scottish Camp before Newark Considered," 129
Goethe, Johann Wolfgang, 90, 101; *Faust*, 101; *Stella*, 90
Gottlieb, Erika, 22, 57
Greene, Robert, 38; *The Pandosto*, 38
Grenville, Lord, 45
Groseclose, Barbara, 217

Haggit, John, 85, 95, 97, 104, 107; *Count de Villeroi: or, The Fate of Patriotism*, 85, 95, 97, 104
Hardy, Thomas, 38
Harrington, James, 118; *Oceana*, 118
Hawthorne, Nathaniel: *The Scarlet Letter*, 23
Haymarket Theater, 106
Hazlitt, William, 13, 39, 59, 60, 61, 64, 67, 68, 69, 70, 71, 72, 73, 74, 75, 103, 104, 107, 146; *Lectures on the Dramatic Literature of the Age of Elizabeth*, 69, 72, 74, 75; *Lectures on the English Poets*, 71
Hegel, Georg Wilhelm Friedrich, 46, 49; *Philosophy of History*, 46
Helvetic Liberty, 27, 109
Heron, Robert, 85; *St. Kilda in Edinburgh; or, News from Camperdown*, 85
Heston, Charlton, 24
Hey, Richard, 85; *The Captive Monarch*, 85
Heywood, John, 67
Hezekia, 85
Hitchener, Elizabeth, 225
Hoagwood, Terence Allan, 16, 20, 22, 23, 208
Holbach, Baron d', 34
Holcroft, Thomas, 14, 27, 38, 43, 68; *A Tale of Mystery*, 27
Holland, Henry Fox, 103
Hugo, Victor, 117
Hume, David, 134, 135, 138; *History of England*, 135
Hunt, Leigh, 60, 73, 146; *The Examiner*, 73, 103
Hunt, Lynn, 163

Inchbald, Elizabeth, 14, 16, 24, 25, 26, 28, 31, 32, 35, 39, 40, 41, 43, 108; *Lovers' Vows*, 26, 32, 35, 39, 40, 41; *The Massacre*, 16, 25, 28, 31, 32, 35, 43; *Nature and Art*, 24; *A Simple Story*, 24

Jacobins, 18
Jacobus, Mary, 57, 136
Jeffrey, Francis, 67, 72
Jerrold, Douglas, 117
John, John St., 27, 87; *The Island of St. Marguerite*, 27, 28, 87, 90, 105

Johnson, Joseph, 29, 35
Johnston, Kenneth R., 17, 18, 19, 30
Jonson, Ben, 67, 102
Julia of Louvain, 90

Keach, William, 219
Kean, Edmund, 63
Keats, John, 59, 60, 63, 72, 76, 77; "Sitting Down to Read *King Lear* Once Again," 59, 60
Kemble, Charles, 140, 141
Kemble, John, 119
Kinnaird, John, 13
Klancher, Jon, 72
Kleist, Heinrich von, 86; *Die Hermansschlacht,* 86
Knowles, James Sheridan, 64, 117
Kotzebue, August von, 35, 39, 40, 41, 74, 76, 86, 90, 106; *Das Kind der Liebe,* 35; *Stranger,* 90
Kucich, Greg, 16, 20, 39

Lamb, Charles, 13, 26, 28, 59, 60, 61, 62, 67, 68, 72, 117, 118, 119, 121, 122, 124, 125, 127, 128, 141, 145, 150, 152; *John Woodvil,* 17, 28, 61, 72, 118–25, 127, 171; "Living Without God in the World," 121; *Mr. H.,* 61; "Newspapers Thirty-Five Years Ago," 125; *Pawnbroker's Daughter, The,* 61; *Specimens of English Dramatic Poets Who Lived About the Time of Shakespeare,* 67
Larpent, Anna Margaretta, 105
Larpent, John, 105, 106, 107, 109
Lewis, Matthew, 13, 59, 103; *Adelgitha; or, The Fruit of a Single Error,* 103; *Alfonso, King of Castille,* 59, 103; *The Castle Spectre,* 32, 35, 103; *Venomi,* 103
Licensing Act, 27, 43, 102, 104
Liddy, G. Gordon, 23
Lloyd, Charles, 121, 122; *Blank Verse,* 121; *Lines Suggested by the Fast Appointed on Wednesday, February 27, 1799,* 121
Locke, John, 118
Lockhart, J. G., 26, 73; "On the Cockney School of Poetry," 73
Lockridge, Lawrence S., 220
London Corresponding Society, 86
London Magazine, 60

Louis XVI (of France), 34, 35, 91, 92, 93, 95, 117, 122, 133, 163, 171, 211
Loutherbourg, Phillippe de, 27

Macaulay, Thomas Babington, 141; *History of England from the Accesion of James II,* 141
McCarthy hearings, 24
McGann, Jerome J., 14, 16, 84; *The Romantic Ideology,* 14
McKenna, Wayne, 119
Mackintosh, Sir James, 121, 122; *Vindiciae Gallicae,* 121
Macready, William, 115, 141, 145
Maid of Normandy, 17, 94, 95, 97
Man for All Seasons, A, 24
Marat, Jean Paul, 94, 95, 100, 105
Marlowe, Christopher, 67
Marryat, Frederick: *Children of the New Forest,* 124, 125
Mary Shelley's Frankenstein, 23
Massinger, Philip, 41, 65; *The Bondman,* 41
Maturin, Charles Robert, 13, 39, 40, 64, 72, 74; *Bertram,* 32, 39, 40, 74
Medwin, Thomas, 63, 132
Mental theater, 27, 34, 57
Middleton, Thomas, 41, 67; *The Changeling,* 41
Milman, Henry Hart, 72, 77
Milton, John, 66, 67, 118, 132
Mitford, Mary Russell, 14, 26, 43, 44, 50, 117, 140, 141, 142, 143, 144, 145, 152; *Charles the First,* 17, 26, 28, 43, 44, 50, 140–45; *Foscari,* 141; *Julian,* 141, 145; *Our Village,* 141; *Rienzi,* 141
Molière, 49; *Le Misanthrope,* 47, 49; *Tartuffe,* 47
Moncrief, William, 117
Monthly Review, 65
Montcrieff, W. T., 98; *Lear of the Private Life,* 98
Monvel, 103; *Les Victimes Cloitrees,* 103
Moore, John, 33; *A View of the Causes and Progress of the French Revolution,* 33
More, Hannah, 93; *Village Politics,* 93
Morning Chronicle, The, 60
Muir, Thomas, 99
Murphy, Arthur, 86; *Arminius,* 86

INDEX

Nelson, Lord, 27
Nerval, Gerard de, 106, 107; *Leo Burckart,* 106, 107
Newton, Richard, 92
Nicholes, Joseph, 17, 18, 19, 30
Nodier, Charles, 74

Ollier, Charles, 137
O'Neill, Eliza, 63
Otten, Terry, 57
Otway, Thomas, 102
Ozouf, Mona, 87

Paine, Thomas, 34, 86, 99, 161, 164, 165, 166, 167, 170, 174, 211; *The Age of Reason,* 166, 173; *Rights of Man,* 86, 161, 164, 166, 167, 170, 174
Palmer, Reverend T. F., 99
Pan Kives Ken Kow! Or, Three Kneelings and Nine Knocks!!! A Dramatic Entertainment in One Act, 29, 30
Pantisocracy, 137
Paulson, Ronald, 88, 91, 92
Peacock, Thomas Love, 63
Perrault, Charles: *Blue Beard,* 35
Peterloo Massacre, The, 134
Philistines; or, The Scotch Tocsin Sounders, 85, 98, 99
Phillip II (of Spain), 160
Pitt, William, 33, 46, 86, 89, 161, 163, 169, 171, 173; *The Rovers; or, The Double Arrangement,* 89
Pixercourt, Rene-Charles Guilbert, 74
Pocock, Isaac, 74, 117; *Miller and His Man,* 74
Poetry of the Anti-Jacobean, 122
Pollin, Burton, 119, 121
Porter, Katherine Anne, 24; *Ship of Fools,* 24
Postman, Neil, 22
Preston, William, 85, 100; *Democratic Rage; or, Louis the Unfortunate,* 85, 100
Price, Richard, 33, 37, 161, 162, 166; *Discourse on the love of Our Country,* 33, 37
Priestley, Joseph, 38
Prince Regent, 130
Purinton, Marjean, 14, 18, 19, 23, 23, 217

Quarterly Review, 66

Radcliffe, Ann, 87
Reform Bill (of 1832), 141, 145
Reign of Terror, 34, 35, 37, 162, 173, 209, 224
Retrospective Review, The, 64, 72
Revolution Society, 164
Richard II, 144
Richardson, Alan, 22, 57, 65, 71; *A Mental Theater,* 71, 77
Robespierre, Isidore Maximilien de, 94, 95, 100, 108, 116, 118, 144, 163, 169, 171, 174, 176, 224
Robinson, Mary, 38
Romantic lyric, 13, 14
Romantic novel, 13
Rousseau, Jean Jacques, 34, 35, 94, 211; *La Nouvelle Eloise,* 92, 94; *The Social Contract,* 211
Rovers, The, 17
Royal Circus, 88
Royalists, 18
Russell, Gillian, 14

Sadler's Wells, 27
St. Bartholomew's Day Massacre, 103
Saint-Just, de, Louis Antoine Leon, 176, 211
Schiller, Johann Christoph Friedrich Von, 27, 28, 35, 36, 39, 40, 45, 61, 101; *Aesthetic Education of Man,* 45; *Cabal and Love,* 90; *Die Rauber (The Robbers,* trans. by Alexander Tytler) 27, 32, 35, 36, 39, 40, 41, 90; *Mary Stuart,* 28, 35, 41; *On Naive and Sentimental Poetry,* 45
Schleiermacher, Friedrich, 41, 42
Scott, Sir Walter, 13, 15, 18, 19, 31, 64, 117, 124, 125, 182–205; *Auchindrane,* 18, 182, 189–98, 201, 202; *The Doom of Devorgoil,* 18, 182, 196, 198–205; *The Eire-King,* 31; *An Essay on the Drama,* 64; *Halidon Hill,* 182, 183; *Macduff's Cross,* 18, 182, 183–89, 193, 201; *The Minstrelsy of the Scottish Border,* 183; *Woodstock; or the Cavalier, a Tale of the Year 1651,* 124
Seditious Meetings Act, 86
Seditious Practices Act, 45
Seneca, Lucius Annaeus, 34
Shadwell, Thomas, 40; *The Libertine,* 40

Shakespeare, William, 17, 28, 59, 60, 61, 62, 65, 67, 68, 75, 76, 100, 101, 102, 116, 117, 119, 144, 189; *As You Like It*, 144; *Coriolanus*, 103, 107; *Cymbeline*, 38; *Hamlet*, 39, 41, 59; *Henry IV, Part 1*, 49; *King John*, 75; *King Lear*, 27, 38, 39, 40, 60; *Julius Caesar*, 24, 25, 28, 38; *Macbeth*, 41, 136; *Othello*, 77; *Richard III*, 60; *The Tempest*, 41, 48, 137; *The Winter's Tale*, 38, 61
Shelley, Mary, 23, 132, 139; *Frankenstein*, 23
Shelley, Percy Bysshe, 14, 19, 27, 28, 29, 30, 41, 49, 50, 56, 63, 76, 77, 101, 103, 104, 107, 117, 126, 131, 132, 133, 134, 135, 136, 137, 139, 143, 144, 145, 146, 152, 208–25; "Address to the People on the Death of Princess Charolotte, An," 219; *The Cenci*, 19, 20, 28, 41, 50, 63, 101, 139, 171, 208–25; *Charles the First*, 17, 28, 63, 132, 133, 136, 139, 140, 141; *A Defence of Poetry*, 40, 50, 101, 136, 208, 213, 220, 223; "England in 1819," 136; "Essay on Christianity," 219; "Feelings of a Republican on the Fall of Bonaparte," 224; *Hellas*, 29, 32; *The Mask of Anarchy*, 136; "On the Punishment of Death," 224; *Peter Bell the Third*, 137; *A Philosophical View of Reform*, 133, 140, 208, 213, 219, 220, 223, 224; *Prometheus Unbound*, 13, 15, 29, 31, 32, 34, 50, 76, 77, 101, 209, 225; *Queen Mab*, 212; "Song to the Men of England," 136; *The Triumph of Life*, 140
Sheridan, Richard Brinsley, 86, 108; *Pizarro*, 86, 108
Siddons, Henry and Sarah, 125, 127, 128
Sidney, Algernon, 118; *Discourses Concerning Government*, 118
Silva, D. M. de, 150
Sophocles, 49; *Oedipus Rex*, 38
Southey, Robert, 28, 29, 87, 116, 118, 119, 122, 137; *The Fall of Robespierre*, 28, 116, 117; *Wat Tyler*, 29
Spa Fields Riots, 104
Spenser, Edmund, 49, 66, 67; *Two Cantos of Mutabilitie*, 49
Staël, de, Madam Anne Louise Germaine, 221

Starobinski, Jean, 103
Steiner, George, 56

Talfourd, Thomas Noon, 115, 141, 142, 145, 146; *Ion*, 115
Tasso, Torquato, 63
Tate, Nahum, 60
Tetreault, Ronald, 218
Theatrical Recorder, The, 68
Thelwall, John, 34, 38, 122
Thompson, E. P., 99
Tieck, Ludwig, 44, 48, 49, 50; *Puss in Boots*, 44, 48, 50
Times, The, 73
Tobin, John, 68; *The Honey Moon*, 68
Treason Trials of 1794, 28, 37
Treasonable Practices Act, 86

Unlawful Assemblies Act, 45–46

Victoria (queen of England), 146
Victoria Theater, 141, 145

Waller, Edmund, 132
Walpole, Horace, 25, 87; *Mysterious Mother*, 87
Warburton, Bishop (William), 132
Watkins, Daniel P., 14, 18, 19, 23, 30, 31, 57
Watson, George, 16, 30, 32, 33; *England Preserved*, 16, 30, 32, 33, 34
Watson, Richard, Bishop of Llandaff, 122
Webb, Timothy, 61, 63, 65
Weber, Henry, 68, 70, 75; *Works of Beaumont and Fletcher*, 75
Wedgewood, Thomas, 86
Wieland, G. M., 29, 30; *Dialogues of the Gods*, 29
Wilkinson, Elizabeth M., 45
William IV, 141
Williams, Raymond, 30
Willoughby, Leonard A., 45
Wilson, John, 72
Wollstonecraft, Mary, 161, 162, 164, 165, 167, 170, 172, 174, 211, 218; *An Historical and Moral View of the Origin and the Progress of the French Revolution*, 161, 162, 164, 167, 170, 174; *Vindication of the Rights of Men*, 162, 167, 172
Woodings, R. B., 138; "Shelley's *Charles the First*," 138

Woodring, Carl, 125; *Politics and English Romantic Poetry,* 125
Wooler, T. J., 29, 30
Wordsworth, William, 15, 28, 34, 40, 63, 77, 85, 104, 115, 116, 119, 131, 137, 146, 150, 151, 152, 153, 162, 164, 165, 166; *The Borderers,* 15, 28, 40, 41, 63, 77, 116, 120, 152, 153, 171; *Letter to the Bishop of Llandaff,* 34, 162, 164, 166; *Lyrical Ballads,* 173; "Ode. 1815," 104; "Preface to *Lyrical Ballads,*" 131